# Stages
of Self

# Stages of Self

## The Dramatic Monologues of Laforgue, Valéry & Mallarmé

BY ELISABETH A. HOWE

OHIO UNIVERSITY PRESS 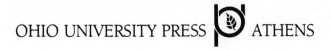 ATHENS

**Library of Congress Cataloging-in-Publication Data**

Howe, Elisabeth A.
    Stages of self : the dramatic monologues of Laforgue, Valéry &
Mallarmé / by Elisabeth A. Howe.
      p.   cm.
    Includes bibliographical references.
    ISBN 0-8214-0953-0 (alk. paper)
    1. French poetry—19th century—History and criticism.
2. Dramatic monologues—History and criticism.   3. Laforgue, Jules,
1860-1887—Criticism and interpretation.   4. Valéry, Paul,
1871-1945—Criticism and interpretation.   5. Mallarmé, Stéphane,
1842-1898—Criticism and interpretation.   6. Self in literature.
I. Title.
PQ439.H686   1990
841'.809—dc20

                                            90-30675
                                             CIP

Ohio University Press books are printed on acid-free paper. ∞

For Michael

# Contents

# Preface

Considerable critical attention has been paid in recent years to the dramatic monologue as a genre, illustrated by reference to the works of various English and American poets. The investigation is rarely extended, however, to poetry written in a foreign language; in the case of French this omission may be partly due to the relative rarity of the dramatic monologue as a form in French poetry. Nevertheless, examples of the genre do exist in French, and the purpose of this study is to analyze them, comparing them to their English counterparts in order to show how they retain the essential characteristics of the dramatic monologue, although modified in a way that conforms to a specifically French dramatic and poetic tradition.

It is a pleasure to be able to record here my gratitude to Richard Sieburth, whose constant encouragement, criticism and advice made this study possible.

A first draft of this book received the joint Book Award for 1989 of the Northeast Modern Language Association of America and Ohio University Press. I am grateful to NEMLA and Ohio University Press for creating this Award, which is a source of encouragement for authors.

I thank the editors of *Nottingham French Studies* for permission to reproduce material from chapter 3 originally published in their journal.

Finally, I wish to express my thanks and appreciation to my husband for his understanding and patience during the writing of this book.

# Introduction

The term "dramatic monologue," though frequently used to characterize poems by English and American poets, is not often applied to French poetry. However, an analysis of various features of the genre leads to the conclusion that the term has relevance not only within the Anglo-American tradition but also for certain poems written in French. Mallarmé's *L'Après-midi d'un faune* and Valéry's *La Jeune Parque*, for example, while being as different from the mimetic, character-revealing dramatic monologues of Browning, Eliot or Pound as Racine is from Shakespeare, can nevertheless be classed as dramatic monologues. They relate, though, to different theatrical and poetic conventions and to a different conception of the dramatic; and they reflect a significant disparity in attitude towards the roles of author, speaker and reader. Laforgue's poems constitute an interesting half-way point between the representational dramatic monologue typical of Browning, which Laforgue ironically undermines, and the more impersonal, universal monologues of Mallarmé and Valéry.

Since the dramatic monologue is not recognized as a genre by French critics (a "monologue dramatique" being essentially a monologue in a stage play), the evaluation of different definitions of this type of poem, in chapter 1, is confined to the Anglo-American field. This review leads to an exploration of the differences between a dramatic monologue and a lyric poem, involving discussion of the lyric "I," the persona, and the question of distance. The dramatic monologue is spoken by a persona who is not the poet; and the setting-up of distance between author and speaker on the one hand, reader and speaker on the other, prevents the reader from identifying with the speaker—as often happens in a lyric poem— or from assuming that author and speaker are one. Distance can be achieved by naming the persona and particularizing him in various ways, in order to establish his separate and recognizable identity.

This chapter concludes with an examination of the language of the dramatic monologue, particularly in its relation to dialogue and to oral discourse generally.

It is impossible to discuss the dramatic monologue without reference to the work of Robert Browning, the acknowledged master of the form in English poetry. His poems serve as a useful springboard and point of comparison for the French poets treated here; several of his most typical dramatic monologues will therefore be examined in chapter 2. Particular emphasis will be laid on his preoccupation with character-revelation and the means used to achieve it, such as the provision of historical or fictitious spatial and temporal contexts. The distance essential to a dramatic monologue is provided partly by these contexts and partly by irony at the speakers' expense—a form of dramatic irony which constitutes one of the many dramatic elements in Browning's poems.

Since many of Ezra Pound's early dramatic monologues resemble Browning's in their portrayal of historical figures, their emphasis on characterization, and their use of spoken language, his poetry is also discussed in chapter 2.

Chapter 3 begins with a brief survey of the tentative approaches towards the dramatic monologue form in French literature prior to the mid-nineteenth century, and then embarks on a study of Laforgue's "Pierrot" poems and *Derniers vers* as dramatic monologues. In Laforgue we witness a move away from a Browningesque unified "I" towards a multiple self. This evolution is accompanied by a preference for stock figures, such as Pierrot and Hamlet, over individuals; for role-playing; and for stereotyped language as against the "genuine" self-expression of a unique personality. Laforgue's use of clichés is examined in the light of Bakhtin's statements regarding the repetitiveness and externality of language—and as a simultaneously mimetic and parodic procedure. This chapter closes with an exploration of the relation between poetry, prose fiction, and the dramatic monologue, with reference to Bakhtin's comments on the literary notion of distance.

In *L'Après-midi d'un faune*, discussed in chapter 4, Mallarmé has created a dramatic monologue totally unlike Browning's in its depreciation of character and deliberate rejection of the realistic and particular in favour of the universal quality of myth and the poetics of suggestion, but which remains dramatic in its portrayal of the "antagonisme" between dream and reality and in its adoption of the forms of dramatic dialogue in the Faun's self-address. It also establishes the distance crucial to the dramatic monologue: by the use of a persona, by the play with fictionality which makes it impossible to know exactly what has occurred, and by Mallarmé's method of suggesting rather than naming. Without impairing its dramatic qualities, the poem illustrates some of Mallarmé's most cherished theories about poetry, such as the relation between reality, poetry and fiction, and the notions of impersonality and self-referentiality. *Hérodiade* and *Igitur*, while not strictly dramatic monologues, also illustrate some of these issues.

Like Mallarmé, Valéry condemns mimetic literature for its necessarily arbitrary portrayal of events and characters, and totally rejects the notion of personality—views examined in chapter 5 in relation to *La Jeune Parque*. The concept of voice, of supreme importance to Valéry, provides at once a source of unity (that of the Parque's central presence) and of disunity, therefore of dramatic conflict: the self is split; one half speaks, the other listens; monologue becomes dialogue. The mind, scene of this "comédie intérieure," can express itself only in language, which comes to it from outside: some of Valéry's statements in the *Cahiers* concerning the "strangeness" of language bear a striking resemblance to those of Bakhtin.

Chapter 6 summarizes various aspects of both types of dramatic monologue analyzed in this study. It also illustrates Browning's move, in some of his later dramatic monologues, away from the representational mode of the *Dramatic Lyrics* and *Romances*. Poems like "Abt Vogler" and "Rabbi Ben Ezra" in *Dramatis Personae* (1864), or *Prince Hohenstiel-Schwangau* (1871) are more universal in scope than the earlier poems, and concentrate less on character-revelation than on an inner debate within the speaker's soul. The linguistic consequences of this evolution are explored.

T. S. Eliot is another poet whose evolution demonstrates even more clearly a move away from the mimetic and particular towards the universal, and away from external characterization towards the exploration of a depersonalized consciousness. His early dramatic monologues invite comparison with those of his youthful model, Laforgue, whereas his *Four Quartets* (although not a dramatic monologue) are more akin to Valéry's *La Jeune Parque*, despite the two poets' differing conceptions of the nature of poetic voice.

The divergent attitudes toward poetic voice of the Anglo-American poets on the one hand, and the French poets on the other, are explored as one possible reason for the relative scarcity of dramatic monologues in French; and this study concludes by noting the connection between the decline of faith in language as an instrument of communication and the demise of the concept of personality.

# CHAPTER ONE

# General Characteristics of the Dramatic Monologue

## I. Origins and definitions

The dramatic monologue form began to flourish in English po-
etry in the mid-nineteenth century, particularly—and quite inde-
pendently—in the works of Browning and Tennyson. Various at-
tempts have been made to establish the origins of the genre, and
examples have been found in the poetry of earlier centuries. Ben-
jamin Fuson discovers sources of the dramatic monologue among
Classical poets. He also claims that over one thousand dramatic
monologues were written, by dozens of different poets, in the early
years of the nineteenth century; and finds another thousand or so
among earlier poets, from Chaucer to Burns, including the Anglo-
Saxon "Banished Wife's Lament," John Skelton's "Boke of Phyllyp
Sparowe" (1508), Burns' "Holy Willie's Prayer" (1799) and Blake's
"The Chimney Sweeper" (1789). As a result of his explorations
among earlier poetry, Fuson concludes that 'My Last Duchess' was
by no means, as some have claimed, the first dramatic monologue.[1]

Robert Langbaum, however, refuses to regard the dramatic

monologue as a traditional genre on the grounds that such a view tends to include too many poems, lyrics in particular. For Lang-baum, the dramatic monologue, a "poetry of sympathy" in which the reader is given "facts from within," belongs to the nineteenth and twentieth centuries and represents a quintessential form of romantic poetry. He takes the view that the romantic poet, no longer able, as in previous centuries, to rely on absolute values or moral standards, posits instead his own experience as a yardstick, and later, by extension, tries—in the dramatic monologue—to enter sympathetically into the subjective experience of others.[2] Yet Blake and Burns, not to mention Chaucer and others, seem to have felt sufficient sympathy with their speakers to compose in their names poems which amount to dramatic monologues, without the benefit of the romantic lyric behind them.

Other critics have looked elsewhere for the origins of the dramatic monologue form. Philip Hobsbaum regards it as arising from stage monologues, and specifically from a growing tendency to value soliloquies above action in the theatre—a tendency he sees as a major reason for the decline of drama after the age of Shake-speare. Individual speeches became more important to both play-wrights and spectators than the plot as a whole, and were often appreciated independently of their context. This gave rise to the publication of various popular anthologies of speeches extracted from plays, such as Dr. Dodd's *The Beauties of Shakespeare* (1752) and Lamb's *Specimens of English Dramatic Poets* (1808)—speeches which can sound very much like the poems we call dramatic mono-logues. Hobsbaum points out that when Lamb's enormously popu-lar *Specimens* came out in 1808, relatively few monologues had been composed, whereas "the next generation, that of Browning and Tennyson, was prolific in the form"; and he posits a probable con-nection between this sudden flowering of the dramatic monologue and "the anthologists' way of reading drama as isolated scenes, as 'beauties.' "[3]

Yet another possible source for the dramatic monologue, accord-ing to A. Dwight Culler, is the monodrama. He distinguishes be-tween monodrama and the dramatic monologue on the grounds that in the former "the passions explored . . . are universal and abstract" whereas in the latter they are "connected with the particular acts and circumstances of an individual, with his deeds and situation."[4] This emphasis on the individual and particular is typical of Browning's dramatic monologues, though whether it is an essential ingredient of the form remains to be seen.

Most attempts at characterizing and defining the dramatic monologue have been based principally, if not exclusively, on a study of Browning's poetry. The author of the *Dramatic Lyrics, Dramatic Romances, Dramatis Personae* and *Dramatic Idylls* never used the term "dramatic monologue," which first appeared, according to Culler, in 1857, and was first applied to Browning's poetry in 1869;[5] however, Browning's insistence on the word "dramatic" in his titles is remarkable. He describes his *Dramatic Lyrics* as being "though for the most part Lyric in expression, always Dramatic in principle, and so many utterances of so many imaginary persons, not mine."[6] In other words by "dramatic" he means, not "exciting; full of conflict, tension, drama," but "objective": the speaker of the poem is not meant to represent the poet. This is the first criterion put forward by all critics seeking to define the dramatic monologue. Fuson, in his attempt at a definition, actually substitutes "objective," for "dramatic," but in fact the term "dramatic," precisely because of its double connotation, seems more appropriate in defining monologues of this type, since both its meanings are relevant. Fuson gives a definition of the "objective" monologue which takes into account both senses of the word "dramatic": "*An objective monolog [sic] is an isolated poem intended to simulate the utterance not of the poet but of another individualized speaker whose words reveal his involvement in a localized dramatic situation.*"[7] Apart from the use of the word "objective" in place of "dramatic," this seems to be a good working definition, implying as it does a monologue dramatic in both senses of the word, complete in itself (unlike monologues in stage plays), and whose speaker is not merely a spectator (as in a first-person narrative poem) but a participant in the drama.

Fuson, however, goes on to list three further ingredients for a successful dramatic monologue: "oral realism," "auditor-focus" and "psychological self-revelation."[8] In the dramatic monologue as realized by Browning, with its accent on character portrayal, it is probably true that the more strongly these features operate, the better the poem, but this does not necessarily make them essential elements for the whole genre. To some extent, Fuson's effort to characterize the dramatic monologue runs into the same problems as an earlier attempt by Ina B. Sessions.[9] Both try to define it according to the presence of certain "ingredients"; Sessions lists seven of them: speaker, audience, occasion, revelation of character, interplay between speaker and audience, dramatic action, and action which takes place in the present. Unfortunately, by no means all dramatic monologues, including some of Browning's best and most well-known poems, present all these characteristics simultaneously.

Langbaum, in his very influential and valuable book *The Poetry of Experience*, abandoned the search for essential ingredients in favour of looking inside the dramatic monologue and considering its "effect, its *way* of meaning." He sees the dramatic monologue as "a poem of experience" in which the experience "has validity just because it is dramatized as an event which we must accept as having taken place, rather than formulated as an idea with which we must agree or disagree." What counts is the reader's sympathy with the speaker and his experience, not his moral assessment of the speaker.[10]

This outline of the "way of meaning" of the dramatic monologue, though interesting, can be criticized on several counts. First of all, it is misleading to suggest that we sympathize with the central figure to such a degree that we waive our moral judgement of him. Langbaum cites "My Last Duchess" in illustration of his theory, but in fact the reader feels, not so much sympathy for the Duke, as perhaps admiration for his poise and control of the situation; and this does not prevent us from judging him. Hobsbaum takes a diametrically opposite view from Langbaum when he says of the dramatic monologue that "characteristically—and, in this unlike most drama—the reader is prevented from sympathising with the protagonist."[11] Indeed, many of Browning's poems invite an adverse judgement of the central character more emphatically than "My Last Duchess": we feel no sympathy at all for the speaker of the "Soliloquy of the Spanish Cloister," for example. And although Langbaum asserts that "the kind of speakers we find in the best dramatic monologues . . . excel in passion, will or intellectual virtuosity—in existential courage, the courage to be themselves," we need only think of Prufrock or Andrea del Sarto to wonder at this statement. When he claims further that the speaker's qualities must "command our admiration in and for themselves, regardless of the moral direction they happen to take,"[12] it is apparent, after his analysis of "My Last Duchess," that he has in mind the Duke from that poem, but how could his affirmation be applied to the monk in the Spanish cloister, or to the Bishop ordering his tomb? In general I would agree with Wayne Booth that "Langbaum seriously underplays the extent to which moral judgment remains even after psychological vividness has done its work."[13] Reading "The Bishop Orders His Tomb at St Praxed's," we may smile at the Bishop's childish enthusiasm for beautiful objects but this does not prevent our condemning his possessive attitude towards them, or his vanity, hypocrisy and greed. Any sympathy the reader feels for Andrea del Sarto does not blind him to the obvious weakness of Andrea's character. To some extent, Andrea may recognize it himself; generally speaking, however, at least in Browning's earlier dramatic monologues, the central characters remain unaware of their own vices and errors of judgement. Philip Drew cites *Cleon* and *Karshish* as "two obvious examples to refute Langbaum's dictum that 'the meaning of the dramatic monologue is what the speaker comes to perceive,' since their main interest lies in what the speaker is unable to perceive."[14]

Indeed, Langbaum himself suggests that "the meaning of the dramatic monologue is in disequilibrium with what the speaker reveals and understands";[15] and since most modern writers on Browning agree that it is usually possible to discern how the poet intends us to judge his characters, at least in the earlier monologues, let us examine the consequences of this latter position, namely that the dramatic monologue depends on the kind of dramatic irony inherent in the "disequilibrium" between what the speaker reveals and what he understands about himself. This assessment does apply very well to poems like "The Bishop Orders His Tomb," "Andrea del Sarto," "The Laboratory," "My Last Duchess," "The Statue and the Bust," "Porphyria's Lover," "Karshish," "Cleon," and other poems from the *Dramatic Romances*, *Dramatic Lyrics* and *Men and Women*. But does it follow that this "disequilibrium" necessarily characterizes the dramatic monologue in general? Langbaum suggests that it does, but this is a very restrictive claim, implying that the main character in a dramatic monologue must have flaws or shortcomings of which he is unaware, i.e., that "most successful dramatic monologues deal with speakers who are in some way reprehensible."[16] Such a statement may accurately describe Browning's best monologues, because it was a formula that worked well for him; but it assumes that the genre must be defined specifically according to Browning's realization of it. The fact that many of Browning's speakers are to some degree reprehensible, and that dramatic irony plays a prominent role in his works, does not necessarily mean that all monologues have to follow this pattern in order to be considered "dramatic." Fuson's definition of a dramatic monologue referred to the speaker's "involvement in a localized dramatic situation"—such as Fra Lippo Lippi's entanglement with the keepers of the peace—which suggests a different type of drama from that emphasized by Langbaum, and there are also of course many instances in Browning's poems of drama in this sense of "exciting," tense situations: in "My Last Duchess," for example, or "The Laboratory," or "Porphyria's Lover." In Tennyson's "Ulysses" the dramatic element is different again, more internal, as Ulysses debates whether to leave Ithaca or stay. While it is therefore appropriate to stress the need for some kind of dramatic element, in order to help distinguish the dramatic monologue from a lyric or a narrative poem, there seems no reason for limiting it to the notion of dramatic irony resulting from the speaker's obliviousness to his own "reprehensible" traits.

The final objection to Langbaum's claim that the dramatic monologue represents a "poetry of sympathy" relying on the effect created by the "tension between sympathy and moral judgment" is that, for this to be a distinctive feature of the dramatic monologue in particular, it should not seem to characterize poetry, or drama, in general. In fact, however, as Park Honan indicates, this effect, "hardly isolates or specially typifies the dramatic monologue. . . . Can it be said, for example, that Macbeth's soliloquies depend any less for their effect than 'My Last Duchess' upon a 'tension between sympathy and moral judgment'?"[17] The novel, too, often relies on such an effect, which is discussed at length by Booth in his *Rhetoric of Fiction*. In the chapter devoted to the issues of sympathy and judgement in *Emma*, he states: "In reducing the emotional distance, the natural tendency is to reduce—willy-nilly—moral and intellectual distance as well."[18] One very effective way of reducing emotional distance is by allowing a character to speak in the first person, and to this extent the tension between sympathy and judgement is as liable to occur in a poem spoken by a reprehensible character as in any other work in which a "villain" speaks in the first person—for example, *Macbeth* or, as Booth points out, *Clarissa*; or *Manon Lescaut*, of which one critic wrote in 1773, "Ce livre est écrit avec tant d'art, et d'une façon si intéressante, que l'on voit les honnêtes gens même s'attendrir en faveur d'un escroc et d'une catin."[19]

Langbaum points out that Browning's speakers, unaware of their shortcomings, do not attempt to know themselves better. Self-analysis and internal debate belong, not in the dramatic monologue, according to Langbaum, but in soliloquy, because "the soliloquist's subject is himself, while the speaker of the dramatic monologue directs his attention outward." Nevertheless, Langbaum treats "The Love Song of J. Alfred Prufrock" as a dramatic monologue, though Prufrock's subject is himself and the poem consists entirely of internal debate. In fact, it is significant that, as soon as Langbaum deals with a dramatic monologue other than those of Browning, his distinction between soliloquy and dramatic monologue weakens considerably: "Prufrock is clearly speaking for his own benefit. Yet he does not, like the soliloquist, address himself; he addresses his other self—the 'you' of the first line . . . Prufrock's other self figures as the auditor."[20] This is precisely what happens in all dramatic monologues which also happen to be soliloquies, i.e., where the speaker is alone: like Prufrock, he addresses his other self, often in the second person.

In another discussion which takes Browning's poems as a model, Loy D. Martin claims that all dramatic monologues "at least fantasize a listener, and this is chiefly what differentiates them from lyrics or extracted soliloquies"; but in soliloquies which are not "extracted," too, such as "Prufrock," the speaker fantasizes a listener, either himself or an absent person or, as in "Tithonus," some other unattainable figure. While apparently insisting that it must have an interlocutor, Martin states that the dramatic monologue "may represent a tenuous but actual exchange, as in 'Fra

Lippo Lippi,' or it may represent the desire for an impossible ex-
change," as in "Tithonus."[21] In fact, however, the exchange in a
soliloquy can in a sense be more "actual" than in "Fra Lippo Lippi,"
since the solitary monologist, simultaneously speaker and listener,
can respond to his own utterance: a phenomenon we shall exam-
ine in more detail in chapters 4 and 5.

In both types of poem, with and without an interlocutor, what
counts is the creation of a certain dramatic tension, through con-
flict either within the character or between what the speaker reveals
and understands about himself. There seems no reason to insist, as
Langbaum does, that only the latter type of conflict characterizes
the dramatic monologue whereas self-analysis belongs in a differ-
ent genre. To do so, or to insist that a dramatic monologue must
have an interlocutor, amounts to saying that only Browning wrote
dramatic monologues: it would exclude not only "Prufrock" but
most of Tennyson's poems, whose protagonists tend to engage in
internal debate, and Pound's, which do not normally assume the
presence of an interlocutor. And if Browning alone wrote dramatic
monologues, the usefulness of the generic term seems questionable.

Many critics since Langbaum have declined to offer a precise
definition of the dramatic monologue based either on objective
criteria or on the concept of sympathy versus judgement. Frances
Carleton asserts that "the dramatic monologue . . . defies a firm
definition," and Roma King that "Browning's short poems . . .
defy rigid classification. . . . Each poem must be judged for what
it is." Other critics deliberately propose very general definitions,
such as Donald Hair's "a combination of the drama and the lyric" or
Honan's "single discourse by one whose presence is indicated by
the poet but who is not the poet himself."[22] This last formula, as
Honan himself points out, would include many works not normally
considered dramatic monologues, such as narrative poems in the
first person like Browning's "The Flight of the Duchess." The
speaker of this poem certainly describes dramatic events, but since
he simply narrates them, without being personally involved, the
poem cannot be—and is not generally—called a dramatic mono-
logue; it is a narrative poem. Fuson is therefore right to insist on the
speaker's own "involvement in a localized dramatic situation."
Again, Honan's definition, by failing to emphasize a dramatic ele-

ment, would include, as he says himself, many lyric poems; and indeed it is often difficult to draw the line between the dramatic monologue and the lyric.

# II. Distinguishing the dramatic monologue from the lyric poem

Regarding the question of voice in literary works, Plato and Aristotle distinguish three main categories, summarized as follows in the article on "Voice and Address" in the *Dictionary of World Literature*:

> a speaker (poet) may (1) speak in his own person, or (2) assume the voice of another person or set of persons and speak throughout in a voice not his own, or (3) produce a mixed speech in which the basic voice is his own, but other personalities are at times assumed and their voices introduced, i.e., directly quoted.[23]

Clearly, the dramatic monologue employs the second of these categories, as the author of the article points out: "The second mode of presentation . . . produced dialogue . . . or, if there be only one assumed voice, 'dramatic' monologue." However, as examples of this structure, he gives both "a monologue of Browning" and "most lyric poetry." This suggests, somewhat abruptly, that there is little or no difference between the voice of a dramatic monologue by Browning and that of a lyric poem—a view apparently echoed by Honan when he says that if his "rather simple" definition, quoted above, "implies that many poems might be considered as both lyrics *and* dramatic monologues, it seems to reflect a truth."[24] He is able to conflate dramatic monologues and lyric poems because of the omission of any dramatic element from his definition; whereas the author of the *Dictionary* article would contend that even lyric poetry is essentially dramatic. For opposite reasons, therefore, it becomes impossible to distinguish between a dramatic monologue and a lyric poem, and indeed this distinction represents one of the main problems arising from discussions of the dramatic monologue. Since the basic reason for the difficulty is that both the dramatic monologue and the lyric are composed in the first person, it would seem advisable to examine the status of the pronoun "I," common to both.

Linguistically, the first-person pronoun (like the second) belongs to a class of words whose precise meaning varies according to the context and which Jakobson classifies as code referring to message. Thus, " 'I' means the person uttering 'I.' "[25] Similarly, Benveniste says of the first-person pronoun (which he terms an "indicator"):

> Each *I* has its own reference and corresponds each time to a unique being who is set up as such.
>    What then is the reality to which *I* or *you* refers? It is solely a "reality of discourse," and this is a very strange thing. *I* cannot be defined except in terms of "locution," not in terms of objects as a nominal sign is.[26]

Clearly, this elusive pronoun is liable to create ambiguity: since it is solely a "reality of discourse" we must rely on the rest of the discourse to define it. In oral speech the identity of the speaker is naturally established by the context, and in some works written in the first person, such as autobiography, the speaker's identity is readily determined. Even in the first-person novel, as Jean Cohen points out, " 'Je' designe un être sans doute fictif, mais qui n'en est pas moins présenté et nommé dans le contexte." He then turns to poetry:

Qu'en est-il maintenant du poème? Qui dit "Je" dans:

Je suis le ténébreux, le veuf, l'inconsolé
Le Prince d'Aquitaine à la tour abolie  . . .

A cette question, le poème ne fournit aucune réponse. Le pronom demeure sans référence contextuelle.

Similarly, the demonstrative adjectives in Baudelaire's "Vois sur ces canaux / Dormir ces vaisseaux," fail to fulfil their normal linguistic function. "Ils désignent sans désigner," says Cohen. In a written context "canaux et vaisseaux devraient faire l'objet d'une autre

mention dans le message. Mais le poème n'en comporte aucune."
And he sees in this linguistic irregularity an essential characteristic
of poetry:

> La carence est délibérée, elle est faite pour frapper d'indétermi-
> nation les êtres et les choses qui peuplent l'univers poétique. Et
> c'est de cette figure, principalement, qu'émane cette impression
> de réalité vague, nébuleuse, irrémédiablement secrète, qui s'at-
> tache à la catégorie même du poétique.[27]

The speaker of a lyric poem has often been equated with the poet
himself, though nowadays it is generally agreed that even in the
most blatantly confessional poetry the poet may adopt a kind of
lyric persona. Käte Hamburger issues this categorical statement:

> there is no exact criterion, neither logical nor aesthetic, neither
> intrinsic nor extrinsic, that would tell us whether we could iden-
> tify the statement-subject of a lyric poem with the poet or not.
> We possess neither the possibility, nor therefore the right to
> maintain that the poet meant the statements in the poem . . .
> as those of his own experience; nor can we maintain that he
> does not mean "himself."[28]

Jean Cohen, too, rejects the identification of the speaker of a lyric
poem with the poet as "simpliste," adding that

> pour débouter une telle preuve, il suffit de se tourner vers la
> deuxième personne, vers ce vocatif poétique qui désigne le des-
> tinataire. Mais d'une manière encore une fois lacunaire:
>
> Mon enfant, ma soeur
> Songe à la douceur.
>
> A qui s'addressent ces mots? A une femme sans doute, mais c'est
> tout ce que le poème nous livre de son identité.[29]

In other words the identity of the person addressed remains as
vague as that of the "I."

Even proper names in a lyric poem can contribute towards the
indeterminacy characteristic of the genre. Cohen again cites
Baudelaire: "Dis-moi, ton coeur parfois s'envole-t-il, Agathe," and

asks "Qui est Agathe? . . . Agathe n'est pas une femme détermi-
née connue de l'auteur, dont il nous déroberait l'identité." Jakobson
defines proper names as code referring to code;[30] the name "Jerry"
refers to a person called Jerry. Therefore, Cohen concludes, the
proper name takes on meaning only if its bearer has been intro-
duced to the reader, either by a description or by being placed in a
particular situation. In the lyric poem, where the identity of the
person named need not be established in this way, the proper
name can remain as vague as the "I" and the "you," a *signifiant* with-
out *signifié*.[31] It is precisely this vagueness which allows the phenom-
enon typical of lyric poetry: the reader's tendency to identify with
the speaking voice, or to attribute it to the poet.

The belated realization that the "I" of a lyric poem does not neces-
sarily refer to the poet led some exponents of the New Criticism to
maintain that all poetry, even the lyric, is basically "dramatic." For
instance, Brooks and Warren lose no time, in their *Understanding
Poetry*, in pointing out that "all poetry, including lyrics and descrip-
tive pieces, involves dramatic organization. Every poem implies a
speaker and therefore the reaction of this person (be it an "I") to a
situation, a scene, an idea." Similarly, Reuben Brower affirms that "a
poem is a dramatic fiction no less than a play," and John Crowe
Ransom claims that all poetry "maintains . . . certain dramatic
features. The poet does not speak in his own but in an assumed
character . . . in an assumed situation."[32] For if the "I" is not the
poet, it must represent, according to this reasoning, a dramatic
speaker, a persona, assuming, like a character in a stage play, an
independent existence of his own. All poetry would, then, belong to
the second definition in the above-mentioned article from the *Dic-
tionary of World Literature*, according to which the poet would
"speak throughout in a voice not his own." Ransom goes so far as to
conclude that any poem "may be said to be a dramatic monologue,"
and that "Browning only literalized . . . the thing that had always
been the poem's lawful form." Yet many critics (and readers) con-
tinue to sense a difference between the lyric poem and the dra-
matic monologue, despite the difficulties they experience in defin-
ing the latter.

A distinction can in fact be made between the lyric poem and the
dramatic monologue. In the former, the identity of the "I" (together

with that of the person addressed and, frequently, of proper names) is so vague, as we saw in Cohen's analysis, that it can easily be taken—rightly or wrongly—to represent the voice of the poet. In the dramatic monologue, on the other hand, the poet, by introducing the speaker to the reader, placing him in a specific context, giving us certain details about his life, deliberately sets him up as a separate entity. The vagueness of the lyric "I" allows the reader to identify with the speaker, adopting the "I" as his own voice, putting himself in the speaker's place. This does not occur with the dramatic monologue, because here the "I" belongs to a specific speaker who is identified or particularized in some way. Nor can this "I" be attributed to the poet, who, by presenting the speaker as Other, clearly signals the distance between them.

One of the most effective signals is the proper name, which here, unlike Baudelaire's Agathe, does represent a definite individual, introduced to the reader and somehow particularized. The majority of speakers in dramatic monologues, whether historical, mythical or fictional, are named; and their names often form part or the whole of the poem's title: "Ulysses," "Fra Lippo Lippi," "Andrea del Sarto," "J. Alfred Prufrock," "Marvoil." The name attached to a dramatic monologue makes it a world seen through the eyes of a particular speaker, specific to him, distorted perhaps. The reader's immediate impulse is to establish the identity of this named speaker, whereas he does not feel the same curiosity about the "I" of a lyric poem. In the dramatic monologue as in the novel, the "apparition d'un nom propre . . . introduit dans le texte une sorte de 'blanc' sémantique," which, for the reader, will gradually acquire meaning.[33] As Michel Foucault says, "le nom propre . . . permet de montrer du doigt, c'est-à-dire de faire passer subrepticement de l'espace où l'on parle à l'espace où l'on regarde."[34] In other words the reader, faced with a proper name introducing a specific individual, is less inclined to feel with him and speak with him, tending rather to examine him from the outside, from "the space where one looks."

The proper name on its own suffices to "objectify" the speaker; but there are also many other signals, or particularizing devices, which can be used to endow him with an independent identity: titles and professions, dates, the characteristics of a particular era, or the atmosphere of a specific place, be it the sixteenth-century Italy of Andrea del Sarto, the mythical Greece of Ulysses, or the twentieth-century drawing-room of J. Alfred Prufrock. Such details serve to place the protagonist in a spatial or temporal context which helps to identify him, for example, as the dying Bishop of Saint Praxed's Church, as a monk in a Spanish cloister, or as a lonely twentieth-century lady surrounded by her lilac, her Chopin and her tea. The dramatic monologue establishes the speaker as an autonomous being with whom the reader may sympathize, or not, but whose voice he cannot adopt as his own—or attribute to the poet—since it clearly belongs to another. The poet has demonstrably opted deliberately to present the poem in a voice other than his own—however close the protagonist's views or thoughts may sometimes be to those of the poet.

Thus dramatic monologues assume a certain separation or *distance* between poet and speaker on the one hand and between reader and speaker on the other, contrasting with the "great lyric poems" which, as Booth comments, "are for the most part written with little or no intended distance between the speaker and the implied author." Conversely, "the deliberate placing of a distance between the poet and his lyric persona effectively dramatizes the substance of the poem."[35] This distance can be engineered in a variety of ways: as well as naming the speaker and/or placing him in a very particularized setting, the poet may create a "moral distance" between speaker and reader through the use of reprehensible characters—a technique often adopted by Browning; or he may establish historical distance, by using a figure from history or myth as speaker. Another, somewhat different, means of distancing the speaker is through the use of irony, which represents a distinctive feature of the dramatic monologues of Jules Laforgue; and T.S. Eliot, following Laforgue's example, employs a similar brand of irony in his early poems.

We may assert, then, that a poem written in the first person but using no "distancing" techniques cannot (*pace* Ransom) automatically be called a dramatic monologue. However, if the creation of distance "effectively dramatizes" the poem, it must also be *seen* to be created, i.e., it must be signalled. The reader's perception of the speaker's autonomy may be uncertain if the signals provided are, deliberately or otherwise, inadequate. It is largely a question of degree: the greater the distance implied, by various means, between both poet and speaker on the one hand and speaker and reader on the other, the more likely we are to assess the poem as a dramatic monologue; when the distance is only slight, or uncertain, we tend to view the poem as a lyric and may identify with the speaker.

In an attempt to distinguish, once again, the dramatic monologue from the lyric, Ralph Rader posits a third category, the "mask lyric," in which the poet expresses, through an "artificial personage," an "aspect of his own subjective situation." Such poems as "Ulysses," "Childe Roland to the Dark Tower Came" and "The Love Song of J. Alfred Prufrock" are, according to Rader, "really a kind of indirect lyric" spoken by an "artificial person projected from the poet" rather than by a "simulated natural person."[36] Such a distinction seems based more on psychological guesswork, however, than on any formal features: how can one tell, from the poem, that Prufrock is not speaking simply for himself but expresses an aspect of Eliot's own "subjective situation"? Rader's distinction ignores, too, the dramatic element, the element of conflict, present in "Ulysses," "Prufrock" and "Childe Roland," which the term "mask lyric" tends to play down. Furthermore, if poems like "Prufrock," "Childe Roland," "Ulysses"—and presumably other monologues by Tennyson—cannot be termed dramatic monologues, we are left with virtually only certain poems of Browning (but not "Childe Roland," for example) in the category of the dramatic monologue proper; and what is the use of a generic term like "dramatic monologue" if it covers only the work of one poet, and not all of that? I would say that poems like "Childe Roland," "Prufrock," and "Ulysses" *are* dramatic monologues and that their speakers differ from, say, Browning's Bishop of Saint Praxed's or Andrea del Sarto not so much in being projections of the poet as in their universality. The speaker of a poem under consideration later in this study, Valéry's *La Jeune Parque*, which Rader would no doubt class as a mask lyric, voices concerns which Valéry reflected on at length; but her significance is as a universal figure rather than as the poet's "mask." The same could be said for Childe Roland or Ulysses. The adoption of a universal figure as speaker precludes the detailed contexts provided in most of Browning's monologues; hence the "irreal, fluid and symbolic scene" which Rader associates with the "mask lyric"[37]—a description that certainly fits *La Jeune Parque*, as well as "Childe Roland." Hence, also, the lack of emphasis on character-portrayal in such poems: a universal or mythical figure does not display specific traits of personality. But this move away from character-portrayal is not confined to the dramatic monologue; in the novel, too, and in drama, the "objective" character has been displaced, in modernist poetics, by a speaker who is simply a locus of consciousness. This progression represents a broad historical evolution and cannot really serve, therefore, to distinguish between two genres or modes, i.e., the dramatic monologue and the "mask lyric."

Alan Sinfield suggests that, like equivalent movements in twentieth-century novels and drama, "modernist dramatic monologue deliberately undermines the naturalistic conception of character." Noting the existence of lyrical dramatic monologues such as those of Tennyson, Sinfield makes an appropriate comparison with drama: just as the latter does not have to be naturalistic, but can be lyrical, so we can expect to find more, or less, lyrical types of dramatic monologue. He concludes that poems like "Tithonus," Eliot's "A Song for Simeon" and Pound's "La Fraisne"—or, we might add, "Ulysses," "Childe Roland," *La Jeune Parque*—"are varieties of dramatic monologue, not some other genre."[38]

Ultimately, in cases where the speaker of the poem is identified only in very vague terms, the reader must decide for himself who is speaking. Such an instance is Mörike's "Lied eines Verliebten," mentioned by Hamburger, in which

> the title's vague reference to "a man in love" can be a more or less transparent camouflage for the empirical I of the poet. In short, despite the role-form the genuine lyric instance may occur in which we can say nothing definite about the relation of the lyric I to the I of the poet.

The amount of distance created by the use of a persona depends on our assumptions regarding his fictionality, as illustrated by Mörike's "Man in Love"; and Hamburger draws a sharp distinction between lyric poetry and narrative prose or drama precisely with respect to fictionality. Her basic position, stated briefly, is that "narrative and dramatic literature afford us the experience of fiction or of non-reality, whereas this is not the case with lyric poetry." Lyric poetry "creates no fictive persons existing in the mode of mimesis as opposed to that of reality." As regards narrative fiction, Hamburger claims that the introduction of an "I" as narrator in a novel destroys fictionality, the mimetic *illusion* of reality, because the narrative act of an "I," whether real or fictive, is in form the statement of a *real* "I." It follows that the first-person novel, according to Hamburger, is not fiction. Like the dramatic monologue (and the ballad), it occupies an intermediary position between fiction and lyric. These "special forms" are

> special with reference to their logical structure, which in the case of the ballad and its related forms is the fictional, and in that of the first-person narrative the statement structure. More precisely, they are special forms because they have "disavowed" their innate structure and gained the right of residing in the respective otherwise-structured genre: the ballad in the lyric, the first-person narrative in the fictional genre.

Like the ballad, the dramatic monologue, or "role poem" (*Rollengedicht*), has the logical structure of fiction but resides in the lyrical genre. It is written in the first person, yet this first person is not, as in a lyric poem, a "genuine statement-subject" but a "feigned" one, a fictional character.[39] Such remarks suggest that the dramatic monologue may have links not only with lyric poetry and with drama but also with the novel, particularly the first-person novel. Conceivably the flowering of the dramatic monologue form in the nineteenth century could have as much to do with the growth of the novel as with the popularity of anthologies of stage monologues.

Hamburger combines the mimetic genres of drama and narrative fiction under the rubric of "epic" in order to oppose them to the lyrical genre with its "real I." The status of the monologue's speaker as a "feigned statement-subject" has important implications for the language of the dramatic monologue, which supposedly belongs to the persona but for which, ultimately, the poet is solely responsible.

# III. The language of the dramatic monologue

Pierre Larthomas points out that, while both monologue and dialogue, in a stage play, communicate something indirectly to the audience, dialogue is also a "moyen de communication entre les personnages," whereas monologue does not have this directly communicative function and is simply "pensée verbalisée." In a typical stage monologue, a character's thoughts are as it were "overheard" by the audience. He analyzes the situation as follows:

> les personnages parlent "comme si c'était vrai"; mais il n'est pas finalement vrai qu'ils parlent; ils semblent parler, mais en réalité récitent, et récitent un texte qui a été écrit pour être récité, étant entendu que cette récitation doit donner l'impression d'être une improvisation, c'est-à-dire le contraire de ce qu'elle est réellement.[40]

The dramatic monologue shares these enigmatic features, for although it is not written to be spoken, it is written to be read as though it were spoken, in the case of poems with an interlocutor, or thought, in the case of soliloquies. Yet at the same time, the reader is aware that the poem's protagonist is not ultimately responsible for his own words.

Perhaps the most characteristic feature of the speech of a dramatic monologue results from this inherent dichotomy between the voice of the poem's speaker and that of the poet, inevitably present. We have seen that this split operates, in Browning's dramatic monologues, to produce the discrepancy between what the speaker reveals and understands about himself, which necessarily implies the presence, within the poem, of a consciousness "beyond what the speaker can lay claim to," namely the "poet's projection into the poem."[41] This split is also apparent on the level of language, even in dramatic monologues where there is no particular emphasis on unconscious self-revelation, simply because the dramatic monologue is a poetic form whereas speakers normally use prose. Rader comments on this with respect to "My Last Duchess":

> If we ask ourselves whether in reading the poem we imagina-
> tively hear the words of the poem as spoken by the Duke, we
> discover of course that we do. If we then ask if we hear the
> rhymes in the poem as part of the Duke's speech, we discover
> that we do not. This small but potent fact suggests even without
> further analysis that the poet's presence in the poem is a funda-
> mental aspect of its form.[42]

Martin, agreeing with this assessment, adds that, in the dramatic
monologue, "language . . . seems to operate both at a level that is
consciously 'poetic' in some traditional sense and at a separate
syntactic, semantic, or merely 'message' level"[43]—a comment tend-
ing to corroborate Hamburger's view of the dramatic monologue as
occupying a position mid-way between lyrical and fictional forms.

These two levels of language can be more or less emphasized,
relative to each other. Although the Duke, for example, speaks in
rhymed couplets, the syntactic line rarely corresponds to the verse
line, so that the "poetic" level of language is played down and the
impression conveyed is almost one of natural speech:

> That's my last Duchess painted on the wall,
> Looking as if she were alive. I call
> That piece a wonder, now: Frà Pandolf's hands
> Worked busily a day, and there she stands.

The effect of natural speech can be achieved not only by the
rhythm, of course, but also by the use of repetitions, interruptions,
relatively simple syntactic structures and vocabulary, and other
devices—devices which tend, paradoxically, to become a matter of
literary convention. Such elements will be analyzed in the chapter
on Browning; meanwhile, an example of the opposite trend, Titho-
nus addressing Eos:

> Once more the old mysterious glimmer steals
> From thy pure brows, and from thy shoulders pure,
> And bosom beating with a heart renew'd.
> Thy cheek begins to redden thro' the gloom,
> Thy sweet eyes brighten slowly close to mine,
> Ere yet they blind the stars, and the wild team
> Which love thee, yearning for thy yoke, arise,

> And shake the darkness from their loosen'd manes,
> And beat the twilight into flakes of fire.

Clearly, not all dramatic monologues attempt to imitate oral speech. Like the dialogue of stage drama, the dramatic monologue can either strive to give, as far as possible, the flavour of spoken language, or forgo any such pretension to oral realism and opt unequivocally for the style of "l'écrit," as do such playwrights as Giraudoux and Claudel. Tennyson's monologues, for example "Tithonus," "Ulysses," "Locksley Hall," are written in an elevated, lyrical, literary style which makes no effort to reproduce the syntax or vocabulary of spoken language. Mallarmé and Valéry also choose a literary rather than a colloquial style; the "split" within a single utterance illustrated by the rhyming couplets of "My Last Duchess" can be felt even more strongly in a poem like *La Jeune Parque* which makes no concessions to oral speech.

Giraudoux gives his chief reason for adopting a "written" style of discourse as the desire to exploit the nuances of written language. In his view the spoken language is poorer, lexically and syntactically, because the speaker does not have time to choose his words carefully or to make corrections, as the author of any written text may do, nor is he generally interested in the style of his utterance, as long as he makes himself understood. Even if he were capable of a more elaborate diction, Larthomas suggests that "une véritable contrainte sociale" prevents him from indulging in it, for fear of being thought pretentious by his listeners. In the language of stage drama, however,

> l'auteur a le temps d'opérer un choix stylistique, s'efforce d'éviter les mots trop usés et les expressions toutes faites, donne à son texte une valeur esthétique, parce qu'il sait qu'il écrit pour un public qui n'a pas, à l'égard des paroles qu'il entend, les mêmes réactions qu'un simple interlocuteur.[44]

We can accept that the characters in a play by Giraudoux or Claudel "ont . . . leur langage . . . qui n'est par le nôtre," because in theatre "il n'y a point d'invraisemblance dès que la vraisemblance n'est point cherchée."[45] The reader of a poem, moreover, does not have the same expectations regarding "vraisemblance" as the spectator at a play, or even the reader of a prose text. If a certain linguistic "invraisemblance" is possible in theatre, where the language is spoken, as if spontaneously, with all the accompanying non-verbal elements of gesture, intonation, facial expression, décor, etc., it is certainly acceptable in the dramatic monologue which, though representing speech or thought, is intended to be read, and read as a poem. Concerning the dialogue genre, Alexandre Lazaridès sums up the situation in a striking formula which also applies to the dramatic monologue: "ce que le dialogue cherche, ce n'est pas tant l'union des contraires, écriture et parole, qu'une substitution hallucinatoire de la parole par l'écriture."[46] We shall see when studying individual poems of Browning, Laforgue, Eliot, Pound, Mallarmé and Valéry, how this substitution operates and to what extent, if at all, the impression of oral speech is produced in writing by each poet.

# CHAPTER TWO

# Self-assertion: Robert Browning and Ezra Pound

## I. Browning

Browning's works can be roughly divided into three main periods. In his early years—up to 1842 when he reached the age of thirty—he wrote several long poems, e.g., *Pauline* and *Sordello*, and plays such as *Strafford, Pippa Passes* and *A Blot in the 'Scutcheon*, none of which was very successful. Indeed, his youthful attempts at poetry and drama clearly represent, with hindsight, early gropings towards a suitable form. The collections of verse from his middle period include most of the dramatic monologues for which he is now well-known—those of the *Dramatic Lyrics* (1842), *Dramatic Romances* (1845), and *Men and Women* (1855), and these are the poems which will concern us in this chapter. His later works, including some of the monologues from *Dramatis Personae* (1864), such as "Rabbi Ben Ezra" and "Abt Vogler," and certain longer poems like *Prince Hohenstiel-Schwangau* (1871) and *Fifine at the Fair* (1872), introduce significant differences in style and construction, which we shall examine in due course.

"The first criterion by which to judge a Browning monologue," affirms Roma King, "is the effectiveness of its characterization." Browning's very failures in stage drama illustrate that his main interest concerned the portrayal of character rather than the development of plot. Thus Edwin Muir points out that he "was concerned with the *dramatis personae* rather than with the play; he set himself to find out what the *dramatis personae* really thought of the play, privately."[1] Browning himself declares in the Preface of 1837 to *Strafford* that the play "is one of Action in Character, rather than Character in Action"—a state of affairs more appropriate to the dramatic monologue than to a stage play.

Browning developed a range of economical and effective techniques for portraying "Action in Character." Of one of his earliest dramatic monologues, "The Bishop Orders His Tomb at Saint Praxed's Church," Ruskin declared that it contained "nearly all that I said of the central Renaissance in thirty pages of the *Stones of Venice* put into as many lines."[2] All the Bishop's sins and vices— hypocrisy, greed, pride, envy, fornication, sensuousness, lack of devotion to his faith, financial corruption, self-centredness—are conveyed in one hundred and twenty-five lines, and the poem is in fact more complex yet, for our condemnation of the Bishop is tempered by a certain amusement at his childishness and unself-conscious ignorance of his own failings. Indeed, it is largely this element of naiveté which encourages the reader to perceive him as a character rather than as simply a typical representative of a certain historical era. A further complication, and the poem's main source of enjoyment, lies in the discrepancy we perceive between the persona's self-image and our own assessment of him.

Browning achieves such vivid and complete characterization, and the simultaneous irony at the character's expense, by his attention to significant linguistic details. The Bishop's emphasis on the rarity of "Peach-blossom marble" or on the size of the "lump . . . of *lapis lazuli*" he has purloined implies that his aesthetic taste is confined to articles obtainable only at great expense. Ironic juxtapositions can also be revealing: "Peace, peace seems all," declares the Bishop, "Saint Praxed's ever was the church for peace; / . . . I fought/With tooth and nail to save my niche, ye know. . . ." Hesitations in the protagonist's speech contribute to the production of a character on a page, disclosing secret motives, as in the Bishop's hasty selfcorrection: "Nephews—sons mine . . . ah God, I know not!" Obsessive repetitions of certain words, such as the Bishop's references to his bath, give away his true concerns. Interjections can say more than the Bishop intends ("Some lump, ah God, of *lapis lazuli*"); as can the comparisons he makes, with Browning's help: the "lump" of *lapis lazuli*, he boasts, is "Big as a Jew's head cut off at the nape, / Blue as a vein o'er the Madonna's breast," lines which emphasize not only his basic covetousness, but also his callous, dismissive attitude towards Jews, and his aesthetic and sensuous approach to matters of religion.

Such details serve to define the Bishop's character and, as Ruskin points out, give the flavour of a whole age. Furthermore, they tend to fix the persona in time and space, providing him with a "realistic" background: the Bishop's typical Renaissance attitudes, together with the date "15—" at the beginning of the poem, establish the era in which he lived, and the various mentions of Italy and things Italian define the place ("Rome" in the subtitle, "Frascati villa," grapes, olives, figs, "popes and cardinals and priests"). Although the Bishop is not named, his church is, and the fact that he is Bishop of Saint Praxed's particularizes him more effectively than a personal name.

In many Browning monologues the speakers are thus pinpointed in space or time by the mention of dates and place-names. "My Last Duchess" is set in Ferrara and the Duke with his "nine-hundred-years-old name" has the pride—and the cruelty—of a noble family of the Italian Renaissance. The mention of the artists Frà Pandolf and Claus of Innsbruck, though the names are invented, adds a touch of apparent realism. "Count Gismond," companion-piece to "My Last Duchess," is subtitled "Aix en Provence." The poem "The Laboratory" bears the sub-title "Ancien Régime," which fixes both the date and the country; its pendant, "The Confessional," takes place in Spain, like the "Soliloquy of the Spanish Cloister." In the poem "Up at a Villa—Down in the City," the respective merits of these locations are debated by "an Italian person of quality."

Loy D. Martin comments on the use of deictics and determiners to denote the speaker's familiarity with the setting in which he is placed. He quotes from "Andrea del Sarto"—and of course hundreds of examples can be found in other poems:

> My youth, my hope, my art, being all toned down
> To *yonder* sober pleasant Fiesole.
> There's *the* bell clinking from *the* chapel-top;
> *That* length of convent-wall across the way
> Holds *the* trees safer, huddled more inside;
> *The* last monk leaves *the* garden.

He points out that this is "an element of style . . . not inherently related to poetic form,"[3] which seems at first glance to contradict Jean Cohen's assertion relative to the specifically poetic function of the demonstrative adjectives in "Voir sur ces canaux / Dormir ces vaisseaux." The difference is, of course, that in the Baudelaire poem no context is given to which "ces canaux" could refer; the country evoked in the poem is an imaginary one (whether or not Baudelaire took his vision of Holland as a point of departure). It is the failure of the deictics, here, to perform their normal demonstrative function, that contributes to "cette impression de réalité vague, nébuleuse," typical of lyric poetry. In Browning's dramatic monologues, however, as in a novel, a context *is* given: the speaker is identified, the place, Fiesole, already mentioned in the poem. The use of deictics and definite articles here serves to place Andrea all the more firmly in his context.

Precise details concerning the speaker's location and era tend to particularize him, endowing him with a separate existence of his own and thereby distancing him from the reader. More specifically, the choice of a genuine historical figure as the poem's speaker "objectifies" him further, since the reader will not be inclined to identify with a character whose objective and autonomous existence is vouchsafed by historical documents—and whose identity cannot therefore be confused with that of the poet either. "Historical perspective is one form of distancing," affirms J. Hillis Miller.[4]

Browning selects from history not the great figures whose attributes and careers are already well-known, but less famous people such as Andrea del Sarto or Frà Lippo Lippi; this choice allows his imagination some freedom to create a fully-fledged "character" from a few known facts. Andrea, a sixteenth-century Italian painter whose work was admired for its faultless technique, was commissioned by Francis I to buy paintings in Italy for the French court, but together with his beautiful wife Lucrezia, spent the money entrusted to him and never returned to France. From this information, Browning has created the lifelike portrait of the weak-willed Andrea, over-fond of his wife, sensing that he has sacrificed his own personal integrity and probably his greatness as a painter for her sake, but ready to accept this situation if she will grant him some token of affection. In this poem, again, references to Italian places (Fiesole) and painters ("Rafael," "Michel Agnolo, "Leonard") and coins ("thirteen scudi for the ruff"), in addition to frequent mentions of King Francis, help to establish Andrea's historical identity. Similarly, Fra Lippo Lippi talks of his employer, Cosimo of the Medici, and his pupil, Guido.

Most of Browning's characters are further particularized by their language. Some use a far more colloquial language than others; some introduce more technical words. Certain speakers pepper their monologues with interjections; Fra Lippi, for example, is known for his "Zooks!"; the monk in the Spanish cloister exclaims "Whew!" and "Forsooth!" Both these characters make exceptionally frequent use of colloquial expressions, even slang such as "Gr-r-r —you swine!" and "gullet's gripe." "He's Judas to a tittle, that man is!" remarks Lippi, and apart from being colloquial, this observation serves to particularize him further: with his artist's eye he constantly picks out faces suitable for certain pictorial subjects:

> I'd like his face—
> His, elbowing on his comrade in the door
> With the pike and lantern,—for the slave that holds
> John Baptist's head a-dangle by the hair.

Very often a speaker's vocabulary reveals his profession or occupation: "Let my hands frame your face in your hair's gold," says Andrea. The Spanish monk finds "a great text in Galatians" and swears by "God's blood." Many of the men of religion use God's name as an interjection ("Some lump, ah God, of *lapis lazuli*") and tend to produce phrases in Latin from time to time ("*Salve tibi!*" "*Iste perfecit opus!*"). The speaker's vocabulary can also reflect his particular preoccupation of the moment, such as the Bishop's extraordinary catalogue of stones: basalt, marble, onion-stone, *lapis lazuli*, travertine, jasper, gritstone.

King points to Andrea's frequent use of "words associated with value: *worth, pay, gold, silver, gain, reward*," as well as to the repetition of words conveying his emotional climate, such as "*silver, dream, quietly, evening, grey, greyness, twilight, autumn*." He also comments on the relatively small number of verbs of action in this poem compared to "Fra Lippo Lippi," reflecting the very different personalities of the two protagonists. Indeed, Lippi produces "numerous words and expressions which are found nowhere else in Browning's poetry" and which "emphasize important aspects of Lippo's personality—his mental alertness, his creativeness, his catholicity—or . . . serve to place him more realistically in his milieu." The number of these words, King concludes, "indicates the care Browning took to make Lippo an individual, and at the same time serves as a warning against too facile generalizations about Browning's diction."[5]

Despite the validity of such distinctions between the style and vocabulary of Browning's different protagonists, however, it remains undeniably true that a basic similarity of diction underlies all their individual utterances, attesting to "the doubleness of language that so emphatically keeps the Victorian poet's own style before us even as each successive speaker reveals the extremities of his own specialized voice."[6] Thus, perhaps, the poet seeks to accentuate the split, characteristic of the dramatic monologue form, between the subject of utterance and the subject of enunciation.

Certainly Browning's characters speak in a conversational idiom; most of his monologues assume a silent auditor, whom the speaker addresses directly. They therefore constitute, in fact, one side of a dialogue, and like the dialogue of a naturalistic drama, they adopt certain features of oral discourse, such as repetitions, colloquial vocabulary, and a very loose, disjointed syntax. In his preference for an intimate, conversational tone, rather than a specifically "poetic" style, Browning foreshadows most modern English and American poets. Eliot appreciated this particular aspect of Browning's work, saying that he was the only nineteenth-century poet "to devise a way of speech which might be useful for others," and that this was largely achieved through his "use of non-poetic material" and his insistence on "the relation of poetry to speech."[7]

Thus the rhythms of Browning's verse, in the poems of his middle period which concern us here, approximate to those of the speaking voice. Pauses occur where the voice would pause, as in the opening of "Andrea del Sarto": "But do not let us quarrel any more,/ No, my Lucrezia; bear with me for once," or that of "My Last Duchess," or the following passage from "Fra Lippo Lippi":

> Who am I?
> Why, one, sir, who is lodging with a friend
> Three streets off—he's a certain  .  .  .  how d'ye call?
> Master—a  .  .  .  Cosimo of the Medici,
> I' the house that caps the corner. Boh! you were best!

The syntax of the speaker's sentences in a Browning monologue is often disrupted, a feature that normally typifies oral as opposed to written language—though if the disruptions and digressions become bewilderingly frequent as in some of Browning's later works, the effect is lost, one feature of oral discourse being its aim of immediate communication to a listener. Oral speech cannot be transcribed directly into a written text: the repetitions, interruptions and half-formed phrases which sound natural in conversation become not only tedious in writing but also unintelligible, partly at least for the lack of supporting intonation, gestures, and facial expressions. Orality can only by signalled by a judicious distribution of its various features—ellipsis, repetition, interruptions, colloquial vocabulary, loose syntax, etc.—a procedure that tends, finally, to become a matter of literary convention.

The frequency of interruptions in the flow of speech, as the speaker changes topic or corrects himself, can be discerned at a glance in Browning's poems from the punctuation: dashes and *points de suspension* abound. The Bishop at St. Praxed's often interrupts himself because of embarrassment:

> Nephews—sons mine  .  .  .  ah God, I know not! Well—
> She, men would have to be your mother once,

Old Gandolf envied me, so fair she was!

. . . . . . . . . . . . . . . . . . . .

Draw close: that conflagration of my church
—What then? So much was saved if aught were missed!

The Duke of Ferrara hesitates in defining what exactly he reproved
in the Duchess:

>                    She thanked men—good! but thanked
> Somehow—I know not how—as if she ranked
> My gift of a nine-hundred-years-old name
> With anybody's gift.

Apart from suggesting "the relation of poetry to speech," Brown-
ing's oral realism, i.e., his use of the rhythms and diction of every-
day speech, in these poems of his middle period, helps to establish
his characters as life-like figures. To this end also he endows them,
very often, with a realistic name and a social occupation or status.
Thus we have an Evelyn Hope, a Count Gismond, a Bishop Blou-
gram; we hear monks and bishops, soldiers, painters; wives, lovers;
dukes, counts, fashionable ladies. He frequently takes his charac-
ters from history, which automatically guarantees their objective,
"real" existence as autonomous entities, independent both of their
creator and of the reader; he gives his speakers specific personality
traits which they reveal in everything they say and sometimes in
their very manner of speaking; and finally, whether or not the char-
acters are historical, he takes care to pinpoint them in space and
time, which particularizes them even further and sets them at a
distance from the reader.

All the realistic detail supplied by Browning paradoxically en-
courages the reader to approach the poem as he would a fiction, a
semblance of life, because the procedure of naming characters and
fitting them into a situation, a time and a place is typically novelis-
tic and mimetic. Thus we find critics asserting that "it is as novels
. . . that many of Browning's poems offer themselves," or "Brown-
ing was not a poet of mythological imagination; the few moments in
which he seems to deserve that name only emphasize his normal
character as a novelist in verse."[8] Dorothy Mermin lists the "novelis-

tic qualities of Browning's dramatic monologues with auditors: many of them "enact an incident . . . elaborately characterize the speaker . . . recount past incidents, and . . . contain the rudiments of a fictional autobiography."[9] Like characters in a novel, Browning's personae have a past, which is revealed to us, and as in a novel (or an autobiography), we attend to the gradual unfolding of the story of the speaker's life (e.g., in "Andrea del Sarto," "The Bishop of St. Praxed's," "Fra Lippo Lippi") or of a particular significant event in his life ("My Last Duchess"). As in a novel, each speaker presents a well-defined, three-dimensional personality: "one whole man," as Pound was later to say of them. Mermin voices the reservation that monologues do not depict character as "a process of becoming," as the novel can, for the monologue "lacks the resources to develop the temporal dimension, the notion of life as a continuing process of growth and change."[10] To a certain extent there is a sense of temporal continuity in Browning's poems; they often begin in mid-stream, with a reaction to an event that has already begun or a speech already made, such as:

> But do not let us quarrel any more . . .
> > ("Andrea del Sarto")
> Draw round my bed: is Anselm keeping back?
> > ("The Bishop Orders His Tomb at
> > Saint Praxed's Church")
> You need not clap your torches to my face
> > ("Fra Lippo Lippi")

This kind of opening gives the reader the impression of butting in on a life which is a continuous process. However, from what we know of Lippi's, Andrea's or the Bishop's past, they have not changed over the years, nor do they develop in the course of the poems. Andrea could well have had similar conversations with Lucrezia before, and could again. Perhaps the dramatic monologue can more justifiably be compared, not with the novel but with the short story, which shares the monologue's limitations in scope; both enact incidents that, in Mermin's words, "can reveal the speaker's character but . . . do not alter it."

Each speaker in a dramatic monologue by Browning has a story to tell about himself; he is involved in a conflict with someone, and sometimes the conflict leads—or has led—to extreme consequences, as in "My Last Duchess," "Porphyria's Lover," "The Laboratory." The speaker's involvement in a drama again distances him from the reader, since in each case the story patently represents the character's own, unique experience. Clearly, the more distinctly the poems are perceived as fictions, the less they will strike the reader as being autobiographical utterances of the poet himself; moreover, Browning has created such a gallery of rogues that the reader is highly unlikely either to identify with them or to assume that they reflect the personality of the author. In other words, in addition to the distance created by particularizing his characters or by choosing historical figures, Browning establishes yet another kind of distance between himself (or us) and his speakers, which could be termed: moral (or ironic) distance.

When Langbaum makes the general assertion that "most successful dramatic monologues deal with speakers who are in some way reprehensible,"[11] he may be going too far in claiming this as an essential feature of the genre as a whole, but the statement does apply to the dramatic monologues of Browning. The Bishop at St. Praxed's, Fra Lippi, Andrea del Sarto, the Duke of Ferrara, the speakers in "The Laboratory" and "The Soliloquy of the Spanish Cloister"—all display either vices or weaknesses of character which the reader cannot fail to notice and condemn. The speakers themselves, however, usually remain unaware of their faults and betray them unintentionally, through their often unspoken assumptions and attitudes, through hesitations and slips of the tongue, or through undue repetition. The Duke of Ferrara tacitly— and arrogantly—assumes that he had every right to deal with his first wife as he wished, and still expects to marry a second time; Andrea's evident pleasure at his wife's smiles—whose significance he misinterprets—illustrates his indulgent attitude towards her and the general gullibility and weakness of character that have ruined his career; the Bishop at St. Praxed's gives away the true facts about himself by his hesitations and slips of the tongue: "Nephews—sons mine . . . ah God, I know not!"; "Did I say basalt for my slab, sons? Black—/'Twas ever antique-black I meant!"

The fact that the speaker's unconscious faults are obvious to the reader shows that the poet has deliberately suggested them by his choice and arrangement of the character's words, by repetition, emphasis, unexpected juxtapositions. In other words, in Browning's dramatic monologues "there is at work . . . a consciousness . . . beyond what the speaker can lay claim to." And this consciousness "is the mark of the poet's projection into the poem; and is also the pole which attracts our projection, since we find in it the counterpart of our own consciousness."[12] Dramatic monologues like those of Browning's middle period involve a certain collusion, then, between author and reader; again this links them to the (traditional) novel for, as John Bayley points out, the "most fundamental thing about characters in fiction is that by a complex process of rapport between the authors and ourselves we know what to think of them." A character is "a product of society and social observation," and his behaviour "is precisely defined and limited by its interrelation with the society he moves in, and which we, as well as moving in, can perceive through the author and his novel as if from outside."[13] Thus Browning, in Clarence Tracy's words, "invites the reader to stand by his side and observe at a . . . distance the antics of the speaker, as he manoeuvres, defends and betrays himself."[14]

It might be objected, and this is a criticism frequently levelled at Browning, that all too often he fails to maintain the distance between himself and his speaker, and uses the latter to present his own views. T.S. Eliot saw this as such an essential feature of Browning's monologues that he chose for this reason alone to class the dramatic monologue in general among works belonging to the second of the *Three Voices of Poetry*, "the voice of the poet addressing an audience" rather than to the third, "the voice of the poet when he attempts to create a dramatic character speaking in verse"— which is surely where the dramatic monologue ought to belong, since its very status as an intermediary genre between lyric and epic forms depends on its creation of a fictive speaker. Eliot claims further that the poet "speaking, as Browning does, in his own voice, cannot bring a character to life" and that "when we read a dramatic monologue by Browning, we cannot suppose that we are listening to any other voice than that of Browning himself."[15] Part of the reason for these claims must be that Eliot does not distinguish between different periods in Browning's works, concentrating exclusively on "Caliban" from *Dramatis Personae* (1864) as an example. If we look, however, at poems from the earlier collections under consideration here, the *Dramatic Lyrics* and *Romances* and *Men and Women*, we find that Browning can and does "bring a character to life." The Bishop at St. Praxed's, Andrea, Fra Lippo Lippi are brought to life as completely as many characters in novels, even if they do not develop in the course of the poems; and the voice we hear is clearly not simply "that of Browning himself" in poems such as the "Soliloquy of the Spanish Cloister," "My Last Duchess," "Andrea del Sarto," "The Bishop Orders His Tomb" and many others. Indeed, as we have just seen, the poet's presence in these poems is felt not because he speaks *through* the characters, as Eliot says we hear him talking aloud through Caliban,[16] in the sense that he voices his own thoughts through their mouths; but because, by his manipulation of their language, he implicitly *criticizes* their attitudes. We therefore hear two antagonistic voices simultaneously— that of the character and that of the poet.

The problem of which Eliot complains arises when the two voices are not antagonistic, when the protagonist's speech coincides with known views of Browning himself. Eliot briefly mentions "Fra Lippo Lippi," saying that here "Browning . . . is speaking in the role of an historical personage." It is true that Lippi expresses views on art—and, by extension, on life—known to have been held by Browning; does this mean, though, that we cannot hear Lippi's voice or sense his individual perspective? On the contrary, his character and voice are established so expertly—by his attitudes to people, his good-humoured self-confidence, his energetic tone, his constant references to monks and priors, his story of his boyhood—that there is absolutely no danger of our taking him solely as a mouthpiece for Browning; the distance between author and protagonist is maintained in spite of the similarity of their views. The collusion between author and reader also remains unaffected, as they smile indulgently at Lippi behind his back, for example, when he hastily corrects himself: "Like the Prior's niece . . . Saint Lucy, I would say."

This author-reader collusion contributes to the dramatic quality of Browning's poems, constituting a type of dramatic irony. In a stage play, dramatic irony occurs when, at a given point in the action, the audience has acquired information regarding a protagonist's situation of which the latter remains ignorant. This is precisely what happens in poems like "The Bishop Orders His Tomb," "The Soliloquy of the Spanish Cloister" or "My Last Duchess," except that here the thing which the speaker fails to perceive usually concerns some aspect of his own charcter—which he alone, nevertheless, reveals. The Bishop is unaware of his own worldliness and hypocrisy, and his vanity makes him more inclined than we are to believe that his "nephews" will carry out his requests; the Soliloquist seems to us spiteful, petty-minded, and vindictive compared to the simple, kindly Brother Lawrence, whereas he himself has a totally different view; the Duke of Ferrara and his first Duchess also inspire in us quite different reactions from the ones the Duke invites.

Drama involves conflict, and the conflict in most of Browning's dramatic monologues of this period lies in this discrepancy between the speaker's apprehension of his situation and the reader's understanding of it. There is no internal conflict, or development, within these characters; on the contrary, they are static, their personalities and their opinions being already fully developed. Rather than struggling with inner conflicts, they tend to be very sure of themselves and strive only to impose their own viewpoint on others. The Bishop of St. Praxed's is not torn by remorse for his attitude to life, he merely wants to have it accepted by others; and the same applies to Fra Lippo Lippi. Langbaum rightly says of such dramatic monologues that "the speaker . . . starts with an established point of view, and is not concerned with its truth but with trying to impress it on the outside world."[17]

The discrepancy between what the speaker unconsciously reveals about himself and the reader's assessment of him represents only one of the dramatic elements in Browning's poetry. The character—named, particularized, endowed with a personality, located in time and space, as in a realist drama—is always placed in a dramatic situation, using "dramatic" now in the sense of "vivid" and "full of conflict." Browning usually depicts a concrete situation depending on external events, such as Fra Lippo Lippi's arrest; the sense of drama may be heightened by the choice of extraordinary happenings like Porphyria's murder or the Bishop's imminent death. The events implied in "The Laboratory," "Porphyria's Lover" or "My Last Duchess" could form the plots of exciting fictional stories or historical dramas. As for conflict, there may be none within the character, but he usually finds himself in a position of conflict with others or in a tense situation whose outcome may have considerable impact on his life—or, in the case of the Bishop ordering his tomb, on his posthumous status. His conflict is not with his conscience but with his nephews; that of the speaker in the Spanish cloister—with Brother Lawrence. Porphyria's lover, having just committed murder, awaits developments; the speaker in "The Laboratory" plans to murder a rival; neither of them is inwardly perturbed by the moral implications of his or her actions. The immediate source of tension in Fra Lippi's situation is his apprehension by the night patrol, but it becomes evident that his nature and life-style also bring him into conflict with the morality of his society—though he himself cheerfully accepts and excuses his own sensuality. Another, related, source of tension consists in the artistic constraints imposed on him.

The "outside world" on which the typical Browning speaker strives to impress an "established point of view" is usually represented by the interlocutor, since Browning's monologues are "spoken": they constitute one side of a dialogue. The introduction of dialogue enhances the dramatic effect of the poem. Dialogue is the distinctive form of stage drama, and Browning attempts to give the flavour of it in his monologues by inserting remarks either directly addressed to an interlocutor or patently prompted by an implied comment or gesture on his part. Thus Andrea addresses Lucrezia when she evidently loses the thread of his story:

> Still, all I care for, if he spoke the truth,
> (What he? why who but Michel Agnolo?
> Do you forget already words like those?). . . .

The Duke of Ferrara reacts to a self-effacing gesture of his interlocutor when he says "Nay, we'll go / Together down, sir," and the Bishop of St. Praxed's has his eye on the movements of the reluctant Anselm:

Draw round my bed: Is Ansel keeping back?

. . . . . . . . . . . . . . . . . . . . . . . . . .

. . . . . . . . . . What do they whisper thee,

Child of my bowels, Anselm?

These asides help to remind the reader of the listeners' presence, and of the fact that the speech of a spoken dramatic monologue, like that of a stage play, is directed towards an interlocutor and therefore aims at an effect, i.e., that of convincing or impressing, of interrogating or informing. A lyric poem is not dramatic in this sense; it does not seek to persuade, it simply *is*, whereas the "dramatic monologue . . . corresponds in its style of address to the dialogue, where each speaker is absorbed in his own strategy."[18]

If the dramatic monologue, in Hamburger's account, hesitates between lyric and epic (narrative and dramatic) forms, those of Browning's middle period definitely lean towards the epic—in contrast with those of Tennyson, for example, such as "Ulysses," which tend towards the lyric.[19]

Indeed, Browning's world in these poems of his middle period resembles that of realist fiction, whether narrative or dramatic, in that it constitutes a "mimesis" of reality, presenting well-defined characters intended to simulate real human beings and recognizable as "individuals" distinct from the author and distanced from the reader. The notion of "character" seems central to fiction: Fernando Ferrara asserts that in fiction "the character is used as a structuring element: the objects and the events of fiction exist—in one way or another—because of the character." In the context of the *nouveau roman*, "Robbe-Grillet's series of objects and Natalie Sarraute's 'tropisms' have all structuring support implicit in a character which is proposed as an eye or an ear and—because of that— is selective, constructive, in short, structuring."[20] But of course, a "character" who is merely an eye or an ear is scarcely a character in any known sense of the word; the eye or ear may structure the fiction, but can we speak any longer of "character"?

Hélène Cixous throws doubt on the notion that "character" is essential to fiction:

"Character" occupies a privileged position in the novel or the play: without "character," passive or active, no text. He is the major agent of the work, at the center of a stage that is commanded by his presence, his story, his interest. Upon his "life" depends the life of the text—so they say. This is why he should not be too mortal. It is therefore disturbing to many that, at the present time, he has disappeared.[21]

And "with the removal of the question of 'character' " in modern fiction, "the question of the *nature of fiction* comes to the fore." For our purposes this brings to the fore also the question of the nature of the dramatic monologue: must it depend, as in the poems of Browning we have been examining, on character-revelation? Cixous adds some further comments about "character" that are very relevant to what we have discovered in Browning:

> If "character" has a sense, then it is as a Figure that can be used in semiotics: the "personage" functions as a social sign, in relation to other signs, within a text which, if it admits of the existence of "character," necessarily goes back to pure representationalism. Such a text is governed by a coding process that assures its communicability; . . . the more "character" fulfills the norms, the better the reader recognizes it and recognizes himself. The commerce established between book and reader is thus facilitated. . . .
> The ideology underlying this fetishization of "character" is that of an "I" who is a *whole* subject . . . conscious, knowable; and the enunciatory "I" *expresses himself* in the text, just as the world is *represented* complementarily in the text in a form equivalent to pictorial representation, as a simulacrum.

Browning's personae may be "split," like those of any dramatic monologue, because they share a voice with the poet, but Browning seems to have believed, at this stage in his career at least, both in the notion of individual personality and in the possibility of conveying it in language, of giving the words in which the "enunciatory 'I' expresses himself." In the poems we have studied, the assumption is that language can communicate a man's inner self, and that the "inner self" does exist. J. Hillis Miller observes that nowadays,

> in the epoch of Gide and Sartre, we are accustomed to the idea that a man may have no given "nature," as does a stone or a tree.

But in Browning's day, and in England, the idea of the indeter-
minacy of selfhood was a scandalous notion, contrary to the tra-
ditional British conviction that each man has a substantial inner
core of self.[22]

He makes the interesting speculation that Browning, while observ-
ing "character" in people all around him and creating it in his dra-
matic monologues, felt that he himself was lacking in it, or at least in
a definite single self:

> Browning's excessive desire for privacy, as well as his decision to
> write dramatic monologues, may be not so much an attempt to
> hide the positive facts of his private life as an attempt to keep
> hidden his secret failure to have the kind of definite, solid self he
> sees in other people, and feels it is normal to have. . . . [We]
> are forced to conclude that his "selfhood" must be defined as the
> failure to have any one definite self, and as the need to enact, in
> imagination, the roles of the most diverse people in order to
> satisfy all the impulses of his being.

If Browning was aware of his own "failure to have any one defi-
nite self," he must have presumed that the same might be true,
despite appearances, of other people. Such an assumption might
certainly be expected to affect the work of a writer of dramatic
monologues, and we shall see in due course that his later poetry
does differ, regarding the question of character and its self-
expression, from the dramatic monologues of the *Dramatic Lyrics,
Dramatic Romances* and *Men and Women*.

Meanwhile, however, it seems appropriate to discuss at this
point the work of a later poet strongly influenced by the Browning
of these three collections, and who also wrote dramatic mono-
logues: Ezra Pound. Much of his poetry leans, like Browning's, to-
ward mimesis, towards fictionality, narrative, and epic—though he
felt, from the start, the impossibility of creating "whole" characters à
la Browning. With the *Cantos*, Pound eventually evolved a more
complex and more modernist approach to the questions of voice
and poetic persona, though even here his Browningesque origins
are evident.

# II Pound

Pound's debt to Browning, in his early career, was so large that he complained he had "caught Browning's manner as if it were a disease."[23] Several poems in the *Personae* of 1909 have a Browning-esque ring, e.g., "Marvoil," "Mesmerism" (addressed to Browning himself), "Famam Librosque Cano" and "Cino." "When Cino images his women speaking," says Thomas H. Jackson, "they speak Browning's English":[24]

> "Cino?" "Oh, eh Cino Polnesi
> The singer is't you mean?"
> "Ah yes, passed once our way,
> A saucy fellow, but . . .
> (Oh they are all one these vagabonds),
> Pest! 'tis his own songs?
> Or some other's that he sings?
> But *you*, My Lord, how with your city?"

Pound certainly approved of Browning's use of natural, everyday language in poetry, rather than the formal style normally considered "poetic" in the nineteenth century. Pound himself had been guilty of adopting such a style, he says, until Ford Madox Ford's adverse reaction to his early poetry, with its "stilted language that then passed for 'good English,' " sent him back to his "proper effort, namely, toward using the living tongue."[25] Subsequently, his poetry came to sound, very often, like speech as reproduced by Robert Browning in his dramatic monologues. In the *Three Cantos* of 1915, Pound addresses Browning directly, beginning with a characteristically abrupt Browningesque colloquialism, "Hang it all, there can be but one *Sordello*!" and using many devices typically employed by Browning to signal oral speech, such as questions directed at the supposed auditor:

> You had one whole man?
> And I have many fragments, less worth?

and interpolations:

> And half your dates are out, you mix your eras;
> For that great font Sordello sat beside —
> 'Tis an immortal passage, but the font? —
> Is some two centuries outside the picture.

Much of Pound's early poetry, especially in the volume entitled
*Personae* (1909, 1926), consists of dramatic monologues; yet he felt
that Browning had achieved so much with his version of the dra-
matic monologue, the "meditative, / Semi-dramatic, semi-epic
story," that he himself could only wonder "What's left for me to do?
/ Whom shall I hang my shimmering garment on?" (*Three Cantos*,
I). Here we witness Pound's concern with finding an appropriate
persona (illustrated, too, by the title *Personae*). Like Browning,
Pound tends to use historical figures, often poets and musicians, as
personae, and many of the poems enact real incidents from their
lives. Even so, Pound's treatment of his speakers differs in some
ways from that of Browning; to start with, he deals not with "one
whole man" as he considered Browning's characters to be, but with
"many fragments," feeling, as he says in the *Three Cantos* of 1915,
that his "beastly and cantankerous age" precludes the portrayal of
"one whole man." Consequently, perhaps, though attracted by his-
torical subjects, Pound is less interested than Browning in charac-
terization for its own sake, in the objective re-creation of life-like
characters embodying the spirit of their age and whom the modern
reader can judge from his perspective. Pound often tends, having
set up such historical figures in *Personae*, to use them as masks for
his own self-expression, as he himself says with reference to this
collection:

> In the "search for oneself," in the search for "sincere self-
> expression," one gropes, one finds some seeming verity. One
> says "I am" this, that, or the other, and with the words scarcely
> uttered one ceases to be that thing.
> I began this search for the real in a book called *Personae*, cast-
> ing off, as it were, complete masks of the self in each poem.[26]

"The 'personae' . . . function as a loudspeaker that reinforces
Pound's own voice," says Christoph de Nagy, commenting on
Pound's use of historical figures to express a "personal attitude":

"While on the one hand he is, as he says in 'Histrion,' a medium through which certain dead poets can manifest themselves, on the other he turns them into masks." The use of masks is normally associated with Yeats, but De Nagy goes on to say that

> Yeats himself did not go beyond using symbolic personages: Aedh, Michael Robartes and Owen Aherne exist merely as masks of Yeats, whereas Marvoil in "Marvoil" and Bertran de Born in "Sestina: Altaforte" are reanimated beings in addition to fulfilling the function of masks.

He suggests that the Poundian persona stands half-way between that of a Browningesque monologue and "a mask in Yeats's sense."[27] This placing of Pound half-way between Browning and Yeats is echoed by Hugh Witemeyer in his book on Pound's early poetry: "By a sort of useful oversimplification," he suggests, "we may think of Yeats and Browning as opposite ends of a spectrum along which Pound's dramatic monologues can be ranged." He quotes Pound's well-known definition of the dramatic lyric, a definition which, he points out, may "be taken as Pound's attempt to distinguish his own practice from Browning's":[28]

> To me the short so-called dramatic lyric—at any rate the sort of thing I do—is the poetic part of a drama the rest of which (to me the prose part) is left to the reader's imagination or implied or set in a short note. I catch the character I happen to be interested in at the moment he interests me, usually a moment of song, self-analysis, or sudden understanding or revelation.[29]

This emphasis on the moment represents a crucial departure from Browning's practice: his characters, though provoked to speak, of necessity, at some specific moment, tend to expand from that moment, using it as a pretext to review a whole lifetime. The moment is not significant in itself, only as a jumping-off point, in "Andrea del Sarto," "Fra Lippo Lippi," "The Bishop Orders His Tomb," "Soliloquy of the Spanish Cloister." Pound, however, likes to concentrate on a moment of "song": of intense emotion or perception, as in "De Aegypto,"

I, even I, am he who knoweth the roads
Through the sky, and the wind thereof is my body.

I have beheld the Lady of Life,
I, even I, who fly with the swallows.

Green and gray is her raiment
Trailing along the wind.

I, even I, am he who knoweth the roads
Through the sky, and the wind thereof is my body.


Other comparatively ahistorical poems in *Personae* include "La Fraisne," "Paracelsus in Excelsis," "The Tree," "Praise of Ysolt," "And Thus in Ninevah," "Night Litany," "The White Stag," "Francesca"; all of which present a given persona's "moment of song" with little emphasis on character or story. Many of the poems, however, resemble Browning's much more closely in their treatment of the persona, portraying a particularized individual in specific circumstances—though, again, concentrating on a certain dramatic moment in the speaker's life. Witemeyer opposes "La Fraisne" and "Marvoil" with their "respective emphases upon an impersonal ecstasy and a concrete historical personality and situation," suggesting that they represent "relatively pure examples of the extremes to be found in Pound's early monologues" and that the "other personae can be ranged between them."[30]

"Marvoil," one of Pound's most Browningesque poems, presents as speaker a genuine historical figure at a specific moment in his life; he is identified both as "Arnaut the less" and as a "poor clerk," in an opening line which somewhat resembles Browning's "I am poor brother Lippo, by your leave": "A poor clerk I, 'Arnaut the less' they call me." Marvoil is precisely located in "this damn'd inn of Avignon," and various other historical names establish the time and the place. The poem offers details concerning a specific—and intrinsically dramatic—incident in Marvoil's life in a language not only essentially spoken in tone, but also characteristically blunt and vigorous, thus enhancing the impression of a "real" speaker:

> Me! in this damn'd inn of Avignon,
> Stringing long verse for the Burlatz;
> All for one half-bald, knock-knee'd king of the Aragonese,
> Alfonso, Quattro, poke-nose.

Forceful language is typical also of Bertran de Born, the speaker in "Sestina: Altaforte," another poem with a Browningesque opening, "Damn it all! all this our South stinks peace." Again we hear a historical personage speaking, and alluding to a well-known contemporary, Richard Coeur de Lion. Dante put De Born in hell, comments Pound in his epigraph to the poem, "for that he was a stirrer up of strife. . . . Have I dug him up again?" The characterization of the belligerent De Born is vivid, if one-sided; but Pound presents other aspects of his personality in other poems, such as "Na Audiart," also from *Personae*, and "Near Perigord" (*Lustra*). In "Na Audiart" we find "the portrait of a detached, sophisticated, and ironic character," who refers, for example, to his own poem about Audiart as "Just a word in thy praise, girl." Witemeyer suggests that this poem "approaches the Browningesque end of our spectrum in being a portrait of some psychological complexity."[31] Like Browning's dramatic monologues, too, it has narrative interest: arising from a specific incident in De Born's life, the poem relates an episode in the "tale of Bertran de Born and My Lady Maent of Montaignac," as Pound points out in his epigraph.

Yet another poem, "Cino," presents a particular speaker in a specific context, and once more the psychological and historical dimensions are significant. Cino the troubadour, Cino "of the wrinkling eyes, / Gay Cino, of quick laughter, / Cino, of the dare, the jibe," walks the open roads of the Italian countryside in the year 1309. He is conscious of his social inferiority in the eyes of the beautiful women whose charms he sings, but simultaneously regards them as inferior in that they do not appreciate art. Nor is he overawed by the lords whom all the women prefer to a vagabond poet: "And all I knew were out, my Lord, you / Were Lack-land Cino, e'en as I am, / O Sinistro." He concludes by rejecting the women as a subject of poetry: "I will sing of the white birds / In the blue waters of heaven, / the clouds that are spray to its sea." As Witemeyer says, Pound here "catches the character at a 'moment of song, self-analysis, or sudden understanding or revelation,' " but "in a definite historical or legendary context."[32]

The very different characteristics, within *Personae*, of the Browningesque poems and the group of more lyrical, ahistorical poems which includes "De Aegypto," and "La Fraisne," suggests a definite duality of purpose in Pound's writing at this stage in his career; a duality implied, also, by his admiration for the work of Rémy de Gourmont, so unlike that of Browning, as the following passage from his essay on Gourmont demonstrates:

> when he portrays, he is concerned with hardly more than the permanent human elements. His people are only by accident of any particular era. . . . Mauve, Fanette, Neobelle, La Vierge aux Plätres, are all studies in different *permanent* kinds of people; they are not the results of environments or of "social causes." . . . Gourmont differentiates his characters by the modes of their sensibility, not by sub-degrees of their state of civilization.[33]

Such an attitude clearly leads in the opposite direction from Browning, and no doubt helped in guiding Pound towards his modernist approach to the question of voice. What matters for Gourmont is not a particular man but "permanent kinds of people," and not a "whole man" but simply a "mode of sensibility," a *"façon de voir."* Gourmont, says Pound, was "intensely aware of the differences of emotional timbre; and as a man's message is precisely his *façon de voir*, his modality of apperception, this particular awareness was his 'message.' "[34] Ronald Bush suggests that Pound's admiration for Gourmont led him to favour the "dramatization of an individual intelligence," adding that, for Pound, "Gourmont's ability to unify an arbitrary conglomeration of subject matter by a sense of antecedent intelligence was uniquely attractive." The *Three Cantos* may have been a "rag-bag" for the modern world to "stuff all its thoughts in," a rag-bag held together, as Bush says, "by the clumsy persona of a *Sordello*-like narrator"; but Pound learned from Gourmont that "a 'rag-bag' of subject matter need not be unified by the external characterization of a speaker. Gourmont imposed the personality of an intelligence on his various works by the inflections of a single sensibility—what we have seen Pound call a *façon de voir* and an emotional 'modality.' " Rather than a character, then, or a mask (still used in the "Homage to Sextius Propertius"), inevitably dependent to some extent on "social and psychological characterization," Pound presents, as narrator of the *Cantos*, "a sensibility—a pervasive but nowhere visible register that [can] absorb images into the unity of an emotional *façon de voir*."[35]

In *The Tale of the Tribe*, Michael Bernstein analyzes Pound's "dilemma of how to use historical figures, how to give speech to others, or, rather, to take on others' voices without thereby losing one's own." The "tale of the tribe" is one definition Pound gives of the *Cantos*, referring to Rudyard Kipling's use of that phrase. Since the tale presents the "deeds of warriors, priests and men of action," the poetry relating such a tale is representational by its very nature: "the 'tale of the tribe' is intentionally directed towards . . . reality, and is expressly fashioned to enable readers to search the text for values which they can apply in the communal world."[36] In his desire to write the tale of a tribe, Pound shares with Browning a leaning towards mimesis and towards narrative which, together with his preference for a disembodied "façon de voir" over the voice of any specific individual, leads him towards the epic.

An epic is a poem including history, states Pound.[37] Like Browning, he had always been drawn to historical subjects, as the many Provençal poets and artists of the *Personae* testify; and the *Cantos* evoke the actions, attitudes and utterances of a multitude of historical figures, famous and obscure, ancient and modern. Bernstein declares that, as "an extended poetical treatment of history in which the data of scientists, anthropologists, and statesmen could figure, *The Cantos* are, quite simply and literally, unique." He suggests an illuminating contrast with *The Waste Land*, which also portrays typical inhabitants of the modern urban environment; but such figures as the ladies in the pub or Mr. Euginedes are, precisely, "*types* of modern decadence; they are 'typical' of their kind, and their historical existence is irrelevant." Furthermore, a poem like *The Waste Land*, "unlike an epic, is intended for the individual reader as a private man, not for the . . . 'citizen.' "[38] The condition that the "proper audience of an epic is not the individual . . . but the citizen" forms one element of Bernstein's definition of the epic poem.

Another important aspect of the epic as defined by Bernstein with reference to Pound relates to the question of poetic voice: "The dominant, locatable source of narration will not be a particular individual (the poet), but rather the voice of the community's heritage 'telling itself.' "[39] Indeed, although the specific facts, stories, personalities mentioned in the *Cantos* have been selected, perforce, by an individual historical author; and although Pound's own voice can sometimes be heard, especially in the Pisan Cantos, "far more sections of the poem are simply given, generated with no locatable or definable narrative source." The impression, at least, is created

> of the tribe's own heritage narrating itself, of the different historical voices addressing us as if without the mediation of one unique narrator or controlling author. It is almost as though the texture of *The Cantos* were designed to illustrate Karl Popper's idea of an "epistemology without a knowing subject," of information objectively existing and available for communal use without necessarily being fully realized in any single individual's competence.

Pound, through his "refusal to indicate a specific narrator," creates the illusion that "History itself, not any one particular author . . . is presenting the factual details of the poem."[40] Nor is any one specific persona ostensibly responsible for them, as in a monologue by Browning: the poetic voice is impersonal in that it is a communal or epic voice, belonging to the "tribe" as a whole—a type of impersonality quite unlike that of Mallarmé and other French poets.

# CHAPTER THREE

# Self-mockery: Laforgue

## I. The dramatic monologue in France

Although it was not until the mid-nineteenth century that the dramatic monologue became popular as a form in England, many examples of the genre can be found in the poetry of preceding centuries, even if these earlier authors, like Browning himself, did not use the term "dramatic monologue." In French literature, how-ever, it is hard to find examples of dramatic monologues before the nineteenth century.

Today, the expression "monologue dramatique" still refers to a monologue in a stage drama, though in the context of mediaeval literature it has a somewhat different connotation while still not implying the type of poem we understand in English by dramatic monologue. In Emile Picot's book *Le Monologue dramatique dans l'ancien théâtre français*, the term refers to a form prevalent in the fifteenth century, involving the performance, by a single actor, often in the street, of a monologue generally comic or burlesque in tone,[1] and presenting, according to Jean-Claude Aubailly, "une véritable recréation psychologique d'un type donné." He distinguishes three "types": *le charlatan, le soldat fanfaron*, and *l'amoureux*. All three types, however, share one common trait: "ce sont d'incorrigibles vantards dont les exploits ne sont pas toujours à la hauteur de la conception qu'ils ont d'eux-mêmes."[2] They betray, by their own words, a discrepancy between their perception of their situation and the reader's understanding of it similar to, if less subtle than, the contrast we noted in Browning's dramatic monologues between what the speaker reveals and understands about himself.

Very popular in the fifteenth century, the *monologue dramatique* suffers a decline in the course of the sixteenth century, when "l'énumération et l'amplification commencent à l'emporter sur l'observation et le drame," and "cette loi qui imposoit au Monologue le développement d'un caractère ou d'une position n'est plus observée."[3] By 1600, and in the seventeenth century, the monologue was restricted to tragedy, "à la triste fin de laquelle il contribua selon ses moyens," in the words of Charles d'Héricault. Within the context of French Classical theatre the monologue was, needless to say, a very different entity from the comic "monologue dramatique" described by Picot; and it also differed in several important ways from monologues on the English stage. Only the principal characters were accorded monologues, which meant, given the usual cast of a classical tragedy, that only kings, queens, princes or other leaders were allowed to speak when alone. The issues debated were correspondingly weighty, with far-reaching consequences, and the tone of the monologue—as of the whole play—was elevated and highly literary, however, impassioned. The very delivery of a monologue or other long speech, in the French classical tradition, was affected by certain conventions foreign to English theatre. Its presentation was static, accompanied by the very minimum of movement and gesture, in order to allow the words themselves to carry their full weight. The declamatory tone in which the *tirade* was delivered emphasized its solemnity and its quality as a quasi-independent "set speech." An otherwise restless audience often paid attention only to the *tirade*, and the liking for long speeches continued well into the nineteenth century; they feature prominently in Romantic drama: "Ce ne sont pas les drames de Hugo qui diminueront le prestige de la tirade; ils ne font que le renforcer."[4]

In view of the popularity, in the theatre, of long set speeches declaimed by one character it seems surprising that there are not more examples of dramatic monologues in French poetry. The *monologues dramatiques* of the fifteenth and sixteenth centuries were printed and can be read as poems, but were clearly intended to benefit from a live performance, and in the field of poetry itself the dramatic monologue has never known in France the kind of vogue it has enjoyed since the mid-nineteenth century in England. In the late eighteenth century, several of Chénier's *Bucoliques* are dramatic in form, representing actual dialogues between two or more characters; his "Jeune Captive" (from the *Odes*) might well be classed as a dramatic monologue, albeit one of a very lyrical stamp, were it not for the last two stanzas which reintroduce the voice of the poet. One or two of his short *Epigrammes* present the utterance of single, mythological speakers.

However, Vigny was undoubtedly justified in claiming to be the first French poet to present, in his *Poèmes antiques et modernes,* "une pensée philosophique . . . sous une forme Epique ou Drama-tique,"[5] since his best contributions to the dramatic form are much more original and impressive than Chénier's. Nevertheless, poems like "Moïse," "La Colère de Samson" or "Le Mont des oliviers" can-not be classed as genuine dramatic monologues, partly because they all comprise introductions or conclusions of varying lengths rather than the totally independent speech of the personae, and partly because these personae so clearly proclaim the poet's own views. While he refrains from expressing his feelings or opinions as openly as a Musset or a Lamartine, Vigny does not conceal his sense of kinship with the figures of Samson and of Christ as he has portrayed them. The conclusions of "La Colère de Samson" and "Le Mont des oliviers" introduce a voice other than that of Samson or Christ indignantly denouncing the betrayal of man by woman in the one poem and by God in the other:

> Terre et Ciel! punissez par de telles justices
> La trahison ourdie en des amours factices
> Et la délation du secret de nos coeurs
> Arraché dans nos bras par des baisers menteurs!
>
> (La Colère de Samson)

> S'il est vrai qu'au Jardin sacré des Ecritures,
> Le Fils de l'Homme ait dit ce qu'on voit rapporté;
> Muet, aveugle et sourd au cri des créatures,
> Si le Ciel nous laissa comme un monde avorté,

Le juste opposera le dédain à l'absence
Et ne répondra plus que par un froid silence
Au silence éternel de la Divinité.

(Le Mont des oliviers)

Though Browning may sometimes be suspected of speaking through his personae, he never abandons them utterly in this way. Vigny uses the historical figures of Moïse, Samson, Christ as symbols to express a nineteenth-century viewpoint; indeed, he says of his "Moïse" that its speaker is not the historical Moses but a figure whose name "merely serves as a mask for a man of all centuries, and a man of modern times rather than of antiquity."[6]

The subject-matter of "Le Mont des oliviers" is also that of Nerval's "Le Christ aux oliviers" which, like Vigny's poems, contains sections of monologue, placed in quotation marks. In Nerval's poem, however, the poet's voice is heard not only at the beginning and end but at several additional points, so that the work comes less close than Vigny's poems to a freestanding dramatic monologue.

Another poet of epic vision and whose *oeuvre* includes several dramatic monologues is Victor Hugo. Some of the monologues are "framed" like "Moïse" or "Le Mont des oliviers," i.e., a short introductory passage referring to the speaker in the third person precedes the monologue itself, which forms the bulk of the poem. "La Vision de Dante," for instance, in *La Légende des siècles*, begins: "Dante m'est apparu. Voici ce qu'il m'a dit," and continues for twenty pages with Dante's first-person utterance. *La Légende des siècles* could be described, like Pound's *Cantos*, as an attempt to capture history through a medley of voices. "Des voix parlaient," begins a poem containing several separate monologues, "Les Sept Merveilles du monde." As a collection, *La Légende des siècles* possesses both epic and dramatic features; most of the monologues are framed by the presence of the epic bard, but there are also some independent monologues, for example, in "Le Groupe des idylles," twenty-two unframed short poems supposedly spoken by various great poets of the past, e.g., Vergil, Petrarch, Ronsard, Shakespeare, Voltaire, Chénier, although their utterances are largely indistinguishable from one another. In fact these poems cannot be called dramatic monologues: in most cases their speakers are identified solely by the name forming the title of each poem; and, more importantly, they are totally undramatic. There is no conflict of any kind in the poems, which mostly celebrate the joys of love; nor is the speaker involved in any specifically dramatic situation, as is the case in Vigny's "Moïse," "La Colère de Samson" and "Le Mont des oliviers."

Vigny, Nerval and Hugo all wrote for the theatre, which could explain their predilection for monologues. French Romantic theatre abounds in declamatory, self-aggrandizing monologues. Even a poem like "El Desdichado" seems to reflect something of this trend, as the speaker announces: "Je suis le ténébreux—le veuf—l'inconsolé; / Le Prince d'Aquitaine à la tour abolie." Again, however, this poem cannot be classed as a dramatic monologue, since the speaker is not actually identified; no matter how closely he is linked, via Walter Scott's *Ivanhoe*, with Richard Coeur de Lion, Richard does not become the speaker of this poem in the way that Andrea del Sarto is the speaker in Browning's poem of that name, or the young Parque is the speaker of *La Jeune Parque*. The Prince d'Aquitaine is not set up as a persona, his title being merely one way of naming the category to which he belongs: that of the "ténébreux," of the "veuf," of "l'inconsolé." We do not feel, reading the poem, that the speaker *is* the Prince d'Aquitaine (or Richard Coeur de Lion), but simply that, in his dejection, he resembles the desolate image created by the line "Le Prince d'Aquitaine à la tour abolie."

Vigny's notion that modern man, and especially the modern poet, needed to don a mask, such as that of Moses in his poem, in order to express himself—or his various different selves—was to become widespread in the course of the nineteenth century. In particular it dominates the poetic output of Jules Laforgue, several of whose poems can be classed as dramatic monologues.

# II. Laforgue

i) From unicity to multiplicity

> Quand j'organise une descente en Moi,
> J'en conviens, je trouve là, attablée,

> Une société un peu bien mêlée,
> Et que je n'ai point vue à mes octrois.[7]

Such is the experience of the speaker of Laforgue's poem "Ballade." "JE est un autre," Rimbaud had written some fifteen years earlier, in the context of his critical remarks about Romantic poetry;[8] Laforgue shares this sense of the "otherness" of the self, insisting indeed on the presence of a multiplicity of "others." According to Warren Ramsey, Laforgue had learned from the philosopher Hartmann "to think of the human individual as an aggregate, a sum of many individuals."[9] Such a viewpoint must clearly affect the nature of the poetic "I," tending to invalidate the notion of the single, unified persona typical of Browning's early dramatic monologues, and of the lyric "I" associated with Romantic poetry. Yet Laforgue had begun writing in a highly Romantic vein: the speaker of the poems collected under the title *Le Sanglot de la terre*, but never published, dwells constantly on his own personal preoccupations: his awe at the vastness of the universe; his shocked awareness of the insignificance and transience of man's life; his horror of death. "Je puis mourir demain" is an oft-repeated phrase, and he hates to think that after death "Tout se fera sans moi!" ("L'Impossible"). These poems are of a philosophical cast, inspired by Laforgue's reading of Hartmann and his knowledge of Schopenhauer;[10] the tone is for the most part one of high seriousness. Meditations on the fate of mankind produce a sense of cosmic despair:

> Eternité, pardon. Je le vois, notre terre
> N'est, dans l'universel hosannah des splendeurs,
> Qu'un atome où se se joue une farce éphémère.

> ("Farce éphémère")

The speaker of these poems pontificates about Man and Life in verse reminiscent of both Hugo and Baudelaire:

> Enfin paraît un jour, grêle, blême d'effroi,
> L'Homme au front vers l'azur, le grand maudit, le roi.

. . . . . . . . . . . . . . . . . . . . . . . .
La femme hurle aux nuits, se tord et mord ses draps
Pour pondre des enfants vils, malheureux, ingrats.
("Litanies de misère")

Already in February 1881 Laforgue expressed "disgust" with this
early verse; by 1882 he was more emphatic: "Je me suis aperçu que
mon volume de vers était un ramassis de petites saletés banales et je
le refais avec rage."[11] The result of this burst of activity in 1883 was
the *Complaintes*, published in 1885.

Ramsey notes, in the majority of the *Complaintes*, "a movement
towards dramatization, a tendency, having its origin in self-
awareness and self-defence, to exteriorize the lyric emotion."[12]
This exteriorization is achieved largely through the use of different
voices, leading away from the straightforward expression of the
personal feeling of a single "I." The disgust Laforgue later felt for the
*Sanglot* poems was undoubtedly partly inspired by their self-
centred mode of writing: in the "Préludes autobiographiques," a
long poem which he insisted on including as a prologue to the
*Complaintes* in order to show what his literary "autobiography" had
been and how his poetic aims had changed, he mocks his former
tendency to see himself as the centre of the universe:

J'espérais
Qu'à ma mort, tout frémirait, du cèdre à l'hysope;
Que ce Temps, déraillant, tomberait en syncope,
Que, pour venir jeter sur mes lèvres des fleurs,
Les Soleils très navrés détraqueraient leurs choeurs.

The themes of the *Complaintes* are often similar to those of the
*Sanglot* poems, but they are treated differently. Instead of the first-
person diction of *Le Sanglot de la terre*, thoughts and feelings are
distributed among many voices belonging to different personae
and expressed indirectly, resulting in a much lighter, less morbid
type of verse, even when the subject is still death. In the poem
"Guitare," from the *Sanglot* collection, a solemn narrating (or ser-
monizing) voice predicts, in alternating alexandrines and octosyl-
lables, the death of a beautiful Parisienne and how soon she will be
forgotten by her contemporaries. No "I" speaks in this poem, but

the address to the lady in the second person presupposes a first-person "shifter," a lyric "I," as the serious-minded speaker of these lines. In the *Complaintes*, however, the very different "Complainte de l'oubli des morts" also treats the theme of the dead being forgotten by the living, but the identity of the poem's speaker radically alters the tone of the poem. Rather than a heavily moralistic accent we hear the more light-hearted, if wistful, voice of the grave-digger, a man with plenty of experience of death, which explains his familiar, almost flippant remarks:

> Les morts
> C'est sous terre;
> Ça n'en sort
> Guère.

He has considerable sympathy for the dead ("Pauvres morts hors des villes!") and his attitude to the living is not without sympathy, though the very nature of his employment represents a threat to them, as he gently points out:

> Mesdames et Messieurs,
> Vous dont la soeur est morte,
> Ouvrez au fossoyeux
> Qui claque à votre porte;
>
> Si vous n'avez pitié,
> Il viendra (sans rancune)
> Vous tirer par les pieds,
> Une nuit de grand'lune!

The introduction of the grave-digger's voice, the shorter lines and choppier rhythms, together with the removal of the Baudelairean emphasis on *pourriture* that we find in "Guitare," transform a slow-moving, trite poem-sermon into a much more original and effective one.

The question of love arises less often than one might expect in the *Sanglot* collection, the "I" of these poems being preoccupied with his own destiny to the exclusion of all else. In one poem, however, "Pour le livre d'amour," he complains that

> Je puis mourir demain et je n'ai pas aimé.
> Mes lèvres n'ont jamais touché lèvres de femme,
> Nulle ne m'a donné dans un regard son âme,
> Nulle ne m'a tenu contre son coeur pâmé.
>
> Je n'ai fait que souffrir. . . . . . . .

This expression of personal distress can easily be read as that of the poet himself. At one point in the *Complaintes* we hear virtually the same phrase, "Nulle ne songe à m'aimer un peu," but the whole tone of this poem, the "Complainte de l'automne monotone," suggests an ironical attitude on the part of the speaker towards himself, a self-awareness which tends, as Ramsey says, to "exteriorize the lyric emotion":

> Automne, automne, adieux de l'Adieu!
> La tisane bout, noyant mon feu;
>  Le vent s'époumonne
> A reverdir la bûche où mon grand coeur tisonne.
>  Est-il de vrais yeux?
> Nulle ne songe à m'aimer un peu.

The words "nulle ne veut m'aimer" recur again in the *Complaintes* but this time in the mouth of a third person, the "lui" of the "Complaintes des pubertés difficiles"—a thin disguise for Laforgue himself perhaps, but a disguise nevertheless, once more indicating a desire to disclaim direct responsibility for the utterance:

> Mais lui, cabré devant ces soirs accoutumés,
> Où montait la gaîté des enfants de son âge,
> Seul au balcon, disait, les yeux brûlés de rages:
> "J'ai du génie, enfin: nulle ne veut m'aimer!"

Laforgue uses various disguises, or masks, throughout the *Complaintes*: the "ange incurable" and the "Chevalier errant," the "roi de Thulé," the "Sage de Paris" and, most of all, Pierrot. Each disguise makes possible the utterance of a new voice. In subsequent collections also, *L'Imitation de Notre-Dame la lune* and the *Derniers vers*, different voices can be heard, speaking, in David Arkell's words, for the "multiple selves of Laforgue and others."[13] It is significant that this move from a unified to a multiple self accompanies Laforgue's choice of a more popular, collective form, since the *complainte* was originally a type of folk-song. Henri Davenson, in his *Livre des chansons*, distinguishes two categories of oral folk-song, "les *rondes* ou chansons à danser que caractérise la présence d'un refrain," and "les *complaintes* ou récits continus" which have affinities with English "complaints" and ballads.[14] Ballads are a form without an author not only because they are often anonymous, but because they specifically aim at objectivity: the "I" of the poet is never mentioned, only that of the various characters. Laforgue seems to be seeking a similar kind of anonymity by attributing his poems to different speakers.

According to Laforgue himself, he first thought of writing poems based on *complaintes* on September 20, 1880, during a celebration in the Place Danfert-Rochereau, when he heard—not of course for the first time—popular songs sung in the street.[15] By the late nineteenth century, the style of the *complainte* had lost the freshness and vigour of the original folk-songs. Davenson is reluctant even to mention the "compositions auxquelles avait fini par se restreindre le nom de complainte," namely "chansons volontairement composées à l'intention du public populaire . . . qui prétendaient descendre du peuple, et qui en fait étaient descendues bien bas." They had become "récits détaillés . . . d'un prosaïsme écoeurant et . . . d'une intolérable tristesse";[16] their sentimentality can be seen reflected in the work of poets such as Richepin. Nevertheless, Laforgue seizes on those aspects of the *complaintes* which suit his purposes. He frequently imitates the popular diction of the *complainte*, for the phrasing, syntax and vocabulary of his second volume of poetry are far removed from the more literary tone of *Le Sanglot*. The songs sung by organ-grinders and other street musicians employed, not the traditional versification of poetry but the rhythms of popular speech, in which mute "e's" did not count as syllables and the hiatus between vowels was filled with a "z" or a "t" sound. Laforgue sometimes adopts these features, as if to emphasize that what we hear is not his voice but the anonymous speech of the "folk," as in:

> Je suis-t-il malhûreux!
> > ("Autre complainte de l'orgue de barbarie")
> C'est l'printemps qui s'amène
> > ("Complainte des printemps")
> Voyez l'homme, voyez!
> .Si ça n'fait pas pitié!
> > ("Complainte du pauvre corps humain")

and in the two poems which he indicates as being variations on actual songs, the "Complainte du pauvre jeune homme" and the "Complainte de l'époux outragé."

Davenson defines *complaintes* as "récits continus," in opposition to the "chanson" or "ronde." Like the ballad, the *complainte* implies narrative, which is, to some extent, a feature of Laforgue's *Complaintes*. Almost all his speakers have a story to tell, usually involving a loss they have sustained and which forms the subject of their lament: a lost love in the "Complainte de la bonne défunte" or the "Complainte des blackboulés," lost innocence in the "Complainte du roi de Thulé," lost wealth and health in the "Complainte des grands pins dans une villa abandonnée." However, the affinity of the *Complaintes* to the ballad is limited, since the latter is essentially a third-person form, whereas the *Complaintes*, as well as Laforgue's later poetry, are written in the first person: they are monologues and many of them, specifically, dramatic monologues.

ii) Dramatic monologue and interior monologue

It is significant that, like Browning, though in a much more modest fashion, Laforgue began his career by attempting to write plays, as well as poetry. In 1882—the year he abandoned the *Sanglot de la terre* poems—he wrote, but did not complete, *Pierrot fumiste*, in which the hero puts on "the same ironic and poignant comic mask" as Lord Pierrot in the *Complaintes*.[17] According to Haskell Block, Laforgue "planned several plays . . . and worked on at least some of them," in 1882–83, as his correspondence shows. Apart from the unfinished *Pierrot fumiste*, however, his only published play, or playlet, is *Le Concile féérique* (1886), a verse drama composed of five poems from the *Fleurs de bonne volonté*, which Laforgue had decided not to publish.

Various critics have noted the basically dramatic impulse of Laforgue's poetry, though few refer to his poems as dramatic monologues. Block talks of the "intrinsically dramatic character of Laforgue's poetry with its complex interplay of several voices," and Ramsey mentions the "dramatic form of the most characteristic *Complaintes*," with their dialogues of "many voices."[18] Not surprisingly, the "many voices" heard in Laforgue's *Complaintes* and later collections often engage one another in dialogue, and dialogue is inherently dramatic, since it constitutes the distinctive form of stage drama. Again it represents a move away from the authoritative discourse of a central "I," allowing room for the speech of others or for internal debate. In some of Laforgue's earlier poems, opposing voices are channelled into an actual dialogue between two speakers like the "LUI" and "ELLE" of the "Complainte des formalités nuptiales." The "Complainte sous le figuier boudhique" boasts four sets of speakers, all named; but more commonly speakers are not designated in this way, the alternations in their speech being indicated by the use of quotation marks, as in the "Complainte des grands pins dans une villa abandonnée." Sometimes the main speaker's words are not enclosed in quotation marks, only those of his imaginary interlocutor, for example in the "Complainte des printemps," the "Complainte des pianos . . ." and *Derniers vers* VIII and IX. Finally, the voices of the dialogue can reflect opposing views solely within the mind of one speaker—the conflicting attitudes of the "société un peu bien mêlée" making up the self:

> Mais, Tout va la reprendre!—Alors Tout m'en absout.
> Mais, Elle est ton bonheur!—Non, je suis trop immense
> Trop chose.
>
> ("Complainte des Consolations")

The frequent suggestion of a dialogue within the mind of one speaker, as in this poem and especially in the *Derniers vers*, reflects the fact that many of Laforgue's speakers are engaged in some form of conflict with themselves, which again contributes an element of drama to his poems, since conflict is in itself essentially dramatic. Indeed, Laforgue's personae are nearly always torn between two opposite impulses: between the desire for love and a mocking rejection of it, as in *Derniers vers* IX; between a feeling of sympathy for

women and an instinctive suspicion of their motives (e.g., in Dv V
and VIII); between a sensual and an ideal love (Dv III and "Com-
plainte de Lord Pierrot"); between patient devotion and impatient
desire ("Locutions des Pierrots, I"). Whereas the speakers of
Browning's early dramatic monologues are not engaged in any con-
flict with themselves, only with the outside world, their freedom
from inner division confirming their status as characters with well-
defined personalities and views, Laforgue's protagonists, on the
contrary, suffer from inner conflicts, doubts and hesitations, and
from a general lack of confidence that makes it hard for them to
establish their own identity. The speaker of Dv III confides:

> . . . j'allais me donner d'un "Je vous aime"
> Quand je m'avisai non sans peine
> Que d'abord je ne me possédais pas bien moi-même.

The dramatic irony in Browning's poems, arising from the dis-
crepancy between the speaker's apprehension of his situation and
the reader's understanding of it, leads to collusion between author
and reader behind the speaker's back; the factor causing the
speaker to distort reality is, very often, simply his own personality,
with its prejudices and blind spots. In Laforgue's work there is still
enough emphasis on character traits for the reader (and the poet)
similarly to judge the speakers—but not behind their backs, be-
cause they forestall criticism by judging themselves, too. Thus the
speaker of Dv IX avoids being labelled as incurably romantic in his
desire to "Faire naître un 'Je t'aime!' " by the irony implicit in the
sheer exaggeration of his wishes:

> Qu'il vienne, comme à l'aimant la foudre,
> Et dans mon ciel d'orage qui craque et qui s'ouvre,
> Et alors, les averses lustrales jusqu'au matin,
> Le grand clapissement des averses toute la nuit! Enfin!

Again, in Dv XII, the patent irony of the speaker's exclamation
"Oh! arrose, arrose / Mon coeur si brûlant, ma chair si intéres-
sante!" shows that although he feels desperate and melancholy, he
is also the sort of sophisticated person who—like the reader and
the poet—finds desperate melancholy ludicrous. The drama in La-

forgue's poems derives more from the internal conflict within the speaker and from the irony that discloses it, than from any discrepancy between his view of himself and our own.

The presence of dialogue in Laforgue's poetry disguises, paradoxically, another essential difference between his monologues and those of Browning. In the majority of Browning's dramatic monologues, the speaker directly addresses a listener, with the poem as a whole representing one side of a dialogue. In most of Laforgue's poems, however, the speakers are alone; any dialogue is purely imaginary, consisting either of comments which the speaker mentally attributes to someone else or words which one side of his personality addresses to another, within the privacy of his own mind. In other words these monologues present, not the speech of a given character to an interlocutor, but his private thoughts, his inner language. For this reason, Laforgue's poems are sometimes referred to as "interior" rather than "dramatic" monologues. J.P. Houston, for example, suggests that the "monologue created by Laforgue is largely an inner one, and if the analogy with drama is appropriate to the monologue invented by Browning, that with the stream-of-consciousness novel is more so in this case."[19] Interior monologue, as practised by Joyce and by Dujardin before him, strives to transcribe in writing the random, fragmentary nature of the "stream of consciousness," of thought as it is formed in the mind. Dujardin asserts that interior monologue represents "un discours antérieur à toute organisation logique"; its form is therefore very simple: "il se réalise en phrases directes réduites au minimum syntaxial." He admits, however, that interior monologue cannot claim to reproduce man's barely-conscious thought-processes verbatim, but can only give the impression of doing so: "Le monologue intérieur ne doit pas donner la pensée 'tout venant,' mais en donner l'impression." This impression is conveyed partly by the use of short "direct sentences" with very loose and abbreviated syntax, and partly by the way the thoughts expressed jump from one subject to another, by a process of free association, often without any apparent logical connection: "Notre pensée court d'un plan à l'autre avec une rapidité qui après coup peut sembler mais n'est pas de la simultanéité; et c'est précisément cette course" à bâtons rompus' dont le monologue intérieur donne l'impression."[20]

Laforgue's *Derniers vers*, in particular, answer to some of these criteria. Written in *vers libres*, where each line represents a unit of meaning, they adopt a loose, elliptical syntax impossible in regular verse:

> Noire bise, averse glapissante,
> Et fleuve noire, et maisons closes,
> Et quartiers sinistres comme des Morgues,
> Et l'Attardé qui à la remorque traîne
> Toute la misère des coeurs et des choses,
> Et la souillure des innocentes qui traînent. . . .
>
> (*Derniers vers* XII)

The paratactic arrangement of this passage, with juxtaposition replacing logical subordination, is typical of the *Derniers vers*, and of the interior monologue, since the barely-formulated thoughts which spring from the stream of consciousness have not yet been ordered by logic. They tend to be linked together by a process of free-association, also found in certain passages of the *Derniers vers*, for example the opening of *Dv* X, where the basic themes—of love-making and marriage—conjure up a variety of unexpected but related images:

> O géraniums diaphanes, guerroyeurs sortilèges,
> Sacrilèges monomanes!
> Emballages, dévergondages, douches! O pressoirs
> Des vendanges des grands soirs!
> Layettes aux abois,
> Thyrses au fond des bois!
> Transfusions, représailles,
> Relevailles, compresses et l'éternelle potion,
> Angélus! n'en pouvoir plus
> De débâcles nuptiales! de débâcles nuptiales! . . .

These characteristics of Laforgue's poetry have led Scarfe to claim not only that he wrote interior monologues, but that he invented the form; in an essay on Eliot, he asserts that Laforgue "invented a new kind of dramatic monologue, usually known as the interior or internal monologue, close to common speech," and implies that Dujardin developed the technique of *Les Lauriers sont coupés* from Laforgue "without acknowledgement."[21] It is true that many lines in Laforgue resemble "common speech" in rhythm, vocabulary and syntax, but at the same time the abundance of scientific, erudite, foreign and archaic words in his poetry destroys the illusion of oral speech, and with it the impression of spontaneity appropriate to interior monologue. In any case, the all-pervading irony of his poetry (to which these verbal juxtapositions contribute) suggests a fully-conscious, deliberate type of writing, irony being the opposite of spontaneous. Furthermore, it is difficult to see how the acoustic effects Laforgue achieves through alliteration, assonance and rhyme can be associated with the supposedly barely-formulated thoughts of the stream of consciousness; or indeed how poetry, which always involves organisational principles of one kind or another, could ever seriously attempt to imitate the disorderly ramblings of the inner monologue.

Though it may be true, then, that certain features of Laforgue's poetry, such as the use of parataxis and of free association, influenced his friend Dujardin to some extent, the claim that Laforgue "invented the internal monologue" is exaggerated. Both interior monologue and poems like Laforgue's *Derniers vers* present a character's thoughts rather than his speech, but there is another important difference between the two, besides the issue of spontaneity. The thoughts of Laforgue's monologues are concentrated on a specific problem or event, unlike the loosely-connected discourse of interior monologue which supposedly records a character's stream of consciousness over a period of time and is not directed solely at a particular topic. Wayne Booth makes this point regarding Stephen's interior monologue in *A Portrait of the Artist as a Young Man*, which "unlike speech in a dramatic scene," does not "lead us to suspect that the thoughts have been in any way aimed at an effect."[22] The discourse of a Laforguian monologue, however, like "speech in a dramatic scene," *is* aimed at an effect. Apart from the poem's effect on the reader, obtained by the deliberate manipulation of rhythms, sounds, or images, and dramatic effects achieved through irony, the speakers themselves have an aim, namely to come to terms with a specific problem or event around which the whole poem revolves. Such problems are, for example, in *Dv* VII—regret

for a lost love; in XI—the faithlessness of women, and how to deal
with it; in X—the conflict between the speaker's need for inde-
pendence and his nostalgia for a "petit intérieur" to share with his
"petite quotidienne"; in V—a call for a change from love as prac-
tised by men and women of the time to the type of love-relationship
the speaker advocates, in which the woman would no longer be
regarded as an "angel," but as man's equal. In these poems, all the
thoughts expressed are in some way relevant to those themes,
whereas in interior monologue the thought "court d'un plan à l'au-
tre," as Dujardin says, reflecting the "course" à bâtons rompus' " of
the stream of consciousness. The content of a Joycean interior
monologue is often very much affected by the subject's surround-
ings, which impinge on his thoughts, but in Laforgue's *Derniers vers*
the speaker's present position is not necessarily mentioned at all; if
so, then it is directly relevant to the problem in hand, as in *Dv* III:

> Or, cette nuit anniversaire, toutes les Walkyries du vent
> Sont revenues beugler par les fentes de ma porte:
> *Vae soli!*

or in *Dv* VII:

> Voici qu'il fait très très-frais
> Oh! si à la même heure,
> Elle va de même le long des forêts. . . .

Laforgue's monologues, then, though they may have some stylistic
similarities with interior monologue, are "aimed at an effect"—that
of examining and attempting to solve a problem which worries the
speaker, or of resolving a conflict within him—and to this extent
they are dramatic.

iii) Dramatis personae

An interest in drama and in the nature of theatrical performance
can be detected in Laforgue's favourite choice of personae, Pierrot
and Hamlet, both taken from the stage and very much aware of
themselves as actors. Both are stereotypes (a certain image of

Hamlet had become a stereotype by the late nineteenth century), both slender, white-faced, tenuous figures, and adepts at playing a part and at playing with language.

The figure of Pierrot—together with those of Gilles the clown, and the *saltimbanque*—had become very popular in French artistic circles by the last quarter of the nineteenth century. Within the theatre, the role of Pierrot had developed from the Pedrolino of the Commedia dell'arte, with the admixture, in the eighteenth century, of some characteristics of the French clown Gilles.[23] His personality seems to have oscillated, over the years, between a tradition that made of him a "lumpish valet," a "rustic good-for-nothing dullard,"[24] and one that allowed him a more lively intelligence. In the paintings of Watteau he appears as a moonstruck, naïve innocent, attired all in white and standing alone, a foolish but sympathetic figure. In the 1830's the part of Pierrot had been played at the Théâtre des Funambules by the great mime Jean-Gaspard (called Baptiste) Deburau, whose performances, acclaimed by the general public, also attracted the attention of literary men. Nodier, Jules Janin, Nerval, Banville and Gautier all wrote about him, and the figure of Pierrot became increasingly popular in literature. Even Flaubert penned a *Pierrot au sérail*. Robert Storey declares that Deburau, as "godparent of the multifarious, moonstruck Pierrots who gradually found their way into Romantic, Decadent, and Symbolist literature," was responsible for "the transmission of the type from the popular to the literary world."[25]

The writers who saw Deburau and, later, his son Charles, play the part of Pierrot, read a great deal into the role, viewing Pierrot in a quasi-tragic light. Gautier suggests that Pierrot symbolized "l'âme humaine encore innocente et blanche, tourmentée d'aspirations infinies vers les régions supérieures,"[26] and Banville evokes a similar yearning for the Ideal on the part of the clown in the final poem of his *Odes funambulesques* (1857):

> Enfin, de son vil échafaud,
> Le clown sauta si haut, si haut!
> Qu'il creva le plafond de toiles
> Au son du cor et du tambour,
> Et, le coeur dévoré d'amour,
> Alla rouler dans les étoiles.

Mallarmé, in the final version of "Le Pitre châtié," describes a similar, though finally more complex, movement upwards and outwards: "J'ai troué dans le mur de toile une fenêtre." The figure of the "tragic clown" was not new; Starobinski points out that it belonged to "une tradition (qui remonte à tout le moins au XVIIIᵉ siècle) selon laquelle l'acteur cache sous son triomphe et ses joies feintes une âme désespérée." Baudelaire renews this tradition by his association of the image of the clown and that of the poet in prose poems like "Une mort héroïque" and "Le Vieux Saltimbanque": "poète des 'deux postulations simultanées,' " says Starobinski, Baudelaire "a conféré à l'artiste, sous la figure du bouffon et du saltimbanque, la vocation contradictoire de l'envol et de la chute, de l'altitude et de l'abîme." Not surprisingly, in the climate of post-Romantic poetry, this Pierrot figure, with his aspirations towards the Ideal, became an *être à part* representing not only the artist in general, but the *poète maudit* or, in Laforgue's term, the *paria*, who feels himself to be an outsider in real life, yet views the "Ideal" as either unattainable or non-existent. "—Certes! l'Absolu perd ses droits, / Là où le Vrai consiste à vivre," exclaims Laforgue's Pierrot in the "Dialogue avant le lever de la lune" from *L'Imitation*. The Pierrot of Verlaine's *Fêtes galantes* is a lively and uncomplicated figure who "Vide un flacon sans plus attendre, / Et, pratique, entame un pâté" ("Pantomime"), but Verlaine was aware of a newer, darker side to Pierrot; a poem from *Jadis et Naguère* illustrates this changing image:

> Ce n'est plus le rêveur lunaire du vieil air
> Qui riait aux aïeux dans les dessus de porte;
> Sa gaîté, comme sa chandelle, hélas ! est morte,
> Et son spectre aujourd'hui nous hante, mince et clair.

Starobinski notes that the Symbolists' Pierrot "amalgame les souvenirs évidents de la *Commedia*, mais encore la silhouette méditative d'Hamlet," an interesting suggestion in view of Laforgue's intense preoccupation with both figures, and one on which Storey bases Pierrot's entire career: "Pierrot's theatrical and literary history is the record of his vacillations between two dramatic and psychological 'types.' At one pole stands his Italian predecessor Pedrolino. . . . At the other stands Hamlet."[27] Within this combination, Pedrolino represents insouciance, comic verve, lack of psychological depth, whereas Hamlet's personality is complex, vulnerable, melancholy, asocial. Both sets of characteristics are typical of Laforgue's "Lord Pierrot," whose utterances alternate between frivolity and serious intensity:

> Ma cervelle est morte.
> Que le Christ l'emporte!
> Béons à la Lune
> La bouche en zéro.
>
> Inconscient, descendez en nous par réflexes;
> Brouillez les cartes, les dictionnaires, les sexes.
>
> Tournons d'abord sur nous-même, comme un fakir!
> (Agiter le pauvre être, avant de s'en servir.)
>
> J'ai le coeur chaste et vrai comme une bonne lampe. . . .
>                    ("Complainte de Lord Pierrot")

His complexity and vulnerability spring from his longing for an Ideal he knows to be unattainable ("ayant pour cible / Adopté la vie impossible"), a longing which in turn arises from his disgust with the everyday life of the "gens nés casés, bonnes gens."

Pierrot's identity as speaker of this poem and the others attributed to him in the *Complaintes* and *L'Imitation de Notre-Dame la Lune* helps to establish the distance characteristic of the dramatic monologue; there is also an element of drama present in the permanent conflict raging within the persona, and in his belligerence towards women. These conflicts, however, are permanent states of affairs; the persona is not engaged in a specific dramatic situation in each poem, as in a dramatic monologue. The nearest we come to that is in a poem beginning *in media res*, as many of Browning's monologues do:

> Elle disait, de son air vain fondamental:
> "Je t'aime pour toi seul!"—Oh! là, là, grêle histoire;
> Oui, comme l'art. . . .
>       (*L'Imitation*, "Pierrots (on a des principes)")

The drama is not allowed to develop, however; five lines later Pierrot has already buried his lady in imagination:

> Mais voici qu'un beau soir, infortunée à point,
> Elle meurt! . . .

Just as he cannot tell a complete story, Pierrot cannot sustain the same self-image for long; expressions of apparently genuine emotion are at once deflated by a mocking voice. Such is the effect of the unexpected "Bis" at the end of the "Complainte de Lord Pierrot":

> —J'ai le coeur triste comme un lampion forain . . .
> Bah! J'irai passer la nuit dans le premier train;
>
> Sûr d'aller, ma vie entière,
> Malheureux comme les pierres. (Bis.)

The fluctuations and contradictions in his personality illustrate a very different view of "character" from that which structures Browning's monologues. With the exception of Andrea del Sarto, the speakers of the Browning poems examined above are totally lacking in self-awareness; confident in the validity of their own views of events and of themselves, they do not engage in self-criticism; moreover, they have distinct personalities which can be recognized by the reader. Pierrot, on the other hand, continually questions his own reactions, so that it becomes impossible to pin him down and define him. His constant irony at his own expense results in the dislocation of his personality. He is troubled, as Storey points out, by "a Hamletic self-consciousness."[28]

The same self-consciousness, irony, and fluctuations from one extreme to another can be seen in another of Laforgue's personae, the speaker of the *Derniers vers*, who closely resembles Pierrot and has strong connections with Hamlet. Two epigraphs from *Hamlet* stand at the head of the collection, the final poem also has its own epigraph from that play, and poem IV ("Dimanches") contains a well-known quotation from *Hamlet*, "Alas, poor Yorick!"

For the Romantics, Hamlet, like Pierrot, came to represent a sensitive, suffering soul in the midst of corruption. Mme. de Staël calls him "l'homme vertueux ne pouvant supporter la vie quand la scélératesse l'environne."[29] To the disillusioned post-Napoleonic generation, the time certainly seemed "out of joint," and the figure of Hamlet was a remarkably appropriate vehicle for the expression of nineteenth-century *mal du siècle*, so much so that Claudel later said that, after Shakespeare, the Hamlet theme "devait attendre deux siècles avant de trouver une atmosphère propre à son développement."[30] The symbolist generation particularly, preoccupied as it was with the Ideal, adopted the figure of Hamlet, along with that of Pierrot. "Shakespeare's spiritually embattled hero," says Helen Bailey, "with his intuition of things undreamed-of in a corrupt and sordid world, found a congenial element in the climate of ideality that nurtured poetry in the last half of the century." Laforgue, she continues, "made Hamlet the symbol of an unrelenting dualism that he knew too well: a longing for the absolute, frustrated by a sense of the accidental and a haunting suspicion that all adds up to nothing."[31] "J'ai cinq sens qui me rattachent à la vie; mais, ce sixième sens, ce sens de l'Infini!" exclaims the Hamlet of the *Moralités légendaires*.

The speaker of the *Derniers vers* shares many of Hamlet's traits: he shows the same inability to reach a decision for which Hamlet is renowned:

> Bref, j'allais me donner d'un "Je vous aime"
> Quand je m'avisai non sans peine
> Que d'abord je ne me possédais pas bien moi-même.
> (*Dv* III, "Dimanches")

> Oh! qu'ils sont pittoresques les trains manqués! . . . .
> (*Dv* X)

Like Hamlet, and like Laforgue's Pierrot, this speaker vacillates between tenderness for a particular woman and contempt for women in general, especially for their provocative behaviour: "you jig, you amble, and you lisp," accuses Shakespeare's Hamlet (Act III, scene 1), and the speaker of *Dv* IV considers that even women's apparently modest gestures are a pose, intended to attract men:

> Oh, pardonnez-lui si, malgré elle,
> Et cela tant lui sied,
> Parfois ses prunelles clignent un peu
> Pour vous demander un peu
> De vous apitoyer un peu!

Hamlet's scathing remarks about human corruption, hypocrisy, and thoughtlessness are also echoed in the *Derniers vers*, for instance in the following passage:

> O bouquets d'oranger cuirassés de satin,
> Elle s'éteint, elle s'éteint,
> La divine Rosace
> A voir vos noces de sexes livrés à la grosse,
> Courir en valsant vers la fosse
> Commune! . . . Pauvre race!
> (Dv V, "Pétition")

Furthermore, like Hamlet, to whom "all the uses of this world" appear "weary, stale, flat, and unprofitable," the speaker of these poems suffers from a general dissatisfaction with life:

> Un spleen me tenait exilé,
> Et ce spleen me venait de tout. . . .
> (*Dv* VII, "Solo de lune")

Laforgue's fascination with Hamlet led him to undertake a trip to Elsinore; from there he dated the "Avertissement" to the collection *Des Fleurs de bonne volonté*, which he never published but parts of which he later used in *Derniers vers*. A Laforguian version of Hamlet is also the hero of one of the *Moralités légendaires*, a Hamlet who closely resembles the speaker of the *Derniers vers* in his attitude towards women, his habit of saying serious things in a bantering tone, his self-irony, and his pessimistic view of life. These similarities tend to corroborate the view that, in the *Derniers vers*, Laforgue has the figure of Hamlet constantly in mind. Never named, the speaker of these poems nevertheless has a recognizable identity; the words are not simply those of a "lyric I" but of a Hamletic persona, if not of Hamlet himself.

Moreover, in most poems of *Derniers vers*, unlike the Pierrot poems of the *Complaintes* and *L'Imitation*, the speaker is involved in a specific dramatic scene or situation. In "Solo de lune" (*Dv* VII), the lonely protagonist, perched on top of a stage-coach, bemoans his separation from his love; he regrets his failure to tell her he loved her, and imagines that now he will spend his life repeating "Si j'avais su"—although, perhaps, if they had married, too, "ne se fût-on pas dit: / 'Si j'avais su, si j'avais su! . . .' " As the coach continues on its way he notices the scenery, and wonders whether she too is wandering about in the moonlight thinking of him. In "Légende" (*Dv* VIII), the partners in an end-of-season romance quarrel and separate. In the imagined drama of "Sur une défunte" (*Dv* XI), the speaker visualizes his lover being unfaithful to him "Avec les nobles A, B, C ou D," supplying their words and setting the scene:

> "Oh, c'est bien Toi, cette fois! . . ."
>
> Il baisse un peu sa bonne lampe,
> Il la ploie, Elle, vers son coeur . . .

—while the speaker himself walks up and down outside watching her window.

Although the setting of these poems is not specified as precisely as in Browning's monologues, they all share an urban background evoking "toute la misère des grands centres." The atmosphere is clearly that of Laforgue's own era, the age of "la phtisie pulmonaire attristant le quartier" and the "statistiques sanitaires / Dans les journaux" (*Dv* I, "L'Hiver qui vient"). The characters on Laforgue's stage require few props; moreover, his personae have no recognizable social status; they are outsiders ("paria" being one of Laforgue's favourite words); and unlike Browning's characters they do not even possess a realistic name. If they have a name at all it is *le roi de Thulé*, Hamlet, Pierrot (or, incongruously, Lord Pierrot): their names are borrowed, not from everyday life but from legend or literature, particularly the theatre; they are not "real," historical figures like many of Browning's, but stereotypes.

The distance essential to a dramatic monologue is achieved in

Laforgue not so much by the particularization characteristic of Browning as by the use of irony, and again, not the dramatic irony typical of Browning, depending on the speaker's being unaware of some aspect of his own situation; Laforgue's protagonists are, on the contrary, totally aware, highly self-conscious. Wayne Booth, in *A Rhetoric of Irony*, divides the concept of irony into two categories: "stable" and "unstable." According to his definition of stable irony as "covert, intended to be reconstructed with meanings different from those on the surface," the reader must reject the literal meaning in favor of a second one determined by his awareness of the "implied author's" "knowledge or beliefs."[32] Such a principle is clearly at work in Browning's dramatic monologues; and the "covert" meaning frequently takes the form of a castigation, since stable irony tends to aim at correcting people or the world. Unstable irony, however, undermines traditional values, and sees "life itself . . . as fundamentally and inescapably an ironic state of affairs."[33] This is the kind of irony we find in Laforgue, and of course in many modern writers; its origins can be traced back to theories of Romantic Irony evolved by Friedrich Schlegel and other German writers towards the end of the eighteenth century. Their ideas arose partly, as D.C. Muecke says, from "the growth of self-awareness, the increasing extent to which men become conscious of being conscious."

Self-conscious and self-critical in the extreme, Laforgue's personae make it impossible for the reader to identify with them, since they are constantly changing, contradicting themselves and undercutting their own finer feelings. Should we accept the "I" who cries wistfully: "Oh! qu'une, d'Elle-même, un beau soir, sût venir / Ne voyant plus que boire à mes lèvres, ou mourir! . . ." or the one who mocks: "Ainsi, elle viendrait, évadée, demi-morte, / Se rouler sur le paillasson que j'ai mis à cet effet devant ma porte" (*Dv* IX)? The "I" who expresses genuine tenderness, as in "Solo de lune," or the one who hints at sexual violence? ("Ah! que je te les tordrais avec plaisir, / Ce corps bijou, ce coeur à ténor" (*Dv* III)). These contradictions and ironic reversals stem from a lack of self-knowledge (the speaker of *Dv* III "ne croit à son Moi qu'à ses moments perdus"), which in turn comes from the feeling of being not whole and single, but multiple, a "société un peu bien mêlée." Such doubts make La-

forgue's personae unsure how to behave in any given situation, so
that they always find themselves playing a role.

Both taken from the stage, Laforgue's Pierrot and Hamlet figures
are fully conscious of their own "theatricality"; they are playing a
part, which means both acting out a role and reciting a text they
have committed to memory. We see Pierrot's physical gestures and
facial expressions—as if in the theatre—during a love scene:

> Ecarquillant le cou
> Et feignant de comprendre
> De travers, la voix tendre,
> Mais les yeux si filous!
> (*L'Imitation*, "Pierrots")

He is "feignant," i.e., playing a part and very much aware of the fact.
To abandon role-playing, for Pierrot, is to arouse cries of:

> Oh! de moins en moins drôle;
> Pierrot sait mal son rôle?
> ("Complainte de Lord Pierrot")

The traditional Pierrot's role was mimed, and his mimicry involved
a repertoire of conventional gestures; Laforgue, of course, has to use
words, but he does so in such a way as to suggest that language, too,
can be merely gesture. His adoption of the set form of the *complainte*
and the stock figure of Pierrot is accompanied by the use of ready-
made language—fixed expressions and clichés; his Pierrots trot
out the stock phrases dictated by convention for use in certain
situations. To women, for example, they address declarations
couched in the rhetoric traditionally associated with love:

> Ange! tu m'as compris,
> A la vie, à la mort!

while thinking:

> Ah! passer là-dessus l'éponge! . . .
> (*L'Imitation*, "Pierrots")

Though Pierrot uses the conventional discourse of love he often shows, by means of ironic exaggeration, that he finds his own speech ludicrous. Thus, while seeming to express his submissive devotion to a lady, he ridicules both his own attitude and his language, by the untoward comparison of the last line:

> Voilà tantôt une heure qu'en langueur
> Mon coeur si simple s'abreuve
> De vos vilaines rigueurs,
> Avec le regard bon d'un terre-neuve.
>            (*L'Imitation*, "Locutions des Pierrots," I)

Like Pierrot, and like Shakespeare's Hamlet, who organizes the "play within a play" and feigns madness, the speaker of the *Derniers vers* is a performer: he adopts various poses, such as that of the "Grand Chancelier de l'Analyse" in *Dv* IV, and imagines how he would act in different situations. In *Dv* X he sees himself married to his "petite quotidienne" but thinking of her as an inaccessible stranger:

> Et puis? L'observer dans le monde,
> Et songer dans les coins:
> "Oh, qu'elle est loin! Oh, qu'elle est belle!
> "Oh! qui est-elle? A qui est-elle?
> "Oh, quelle inconnue! Oh, lui parler! Oh, l'emmener!"

In *Dv* XI he pictures the scene in which his beloved is being unfaithful to him while he wanders around outside; this is followed by an alternative episode where he pities both himself and her:

> Je me dirai: Oh! à cette heure,
> Elle est bien loin, elle pleure,
> Le grand vent se lamente aussi,
> Et moi je suis seul dans ma demeure,
> Avec mon noble coeur tout transi  . . .

Again, as with Pierrot, role-playing is accompanied by an addiction to an appropriate type of rhetoric—usually, as here, that of love ("mon noble coeur tout transi"). The Hamlet of the *Moralités Légen-*

*daires* plays the role of *l'Incompris* for the benefit of the young girl whose canary he has deliberately killed:

> —Oh! pardon, pardon! Je ne l'ai pas fait exprès! Ordonne-moi toutes les expiations. Mais je suis si bon! J'ai un coeur d'or comme on n'en fait plus. Tu me comprends, n'est-ce pas, Toi?
> Oh monseigneur, monseigneur! balbutie la petite fille. Oh! si vous saviez! Je vous comprends tant! Je vous aime depuis si long-temps! J'ai tout compris . . .
> Hamlet se lève. "Encore une!" pense-t-il.

This "Encore une!" shows clearly that Hamlet has deliberately been using the conventional discourse of love in order to test the girl's reaction; her reply is equally banal, but in her case it is "sincere": unaware that her words have been spoken thousands of times before and will be again, perhaps by herself to someone else, she does not realize that Hamlet has no faith in them. Laforgue's women have no distance on their language: they say what they mean, or what they think they mean. Humming their "stériles ritournelles," they ignore the fact that "La vie est vraie et criminelle."

Despite their mockery of women's readiness to accept the stereo-typed roles offered by society, Hamlet and Pierrot find themselves acting out similarly conventional roles. They are both supremely aware of themselves as unique individuals ("—Et, au fond, dire que j'existe! Que j'ai ma vie à moi!" exclaims the Hamlet of the *Moral-ités*); like Baudelaire's dandy they experience "le besoin ardent de se faire une originalité";[34] yet they are obliged to "vivre de vieux compromis," as Lord Pierrot puts it in his "Complainte." Part of their difficulty in asserting their personality stems from a lack of self-knowledge ("je ne me possédais pas bien moi-même"), but another important factor is their realization that language simply does not allow one to be original. The uniqueness they both feel can only be expressed with the "words, words, words" of other people. Laforgue's poetry abounds, therefore, in clichés, in the banal, stereotyped phrases of a sophisticated group of people playing endless love-games, asserting that "On n'aime qu'une fois," accus-ing one another: "Assez! assez! / C'est toi qui as commencé" (*Dv* VIII), or assuring one another that "Je t'aime pour toi seul" ("Pierrots (on a des principes)"). In the section of the *Mélanges posthumes* entitled "Sur la femme" the following passage appears, under the sub-heading "Première entrevue d'aveux":

> Dès qu'on s'est bien dit et dûment déclaré "je t'aime," un silence, presqu'un froid. Alors, celui des deux qui est destiné à s'en aller plus tard (c'est fatal) commence ses inutiles litanies rétrospectives: "Ah! *moi*, il y a longtemps déjà! . . . Tenez, vous ne saurez jamais! . . . Oh! la première fois que je vous vis . . . etc."[35]

Such "litanies" are typical of Laforgue's speakers: the girl in *Derniers vers* IX talks of her "vie faite exprès," and affirms: "ma destinée se borne . . . / A te suivre" because "c'est bien toi et non un autre." If Laforgue's personae all have similar voices, it is because the things they say tend to be what they have heard other people say. Many of their phrases sound like the refrains of popular songs, a genre with which the *Complaintes* were of course closely associated. In the "Complainte des Blackboulés" we read: "L'orchestre du jardin jouait ce 'si tu m'aimes' / Que vous savez"; and the refrain of the "Complainte des pianos" was taken from a popular song of the time: "Tu t'en vas et tu nous laisses, / Tu nous laiss's et tu t'en vas. . . ."

Pierrot, being a comic figure, likes to give an unexpected twist to the conventional phrases he proffers. In the famous "Autre Complainte de Lord Pierrot," the lady's banal exclamation "Ah! tu ne m'aimes pas; tant d'autres sont jaloux!" is countered by Pierrot with another, totally inappropriate, cliché: "Merci, pas mal; et vous?" Similarly, to the lady's accusation " 'Ah! tu te lasseras le premier, j'en suis sûre,' " Pierrot responds with a stereotyped expression from another context but which makes admirable sense here, too: "Après vous, s'il vous plaît!" The twist which Pierrot gives to banal, stereotyped phrases empties them of any last shred of meaning they may have had when used in their normal context; they become as hollow as the refrains like "tir-lan-laire" or "diguedondaine" in the songs Laforgue was imitating in the *Complaintes*. The implication must be that language, like the conventional gestures of mime, is habitual. The automatic responses of people's daily exchange are pure ritual, devoid of profound content, revealing and communicating nothing of value.

Pierrot and Hamlet both confront the problem of how, using language, to break out of the established patterns of language, and the answers proposed are extreme. One is to indulge in the type of word-play practised by Pierrot, ironically twisting the meanings of words; ultimately this remains unsatisfactory, however, since it precludes any meaningful communication with an interlocutor. A second possibility is silence: "rien n'est pratique que se taire, se taire, et agir en conséquence," says the Hamlet of the *Moralités*. ("Agir" would be another way of expressing oneself, but a notoriously difficult one for Shakespeare's Hamlet and Laforgue's; as Albert Sonnenfeld says, for Laforgue's Hamlet, "action means acting," i.e., once again, the repetition of a role.)[36] Silence is also the solution adopted by Laforgue's *Pierrot fumiste*, in that he offers no explanation for his peculiar conduct to his bride; the role of Pierrot was traditionally silent, of course, being mimed. The alternative to silence is death, which befalls both Shakespeare's and Laforgue's Hamlets; and death means silence, as the former's dying words proclaim.

Language, then, plays a large part in the dislocation of the notion of personality that we witness in Laforgue; his poetry conveys the impression that character *is* the stereotyped phrases in which it expresses itself. Unlike the three-dimensional characters of Browning, carefully constructed by the accumulation of realistic detail, Laforgue's personae only possess certain recognizable traits—jealousy, faithlessness, timidity, tenderness, brutality, sentimentality—endlessly repeated and, through irony, endlessly negated. Laforgue's universe is one of repetition; instead of presenting an authentic, unique self, his speakers demonstrate that the "I" is a place where repetitions are gathered: "Mais tu ne peux que te répéter, ô honte!" exclaims the "paria" of "Simple agonie" (*Dv* VI). One can only repeat oneself and repeat the words of others.

Michael Riffaterre suggests that to make a literary character speak in stereotyped phrases almost automatically deprives him of personality because they imply conformity to ready-made attitudes or standards:

> La formule figée, parce qu'elle est inséparable de certaines attitudes sociales ou morales, sert à l'auteur à situer son personnage: il n'a qu'à mettre sur ses lèvres les modes verbales d'un milieu donné. . . . Recueillir des automatismes, c'est choisir délibérément de voir l'homme sous un mauvais jour, dans les com-

portements sociaux ou mentaux par lesquels il abdique sa
personnalité.

These statements appear in Riffaterre's essay on "Le Cliché dans la
prose littéraire," but they apply equally well to Laforgue's poetry.
Similarly, John E. Jackson speaks of the "usure du langage chez
Laforgue" and suggests that "Les mots sont en voie, pour lui, de
perdre leur *créance sémantique*. Ils sont formules, stéréotypes, c'est-
à-dire omnitude autonome, désinvestie de presque tout répondant
au *moi* qui les profère."[37] The cynical attitude of Laforgue's male
speakers exposes the clichés for what they are: trite, empty phrases
passed from mouth to mouth but devoid of any true meaning—the
sort of phrases collected by Flaubert in his *Dictionnaire des idées
reçues*, or, more appropriately since the context is almost always
one of love, by Roland Barthes in his *Fragments d'un discours
amoureux*. According to Laforgue's men, "love" is largely a matter of
being in love with the discourse of love. Thus the speaker of "Sur
une défunte" (*Dv* XI) suggests that a woman can make the same
declarations indifferently to "les nobles A, B, C, ou D," to any of
whom she will say:

> "Oh, tes yeux, ta démarche!
> "Oh, le son fatal de ta voix!
> "Voilà si longtemps que je te cherche!
> "Oh, c'est bien Toi, cette fois! . . ."

The man implies that these are simply empty verbal formulas which
can be reproduced at will, as they are in so many of Laforgue's
poems, either deliberately—by the men, or unconsciously—by the
women. Here as elsewhere Laforgue emphasizes the sheer auto-
matism of a language that nevertheless purports to speak the heart:
never original, the discourse of love is always a repetition of what
someone has said previously, and cannot therefore represent the
authentic expression of the unique Self. Along with the notion of
love, this view of language as repetition undermines the very con-
cept of interiority itself: for, since words are always exterior, re-
peated, overheard, the individual can never possess language,
which remains outside him, belonging to others as well as himself.

iv) Dialogical utterance in the dramatic monologue

Needless to say, the notions of repetivity and externality apply not only to the language of love but to language in general; they are central to the influential theory of intertextuality, or dialogical discourse, outlined by Bakhtin, who stresses that no single utterance can claim to be totally individual or unique. The words we use, he says, have been used by others and are inevitably impregnated with their intentions: "Le langage n'est pas un milieu neutre. Il ne devient pas aisément, librement, la propriété du locuteur. Il est peuplé et surpeuplé d'intentions étrangères."[38] It follows therefore that "tout énoncé se rapporte aussi à des énoncés antérieurs, donnant ainsi lieu à des relations *intertextuelles* (ou dialogiques)."[39] This is the case not only in works of literature but, as Bakhtin points out, in everyday speech, where the social context plays an important role: "Aucun énoncé en général ne peut être attribué au seul locuteur: il est le *produit de l'interaction des locuteurs* et, plus largement, le produit de toute cette *situation sociale* complexe, dans laquelle il a surgi."[40] Stereotyped expressions offer a privileged, extreme illustration of this state of affairs. At the end of Dv III ("Dimanches"), the speaker temporarily adopts a motherly, protective attitude that expresses itself in clichés and makes light of the sufferings of the "pauvre, pâle et piètre individu" recounted earlier in the poem:

> —Allons, dernier des poètes,
> Toujours enfermé tu te rendras malade!
> Vois, il fait beau temps tout le monde est dehors,
> Va donc acheter deux sous d'ellébore,
> Ca te fera une petite promenade.

In lines 2–3 and 5 we can hear, as well as the poet's voice, that of any mother talking to her child, and the speaker parodies this voice while at the same time offering a valid comment on his own behaviour. He is temporarily looking at himself from the outside, or as Bakhtin puts it "avec les yeux d'un autre homme, d'un autre représentant de [s]on groupe social ou de [s]a classe."[41] The resulting speech is "double-voiced," or "dialogical," i.e., it is an utterance in which two voices can be heard, even though only one speech act is involved.

This deliberate "quotation" of stereotyped phrases represents an essentially parodic gesture; indeed, as Claude Bouché points out, the idea of intertextuality is crucial to parody, since the parodic text constitutes, by definition, a text constructed with other texts; in other words, "appliquée à la parodie, la méthode intertextuelle n'est plus seulement une option parmi d'autres possibles."[42] All texts are "intertextual" but some are deliberately and systematically so, particularly those which employ parody and related devices, all of which can be defined as "des formes, plus ou moins littérales . . . de la *citation*." One of them is "la stéréotypie," involving the multiple, diffuse referent of a *discours*, rather than a particular text:

> Avec la stéréotypie, on débouche sur le vaste domaine des poncifs et des "topoï", des clichés et des lieux communs. . . . Styles éculés et situations-types se rencontrent un peu partout: dans les livres, certes, mais aussi dans les journaux, la publicité, les messages politiques, le langage de la rue, bref, dans tout ce qui est manifestation écrite ou orale collective.

It is "stéréotypie" of this diffuse type which forms the main thrust of the parodic impulse of Laforgue's poetry, though parody of specific texts does occur in his work, in the *Moralités légendaires*, and Bouché devotes a section of his book on Lautréamont to a thorough analysis of Laforgue's "Hamlet" as a typical example of parody. Parody of literary stereotypes and conventions, as well as of the "lieux communs" of everyday speech and in particular of amorous discourse, abounds in both the poetry and the *Moralités*.[43]

Distinguishing between pastiche and parody, Bouché states that pastiche imitates only the style of a text, whereas parody can deal with any aspect of it; he relates this to a similar distinction between *cliché* and *lieu commun*, quoting Rémy de Gourmont: "cliché représente la matérialité même de la phrase; lieu commun, plutôt la banalité de l'idée." Riffaterre too emphasizes that a cliché must be a set figure of speech:

> la stéréotypie à elle seule ne fait pas le cliché: il faut encore que la séquence verbale figée par l'usage présente un fait de style, qu'il s'agisse d'une métaphore comme *fourmilière humaine*, d'une antithèse comme *meurtre juridique*, d'une hyperbole comme *mortelles inquiétudes*, etc.[44]

Laforgue plays with clichés of this type frequently in the *Moralités*; sometimes he "renews" them by altering one or more words; or he deliberately underscores them, for instance when "le cliché 'public houleux' " is said to come into Hamlet's mind as he surveys the scene in the theatre, or when, Lohengrin having dismissed his swan, the narrator declares: "Oh, sublime façon de brûler ses vaisseaux!" The poetry, however, offers far more examples of *lieux communs*: stereotyped expressions which are not figures of speech; Laforgue is concerned not only with their "style" or form but with the attitudes they betray, with the mentality of the speakers who proffer them so uncritically. Ruth Amossy and Elisheva Rosen claim that "le lieu commun . . . renvoie à une stéréotypie de la pensée et non de l'unité discursive"—though in practice the two tend to go hand in hand, stereotyped language reflecting "stéréotypie de la pensée." The ironic quotation of clichés or *lieux communs* can be a useful device for suggesting criticism of the assumptions underlying them. As Amossy and Rosen say of *Eugénie Grandet*, "C'est souvent à la faveur d'un jeu de mots ou d'un emploi ironique du cliché que certaines valeurs consacrées se voient tournées en dérision."[45] Laforgue's love-sick ladies are condemned out of their own mouths by the platitudes they utter.

The deliberate quotation of banal expressions tends, as Riffaterre suggests, to become "un signal, un indice de l'ironie ou de l'humour." However, phrases used in this way must themselves be marked or signalled lest the reader should accuse the author "d'avoir inconsciemment employé ces clichés que justement il prête à ses personnages."[46] These marks of distanciation can be typographical, as in the case of italics or the quotation marks and *points de suspension* so frequent in Laforgue:

> . . . le pur flacon des vives gouttes
> Sera, *comme il convient*, d'eau propre baptisé.
> > ("Complainte des pianos . . .")
> Oh! ce fut pour vos cors, et ce fut pour l'automne,
> Qu'il nous montra qu' "on meurt d'amour"!
> > (*Dv* VI)

Or they can involve exaggeration, repetition or accumulation. In *Dv*

IX, the speaker parodies the utterance of an intense, passionate young girl; his voice can be heard through hers because of the sheer exaggeration of her claims:

> "Pour moi, tu n'es pas comme les autres hommes,
> "Ils sont ces messieurs, toi tu viens des cieux.
> "Ta bouche me fait baisser les yeux
> "Et ton port me transporte
> "Et je m'en découvre des trésors!" etc.

A certain weakness in the logic of the girl's argument also indicates irony:

> "Tu me demandes pourquoi toi et non un autre,
> "Ah, laisse, c'est bien toi et non un autre.

> "J'en suis sûre comme du vide insensé de mon coeur
> "Et comme de votre air mortellement moqueur."

The man's mocking voice can be heard distinctly in this unconvincing choice of comparisons, as well as the insistent acoustic repetitions he puts into the girl's mouth (*port, transporte, trésors; pleure, soeurs, peur, meure*).

The quotation of stereotyped expressions such as those proffered by the girl in this poem represents at once a mimetic and a parodic procedure: mimetic in that it imitates the language a naive young girl might use in reality; parodic in that the speaker of the poem clearly views her utterances in an ironic light, passing, as Riffaterre says, "du portrait à la charge."[47] This tendency for the quotation of clichés to slide from mimesis into parody is explored by Amossy and Rosen. In the realist novel—as in Laforgue's poetry—the use of clichés helps to establish the feeling of "reality," since they inject into a literary text the discourse of a "texte culturel extérieur au récit," namely that of everyday life.[48] Judiciously placed, therefore, "le cliché assure la crédibilité de la narration en la conformant au savoir du public et, conséquemment, en provoquant une reconnaissance confondue avec la connaissance du réel." However, the artificiality of this procedure becomes evident when the "device is bared"—when it becomes a parodic gesture (marked, typographically or otherwise, as in the examples from Laforgue quoted above):

> Le cliché ne contribue néanmoins à consolider l'édifice du vraisemblable qu'en le marquant du sceau de la conventionnalité. Le procédé, en effet, se laisse aisément reconnaître et la figure originellement destinée à "masquer les lois du texte" tend précisément à les exhiber. . . . Le même fait de langage se voit dès lors attribuer, à des niveaux différents, deux fonctions inverses: d'une part le cliché renforce une.vérité commune, renvoie à un savoir préétabli, "naturel"; de l'autre, il en dénonce la conventionnalité et la facticité.

On this second level the cliché also implies an awareness of the conventionality of language itself; it reminds us that "toute *mimesis* passe par un rapport aux modèles: modèles rhétoriques, modèles idéologiques, qui fournissent les codes de la (re)production du 'réel.' "[49] This property of the cliché, or of "la stéréotypie," accentuates the feeling we have, reading Laforgue, that his is a universe of words eminently conscious of itself as such, aware of its own non-referentiality. As Bouché says of the *Chants de Maldoror*, Laforgue's works, written within fifteen or twenty years of Lautréamont's, "se situent à la croisée de ces mouvements multiples qui ne cessent de ramener l'écriture à elle-même."[50] Laforgue's constant repetition of empty verbal formulas, whether of a literary or an everyday type, inevitably suggests that there is nothing *but* "words, words, words." "A mesure que la répétition se répète," says Shoshana Felman of Flaubert's *Un Coeur simple*, "le signe linguistique se décale à la fois de son sens et de son référent"; she concludes that the function of clichés is "de nous forcer à réfléchir l'*arbitraire* du signe, qu'ils mettent en évidence, en dénonçant du même coup l'illusion réaliste et référentielle."[51]

A distinction can be made on these grounds between Laforgue and Browning who, at least in the early monologues under discussion above, is still attempting a "genuine" mimesis of reality. If his characters speak in clichés or stereotyped phrases it is on the mimetic level, in order to give an *effet de naturel*, the flavour of oral speech. Laforgue, on the contrary, sets up the spoken effect only to destroy it again; his speakers constantly mix clichés with technical or intellectual words, oral syntax with literary turns of phrase, as in this example from "Ballade": "Allez, c'est bon. Mon fatal polypier / A distingué certaine polypière," or in "Autre complainte de Lord Pierrot" when Pierrot says ". . . .d'un oeil qui vers l'Inconscient s'emballe: / "Merci, pas mal; et vous?" The ironic mixing of literary and colloquial contexts tends to deflate the pretentiousness of the more formal style, while at the same time the intrusion of learned words or literary phrases into colloquial speech destroys any *effet de naturel*. The constant juxtaposition of two different lexical codes, the familiar and the erudite, emphasizes the basic premise that nothing is whole, integral, true to itself—neither a man's language nor his "character." Browning, on the other hand, still assumes that language can communicate a person's essential self, or his own view of it; that one can know someone else through language. Furthermore, since Browning's characters mean more or less what they say (even if the *reader* understands more, or differently), their language requires no marks of distanciation such as the conscious exaggeration employed by Laforgue's speakers, who parody not only the speech and attitudes of others but also their own. The man who mocks at the love-lorn girl of *Dv* IX taunts himself, too, for wanting the experience evoked in the first lines to come about. This is revealed by the emphatic tone of his own speech:

> Oh! qu'une, d'Elle-même, un beau soir, sût venir
> Ne voyant plus que boire à mes lèvres, ou mourir! . . .
>
> Et alors, les averses lustrales jusqu'au matin,
> Le grand clapissement des averses toute la nuit! Enfin!

The self-irony evident in these lines accomplishes a definite distancing effect, since it is impossible for the reader to identify with a character who is ironic at his own expense, who has a "dialogical relationship," as Bakhtin terms it, to his own speech:

> It is possible to have dialogical relationships to one of our own
> utterances, to its individual parts, and to an individual word
> within it, if we in some way separate ourselves from them, if we
> speak with an inner reservation, if we maintain *distance* from

them, as if limiting or dividing our authorship in two (my emphasis).[52]

Self-parody involves just such an "inner reservation," and this type of "dialogical relationship" occurs frequently in the poems of Laforgue. In the despairing exclamation of Dv XII: "Oh! arrose, arrose / Mon coeur si brûlant, ma chair si intéressante!" we can hear both a genuine cry of distress and, thanks to the repetitions of "si" and "arrose," and the use of the word "intéressante," the mocking comment of a speaker who disapproves of self-pity and melodramatic gestures. This self-parody effectively distances the speaker from his own speech, which he seems to regard as a text on which to comment, or as the words of another.

According to Bakhtin, such distanciation is the antithesis of poetic language: "Le langage du poète, c'est son langage à lui. Il s'y trouve tout entier, sans partage. Il utilise chaque forme, chaque mot, chaque expression dans leur sens direct ("sans guillemets", pour ainsi dire)."[53] Laforgue, however, handles almost every word with "guillemets." Quite apart from using quotation marks simply to denote direct speech (which is not what Bakhtin has in mind), he continually employs words, especially stereotyped expressions, in a way which suggests that they are quotations and that their significance can alter according to the speaker—or indeed for one and the same speaker. Language thus becomes not merely the means of representation but the very object of representation. For Bakhtin, this phenomenon is typical of prose and specifically of the novel: "Le langage, dans le roman, ne fait pas que représenter: il sert aussi lui-même d'objet de représentation.[54] In this way speaker, author and reader are all distanced from the act of utterance, whereas in poetry, Bakhtin insists: "Chaque mot doit exprimer spontanément et directement le dessein du poète; il ne doit exister aucune *distance* entre lui et ses mots" (my emphasis).[55]

If, then, an essential characteristic of the dramatic monologue is the postulation of a certain distance between the poet and the speaker of the poem, this feature would indicate for Bakhtin a close connection between the dramatic monologue and prose. Indeed, since the voice we hear in the dramatic monologue belongs simultaneously to the poet and the speaker, it clearly constitutes an inherently "dialogical" form. In Laforgue's poems, as we have seen, there is a further "split," within the speaker's utterance, resulting from his ironic stance in regard to both his own speech and that of his interlocutors.

Bakhtin considers that dialogical utterances belong almost exclusively to prose because (lyric) poetry presupposes stylistic unity: "pour la plupart des genres poétiques l'unité du système du langage, l'unité (et l'unicité) de l'individualité linguistique et verbale du poète, sont le postulat indispensable du style poétique." The very rhythms of poetry, he claims, discourage "bivocal" or "plurivocal" speech: *"Le rythme, en créant la participation directe de chaque élément du système d'accentuation à l'ensemble . . .* raffermit et resserre plus encore l'unité et le caractère fermé et uni du style poétique et du langage unique postulé par ce style."[56] This is an interesting comment in view of Laforgue's experimentations with rhythm in the *Complaintes* and *L'Imitation de Notre-Dame la lune* and his eventual adoption in *Derniers vers* of the *vers libre*.

However, Bakhtin allows that the work of certain poets does admit of "plurilinguisme," and he lists these exceptions in a footnote: Horace, Villon, Heine, I. Annenski—and Laforgue; "si hétérogènes que soient ces phénomènes."[57] No doubt he could have added Browning to this list. Elsewhere, Bakhtin mentions "the 'prosaic' lyric of Heine"—whom Laforgue admired,[58] and with whose ironic style his own verse clearly has a remarkable affinity—as an example of one of the "rare and isolated cases" in the nineteenth century of "[poetic] works which do not reduce their entire verbal material to a common denominator," and he adds that "the drastic 'prosification' of the lyric occurs only in the 20th century."[59] For Bakhtin, then, Laforgue belongs to a group of poets who, in exploiting the resources of dialogical speech, have adopted a technique normally reserved for prose.

Bakhtin's suggestion of a link between prose and the dialogical utterance characteristic of the dramatic monologue is summarized as follows by Todorov:

> Le poète assume son acte de parole, qui est dès lors une énonciation au premier degré, non représentée, sans guillemets. Le pro-

sateur représente le langage, introduit une distance entre lui-
même et son discours.[60]

The reasons for the opposition between poetry and prose, he says,
lie in the fact that "le poème *est* un acte d'énonciation, alors que le
roman en représente un." Todorov comments, very appropriately,
on the similarity between Bakhtin's opposition of poetry and prose
and the distinction drawn by Käte Hamburger some twenty years
later between the lyric and narrative genres. She regards the lyric
poem as "the statement of a genuine statement-subject"[61] (cf. "le
poème *est* un acte d'énonciation"), whereas the novel or drama
*represents* a fictional world, a semblance of life, like the dramatic
monologues of Browning. Certainly the realistic detail in Brown-
ing's early monologues invites the reader to approach them as he
would a fiction, and this tendency is encouraged by the presence of
elements that point towards a plot, in poems like "Porphyria's
Lover," "The Laboratory," "The Bishop Orders His Tomb." Laforgue
provides much less in the way of realistic detail or plot, but the
novelistic feeling remains to some extent, thanks largely to his play
with voices.[62]

The move away from mimesis which emerges from a comparison
of Laforgue's dramatic monologues with those of Browning's early
and middle periods accompanies a general devaluation of the no-
tion of personality. Much less idiosyncratic than the Browning-
esque persona, the "I" in Laforgue sees itself not just as split into two
but as adopting a multiplicity of poses and playing a succession of
different roles over and over again. All the Self can do is repeat itself;
it is as intertextual as its language. And the constant repetition of
clichés by Laforgue's personae suggests that their words reflect no
"real" personal feeling; that their language refers, in fact, to no real-
ity beyond itelf.

The question of mimesis in relation to the work of art—or, on the
contrary, of the latter's self-sufficiency—becomes crucial when we
approach the work of Mallarmé. Commenting on Mallarmé's "Mim-
ique," itself a commentary of Paul Margueritte's play *Pierrot assassin
de sa femme*, Derrida states that:

rédigeant et composant lui-même son soliloque, le traçant sur la

page blanche qu'il est, le Mime ne se laisse dicter son texte de-
puis aucun autre lieu. Il ne représente rien, n'imite rien, n'a pas à
se conformer à un référent antérieur dans un dessein d'adéqua-
tion ou de vraisemblance.[63]

Mallarmé's own summary of Margueritte's play, "La scène n'illustre
que l'idée, pas une action effective,"[64] is also an admirable descrip-
tion of his poem L'Après-midi d'un faune—arguably the first dra-
matic monologue written in French, since it was conceived in 1865
and first published in 1876, nine years before the Complaintes.

# CHAPTER FOUR

# Self-questioning: Mallarmé

To a greater extent than Laforgue, and perhaps even than Browning, Mallarmé was passionately interested in theatre, although the only work he ever tried seriously to have staged was the "Monologue d'un faune," as *L'Après-midi d'un faune* was originally entitled. In its final form this poem represents the first true dramatic monologue in French and the only one in Mallarmé's output,[1] though the "Scène" from *Hérodiade* (originally conceived as a three-act tragedy) possesses various features of the dramatic monologue despite its dialogue form.

In a letter to Cazalis, Mallarmé said of the "Monologue d'un faune," "je le fais absolument scénique, non *possible au théâtre*, mais *exigeant le théâtre*"; yet a glance at the work reveals that, despite a few stage directions such as "Frappant du pied," "A grands pas," "Le front dans les mains," the "play" is basically static and lacking in "l'anecdote nécessaire que demande le public,"—the reason given by Banville and Coquelin *aîné* for refusing to stage it.[2] In studying *L'Après-midi d'un faune* we shall need to examine Mallarmé's views on theatre—views that allowed him to consider a work like the "Monologue d'un faune" as "absolument scénique"; and in so doing we shall come across the same two theatrical figures beloved of

Laforgue: Pierrot and Hamlet, both intimately bound up with Mallarmé's conception of theatre.

# I. Mimesis, fictionality and myth

As early as 1862, in a letter to Cazalis, Mallarmé applied to himself the image of a despondent, inactive Hamlet:

> Que vous serez désillusionné quand vous verrez cet individu maussade qui reste des journées entières la tête sur le marbre de la cheminée, sans penser : ridicule Hamlet qui ne peut se rendre compte de son affaissement.[3]

Perhaps it is this vision of Hamlet, with his hesitancy and inability to act, which leads the "pitre châtié" to describe himself as "reniant le mauvais / Hamlet," since he, the clown, has, on the contrary, just taken a decisive step. Another derogatory reference to Hamlet appears in the first version of Mallarmé's early poem "Le Guignon" (1862), where he appears as a symbol of the *poète maudit*:

> Quand chacun a sur eux craché tous ses dédains,
> Nus, assoiffés de grand, et priant le tonnerre,
> Ces Hamlet abreuvés de malaises badins
>
> Vont ridiculement se pendre au réverbère.[4]

Mallarmé's Hamlet, like Laforgue's and like the *poète maudit*, is in search of an Ideal (cf. "assoiffés de grand"), and this preoccupation becomes much more pronounced in the next work which introduces—but does not name—the figure of Hamlet, *Igitur*. Charles Chassé points out that in *Igitur* "la silhouette du prince danois se détache continuellement dans le filigrane du récit"; Claudel, in "La Catastrophe d'*Igitur*," draws a parallel between this work and *Hamlet*; and Dr. Bonniot refers to Igitur as a "sorte d'Hamlet plus impersonnel."[5] Furthermore, Mallarmé apparently intended, at a later point in his career, to write a play entitled *Hamlet et le vent*, and Haskell Block points out the similarities between the little we know of this work, and *Igitur*.[6]

Igitur offers an interesting contrast with Laforgue's Hamlet, a sensitive soul, tempted by the Absolute and scathing of the world around him, but at the same time living in the world, adopting conventional masks and poses. A Hamlet who has gone one stage further, Igitur renounces the world completely, to live alone in his tower pondering essential questions: the Absolute and infinity, Time and le néant, necessity and chance, life and death, the contingency of the Self. And whereas Laforgue's Hamlet suggests a dislocated character, torn between different versions of himself, Mallarmé's Igitur is totally devoid of character. One can attribute to him only a certain nobility of purpose, suitable in a hero. For while Laforgue, the mythoclast, tends to poke fun at Hamlet (as at any "hero"), there is no denying his heroic status for Mallarmé, or his importance as representative of the supreme Hero.

"Le héros," says Mallarmé of Hamlet, "—tous comparses, il se promène, pas plus, lisant au livre de lui-même, haut et vivant Signe . . ." (p. 1564). The hero as conceived by Mallarmé is not a character, but a Sign or symbol. In fact Mallarmé deplored the tendency of realist drama to depict everyday people in everyday situations; after a performance of Sardou's Le Crocodile he complains:

> Appuyant sur des moi de rencontre, nommément il en fait Monsieur un tel, Madame une telle et satisfait à la badauderie sans présenter, d'après la haute esthétique, plutôt d'essentielles figures.(p. 337)

Essential figures do not have names like "Monsieur un tel" but "Hérodiade" or "Igitur," and they belong to the realm of the Absolute: Mallarmé proclaims "avec dandysme" his own "incompétence, sur autre chose que l'absolu" (p. 330). He spurns plays imitating real life, in favour of "la pièce écrite au folio du ciel et mimée avec le geste de ses passions par l'Homme" (p. 294), for, ideally, as he declares in "Mimique": "La scène n'illustre que l'idée, pas une action effective" (p. 310). The text entitled "Mimique" evaluates Paul Margueritte's play Pierrot assassin de sa femme and in it Mallarmé describes mime as the "genre situé plus près de principes qu'aucun!" Pierrot, the mime, does not enact an "action effective," a mimesis of reality, but by his gestures alludes to an action: "Tel opère le Mime,

dont le jeu se borne à une allusion perpétuelle sans briser la glace"
(p. 310). By his "allusion perpétuelle," the mime installs "un milieu,
pur, de fiction" rather than imitating reality. Derrida, commenting
on "Mimique," remarks that

> rédigeant et composant lui-même son soliloque, le traçant sur la
> page blanche qu'il est, le Mime ne se laisse dicter son texte de-
> puis aucun autre lieu. Il ne représente rien, n'imite rien, n'a pas à
> se conformer à un référent antérieur dans un dessein d'adéqua-
> tion ou de vraisemblance.[7]

All these comments apply admirably to the Faun as well as to
Pierrot. Like the mime, by suggestion and allusion, the Faun "in-
stalle . . . un milieu, pur, de fiction," a space in which nymphs
appear. The question as to whether these nymphs were real, a
dream, or an illusion of his "sens fabuleux" is deliberately left unre-
solved. In the "Monologue d'un faune" they were certainly real, es-
caping from his arms as the "play" began—though the Faun still
asked himself whether they were a dream or an illusion, doubts
which were dispelled by the discovery of "une morsure / Féminine"
on his fingers. However, the fact that they were intended as real in
the first version proves nothing about their status in the final one.
The Faun clearly remains undecided. "Aimai-je un rêve?" he asks,
recalling the question of an illustrious predecessor, Faust, who in
very similar circumstances, enticed by nymphs, asks

> Why, do I dream this? Recollect it?
> This blissful sight was mine before.[8]

Here, though, the reader knows Faust has seen them in a dream,
whereas with the Faun we cannot tell. He goes on to consider the
possibility that the nymphs were an illusion, engendered by the
sound of water or the feel of the hot wind in his fleece; but then he
remembers that there is—or was—no water in the vicinity other
than the notes sprinkled by the flute, no wind other than his breath
or the "souffle artificiel / De l'inspiration"; so the possibility of an
illusion based on these phenomena is ruled out, though not, of
course, that of an illusion due to some other cause. As for the theory

that they were a dream, the Faun seems at first to opt for this explanation, since he sees

> . . . maint rameau subtil, qui, demeuré les vrais
> Bois mêmes, prouve, hélas! que bien seul je m'offrais
> Pour triomphe la faute idéale de roses.

Nevertheless, the fact that the woods are real does not in itself prove that the nymphs were unreal or that he was therefore "bien seul";[9] unless, perhaps, he has a mental picture of the nymphs in some other setting—that of his dream. However, the Faun then immediately goes on to consider the theory of an illusion, which suggests he is not convinced the nymphs were a dream. Furthermore, the final line of the poem, "Couple, adieu, je vais voir l'ombre que tu devins," implies that the couple *became* a shadow: if they were merely figures of a dream in the first place they were never anything but shadows ("A dream itself is but a shadow"), whereas if they were real but escaped him, then they became mere shadows in his memory. Finally, Mallarmé evidently intended the nymphs to speak a dialogue while the Faun slept,[10] which suggests he thought of them as real, however undecided the Faun may have been—unless, of course, he planned that the dialogue should take place within the context of the Faun's dream. . . . Ultimately the nymphs' status must remain ambiguous because what matters is the Faun's reaction to this very uncertainty.

The Faun is plainly conscious—like Faust—of the tragic discrepancy between a man's dreams and his life, of "l'antagonisme de rêve chez l'homme avec les fatalités à son existence départies par le malheur," which is the subject of *Hamlet* and indeed, according to Mallarmé, the only subject (p. 300). The Faun responds by installing, like the mime, "un milieu, pur, de fiction" through constant allusion to the objects of his desire ("je vais parler longtemps / Des déesses"), whatever their ontological status. As Kravis points out, the phenomenon of allusion is a "phenomenon of fiction, since what is visible never appears to be 'the real thing', but only anticipation or recollection of it."[11] Anticipation and recollection are the stuff of which *L'Après-midi d'un faune* is made, in a synthesis that Mallarmé, in "Mimique," calls "un hymen (d'où procède le

Rêve) . . . entre le désir et l'accomplissement, la perpétration et
son souvenir" (p. 310). The Faun, moreover, is an artist and there-
fore aware, like the poet, of the drama inherent in the complex
relation of fiction to reality, as his reference to "confusions/
Fausses" in the following lines implies:

> Mais, bast! arcane tel élut pour confident
> Le jonc vaste et jumeau dont sous l'azur on joue:
> Qui, détournant à soi le trouble de la joue,
> Rêve, dans un solo long, que nous amusions
> La beauté d'alentour par des confusions
> Fausses entre elle-même et notre chant crédule.

This evokes a kind of musical fiction, the transformation of the real
world ("La beauté d'alentour") into a song—or a poem. Again, an
awareness of the close links between fiction and the "real" would
emerge from a further possible interpretation of the final phrase of
the poem, "l'ombre que tu devins," which could refer to the shadow
the nymphs became as subjects of the Faun's song (or fiction, or
poem), in which he has "perpetuated" them. The preceding words,
"Je vais rejoindre," would then project the Faun himself into a fic-
tion, at a different level, that of Mallarmé's poem, implying a con-
sciousness on the Faun's part of himself as the subject of that poem.

The way the poem divides into sections also helps to convey an
impression of fiction. The parts of the poem set in italics represent
the Faun's reconstruction of the day's events, whether in reality or
in a dream, whereas the sections in Roman type record his thoughts
on the subject "now," in the afternoon. However, this isolation of
the italicized sections gives them the appearance of a fictional story
told by the Faun, especially as they are introduced by the verb
"CONTEZ," in capitals. There is more realistic detail in the itali-
cized passages, apparently supplied by the Faun's memory of actual
events, but also tending to strengthen the impression of a fiction:

> . . . . . . . . . *sur l'or glauque de lointaines*
> *Verdures dédiant leur vigne à des fontaines,*
> *Ondoie une blancheur animale au repos.*
> . . . . . . . . . . . . . . . . . . . . . . . . .
> *Je les ravis, sans les désenlacer, et vole*

*A ce massif, haï par l'ombrage frivole,*
*De roses tarissant tout parfum au soleil. . . .*

As we saw in Browning, the accumulation of realistic detail tends, paradoxically, to reinforce the impression of a fictional story, but a vast difference exists between the two poets' attitudes towards fiction: Browning places each story into the mouth of a realistic character who tells it as if it had actually happened to him, whereas in the *Faune* both the poet and the Faun himself are patently conscious of the problematic relation, particularly in literature, of appearance to reality, fact to fiction, words to the objects they represent. In fact the Faun's relation to his dream (or memory, or experience), involving doubts as to the very existence of the nymphs, i.e., of a referent, duplicates the reader's relation to the poem as he asks himself how to interpret this Faun and reflects on the possibility of moving from word to referent. Poetry uses words, which denote real objects, and yet, according to Mallarmé, it uses them in such a way as to render only the "notion pure" of an object while the thing itself almost vanishes:

> A quoi bon la merveille de transposer un fait de nature en sa presque disparition vibratoire selon le jeu de la parole, cependant; si ce n'est pour qu'en émane, sans la gêne d'un proche ou concret rappel, la notion pure (p. 368).

Kravis, commenting on this passage, states that

> The words set up a series of vibrations that cause reality almost, but not quite, to disappear. . . . 'La notion pure' does not cause reality to 'abdicate', but sets up a pattern of virtual, literary time, which merely sets reality on a different plane. . . . The written notional reality is . . . like the reality of a dream that one seems to see clearly enough to be convinced that it exists, but which can never be reached or verified: the sense of its presence is its only guarantee.[12]

The Faun's dream epitomizes this phenomenon. Furthermore, the "notion pure" emanating, with the help of words, from "un fait de nature" fascinates the Faun, as his celebration of empty grape skins illustrates:

> Moi, de ma rumeur fier, je vais parler longtemps
> Des déesses; et par d'idolâtres peintures,
> A leur ombre enlever encore des ceintures:
> Ainsi, quand des raisins j'ai sucé la clarté,
> Pour bannir un regret par ma feinte écarté,
> Rieur, j'élève au ciel d'été la grappe vide
> Et, soufflant dans ses peaux lumineuses, avide
> D'ivresse, jusqu'au soir je regarde au travers.

"A la plénitude réelle du raisin," comments Jean-Pierre Richard,

> succède le plaisir imaginaire d'un fruit vide, refabriqué par une
> *feinte*, empli par le souffle tout artificiel d'une invention humaine.
> Privé de suc, le monde est "regonflé" par l'activité mensongère de
> l'esprit. A cette activité on comprend que les choses servent
> seulement ici de support matériel, ou de prétexte. Tout ce que
> nous trouverons en elles, nous l'y aurons nous-mêmes introduit.

However, if everything is "mensonge issu de nous, qui nous prouvera que le vécu le plus aigu a été autre chose qu'un rêve?"[13] The Faun's search for proof can only be inconclusive. Evidently his "sens fabuleux" are fabulous not only in the sense of belonging to fable or myth (and in the sense of "prodigious"), but also strongly connote the etymological meaning of "creative of fables," i.e. fictions. Indeed, he utters this phrase at the very moment when he is considering the possibility that the Nymphs were his own fictitious creation: ". . . ou si les femmes dont tu gloses / Figurent un souhait de tes sens fabuleux!"

Uncertainty as to the reality of events in the *Faune* highlights another aspect of fictionality, and another drama: that of the Self. If what the Faun relates actually happened, then he is one kind of person: aggressive, impulsive, impatient; if, on the other hand, it was merely a dream, he can be seen as quite another type: sensuous still, but perhaps more self-contained, reflective: a dreamer, still anxious to fulfill his desire but not necessarily capable of attempting a double rape. As Richard says of Mallarmé's Hamlet, "qui se débat sous le mal d'apparaître" (p. 299), the Faun "figure la difficulté que toute âme authentique éprouve à être pleinement elle-même, il illustre l'hiatus qui sépare la pensée de la vie, l'être de la conscience d'être."[14] We have seen Laforgue's speakers experiencing the same problem and deliberately creating fictitious images of themselves by successively playing different roles; in the *Faune*, the hint at fiction is more subtle, since it remains unclear whether the Faun invented his story or whether it actually happened. But even if it did happen, the italics and the "CONTEZ" imply, there would still be an element of fiction involved, because the act of narrating events—and dreams—always tends to fictionalize them. A man's personality depends on the stories he tells about himself: the Self is, ultimately, a fiction. Part of the attraction of Hamlet for Mallarmé must have been his preoccupation with language, his awareness that a self can be created with nothing but "words, words, words." Philippe Sollers, speaking of Mallarmé, declares that "il n'y a pas de sujet en soi . . . puisque le sujet est la *conséquence* de son langage."[15] The subject attempts to prove his existence by telling stories about himself, and perhaps, in the case of the Faun, inventing them.

Mallarmé states specifically that everyone possesses a multiplicity of selves, which facilitates the mental acting-out of fictions: "A la rigueur un papier suffit pour évoquer toute pièce: aidé de sa personnalité multiple chacun pouvant se la jouer en dedans" (p. 315). This process is also made easier by the nature of the Mallarmean hero: not a specific character but a "Type sans dénomination préalable" (p. 545), Man in general rather than a particular man.[16] Such a preference for the general or universal clearly represents the opposite viewpoint from that of Browning, whose dramatic monologues usually aim to define and particularize a specific individual.

The universal "Type" favoured by Mallarmé can best be found in the world of myth, as Mallarmé himself points out: "les Mythes . . . Le Théâtre les appelle, non: pas de fixes, ni de séculaires et de notoires, mais un, dégagé de personnalité, car il compose notre aspect multiple" (p. 545). He comments, specifically, on the mythical status of Hamlet: "avance *le seigneur latent qui ne peut devenir,* juvénile ombre de tous, ainsi tenant du mythe" (p. 300). There is a Hamlet in everyone, and his drama has a universal significance which makes it appear

le spectacle même pourquoi existent la rampe ainsi que l'espace doré quasi moral qu'elle défend, car il n'est point d'autre sujet, sachez bien : l'antagonisme de rêve chez l'homme avec les fatalités à son existence départies par le malheur. (p. 300)

The Faun, too, is a mythical being rather than a specific "character." His urge to satisfy his sexual appetite represents not a character trait but an instinct fundamental to the whole of the human and animal world. As for his artistic propensities, they constitute a mark of genius, unconnected with character. The Faun represents not a personality in his own right but a symbol of the poet and a generic symbol of "man, both as a sensual and spiritual being, torn by the conflict of dream and actuality,"[17]—engaged, then, in the same univeral drama as Hamlet, the "antagonism" of dream and fate. Nevertheless, the Faun's presence, his preoccupations, dominate the poem; and his persona, despite its lack of character traits, guarantees the poem's status as a dramatic monologue rather than the utterance of a lyric "I."

Mallarmé's other heroes are also far from being exercises in character study. Igitur, totally preoccupied with abstract questions, shows no evidence of personality beyond this. As for Hérodiade, she is, or declares herself in the "Scène" to be: cold, narcissistic, proud, sterile, self-sufficient; but Mallarmé deliberately carries these traits to such an extreme as to make her totally incredible as a realistic character. Rather she is a figure or a Type, an "haut et vivant Signe," the symbol of absolute and self-sufficient Beauty. In Hérodiade, says Gardner Davies, Mallarmé "cherche à évoquer non point un individu doué d'une beauté resplendissante par comparaison aux autres, mais un symbole de la beauté tout court."[18] Hérodiade may be young, beautiful, noble (as well as proud, cruel, self-centred and self-sufficient); she may be described physically (to some extent); psychologically motivated (however obscure her motives); nevertheless, she is not a "character," partly because she carries her attributes to such extremes, and partly because she inhabits a space totally divorced from reality. She has no social role, and she is not linked to any time or place, except the mythical, Biblical time epitomized by her name.

The pin-pointing of protagonists in time and place helps to define or characterize them, as we have seen in Browning. From the details Browning supplies, the reader is invited to construct a whole (a "whole" character and a "whole" world which he inhabits)—to fill in the gaps, flesh out the character and imagine a context for him, a fictional or historical world containing his moment of dramatic utterance. Mallarmé, on the other hand, deliberately omits context, which frustrates our attempts to reconstruct a "whole" character as referent. And yet with his inclination towards the general and the universal, Mallarmé actually deals with much greater "wholes": rather than portraying specific characters set in a particular context, his ideal theatre would represent a vaster scenario, "la pièce écrite au folio du ciel et mimée avec le geste de ses passions par l'Homme," in which case it matters little at what precise point on earth "l'Homme" conducts his performance. The tower in *Hérodiade* could be anywhere (though we are aware of the Biblical tradition); and *L'Après-midi d'un faune*—which evokes the myth of Pan and Syrinx—takes place somewhere in Sicily, in view of Mount Etna, against a backdrop of lake, woods, roses. No more is necessary, and Etna could be dispensed with but for its symbolic value at the end of the poem. *Igitur*, which according to Mallarmé requires a mental staging on the part of the reader ("Ce Conte s'adresse à l'Intelligence du lecteur qui met les choses en scène, elle-même" (p. 433)), contains no indications at all as to place or epoch; the inner drama enacted in it, though a "drama of cosmic proportion,"[19] requires little in the way of props. Igitur's room, at the top of a high staircase, might evoke that of Laforgue's Hamlet in the *Moralités*, were it not for the furnishings: Laforgue's room is full of bric-a-brac whereas in *Igitur*, apart from "la pâleur d'un livre ouvert que présente la table," we discern only a "mystérieux ameublement," "une douteuse perception de pendule."

*Igitur* abolishes time as well as place: it takes place at midnight, "l'heure zéro," in Schérer's words, "l'heure qui . . . abolit le temps"; the hour of midnight "nous sort de l'écoulement temporel en nous introduisant au temps retrouvé, ou à l'éternité."[20] Mallarmé's attitude towards the question of Time leads him to choose not historical characters, as Browning often does, but figures of myth, belonging to all time, such as the Faun, Hérodiade and Hamlet-Igitur. He points out that it is a mistake to try and pinpoint the universal drama of Hamlet in space or time, for instance

by playing it in sixteenth-century costume, because "cela date, trop
*à coup sûr*, et . . . le choix exact de l'époque Renaissance spirituel-
lement embrumée d'un rien de fourrures septentrionales, ôte du
recul légendaire primitif . . ." (p.300). The Faun, too, benefits
from a "recul légendaire primitif" which establishes him as a mythi-
cal being, a *figura* rather than a character.

Kravis mentions the "virtual, literary time" of Mallarmé's poetry, a
time that "sets reality on a different plane."[21] Mallarmé himself ex-
plores this concept in the text "Mimique," which is very relevant to
*L'Après-midi d'un faune*:

> "La scène n'illustre que l'idée, pas une action effective, dans un
> hymen (d'où procède la Rêve), vicieux mais sacré, entre le désir
> et l'accomplissement, la perpétration et son souvenir: ici
> devançant, la remémorant, au futur, au passé, *sous une apparence*
> *fausse de présent*."

The "milieu, pur, de fiction" installed by the mime is set up in an
apparent present, the present of the book, poem or performance.
Like the Pierrot of Margueritte's play, the Faun stands "entre le désir
et l'accomplissement, la perpétration et son souvenir": his desire
for the nymphs frustrated, he seeks to "perpetuate" them in his
memory, "ici devançant, la remémorant, au futur, au passé, sous
une apparence fausse de présent." His memory of them is so
strong—or their presence so recent—that even "now," in the pres-
ent from which he considers their status as possibly dream or illu-
sion, "Leur incarnat léger . . . voltige dans l'air." He refers back to
the past, in the past tense ("Aimai-je un rêve?" "bien seul je m'of-
frais"), then returns to the present with "les femmes dont tu gloses";
but the tense of the passage following this (11.10–22) is deceptive:
"Faune, l'illusion s'échappe des yeux bleus / Et froids, comme une
source en pleurs, de la plus chaste," he declares, as if the nymph
were present now and the illusion "escaping" now; but in fact he is
referring to the past "sous une apparence fausse de présent" and
continues to do so throughout several lines which at first sight ap-
pear to denote his present time, the time of "tu gloses":

> . . . . . . par l'immobile et lasse pâmoison
> Suffoquant de chaleurs le matin frais s'il lutte,

> Ne murmure point d'eau que ne verse ma flûte
> Au bosquet arrosé d'accords; et le seul vent
> Hors des deux tuyaux prompt à s'exhaler avant
> Qu'il disperse le son dans une pluie aride,
> C'est, à l'horizon pas remué d'une ride,
> Le visible et serein souffle artificiel
> De l'inspiration, qui regagne le ciel.

But the themes of water and wind introduced in these lines presumably belong to the (past) time of the nymphs' presence, since it was they who evoked those ideas, the one nymph being (possibly) like "une source en pleurs" and the other "Comme brise du jour chaude dans ta toison." The phrase "matin frais," too, seems to imply that the adventure with the nymphs took place in the morning and that this whole passage refers to it, therefore, in a kind of "historic present."

The parts of the poem set in italics, on the other hand, are in the past tense; when the present is used, it unequivocally represents a historic present evoking the past:

> . . . *je coupais ici les creux roseaux domptés*
> *Par le talent; quand* . . . . . . . . . . .
> *Ondoie une blancheur* . . . . . . . . .
> . . . . . . . . . . . . . . . . . . . . . .
> *Mon oeil, trouant les joncs, dardait chaque encolure*
> *Immortelle, qui noie en l'onde sa brûlure.*

The three lines following the first italicized section, beginning "Inerte, tout brûle dans l'heure fauve," could, again, refer in the present tense to the past—to the moments immediately succeeding the flight of the nymphs; and after the second italicized section the verb "délaisse" clearly refers to the past:

> . . . . . . . . . . . . . . . la timide
> Que délaisse à la fois une innocence, humide
> De larmes folles ou de moins tristes vapeurs.

The Faun's tendency to muse "au futur, au passé, sous une apparence fausse de présent" underlines another basic difference be-

tween the poetry of Browning and that of Mallarmé, even when
both are writing dramatic monologues. In Browning's poems we
attend to the gradual unfolding of events as the narrative pro-
gresses; there is a definite temporal sequence, and past events are
narrated either in the past tense or in an unambiguous historic
present. A poem by Mallarmé, on the other hand, demands to be
read as a whole belonging to a "virtual, literary time," rather than as
a chronological sequence; all its parts are interconnected. This is
true not only of his short poems, but of the *Faune* and even, or
especially, of *Un coup de dés*. The italicized sections from the *Faune*
standing on their own would form a narrative with a temporal se-
quence, but Mallarmé has deliberately sought to avoid this by the
interruptions, the play with tenses, and the uncertainty as to the
reality of the events described. It is as if Mallarmé's—and the
Faun's—awareness of an all-embracing fictionality, and of the
"confusions / Fausses" it can involve, has subverted the Faun's at-
tempt to set up a specific narrative.

The structure afforded by chronological narrative in a dramatic
monologue by Browning is replaced in the *Faune* by a different
kind of structure, one which guarantees that all parts of the poem
are interconnected, on several levels. Thematic motifs recur, with
subtle variations; for example the repeated references to heat (11.
13–15, 32, 64, 73–74, 106–09) and the heat of the Faun's desire
(11. 77, 85, 103); light (11. 24, 36, 60, 67, 77) and shade ("ombre"
with its multiple meanings, discussed by Cohn)[22]; water (11, 11, 17,
28, 66–67); and many other faint echoes too numerous to mention,
e.g., the roses of lines 7 and 73 or the tears of lines 11 and 81. On
the level of sound, frequent alliterations link words and images
together. Further structural patterns are created by the careful posi-
tioning of individual words, such as the "je" at the fourth syllable in
the first and last lines and correspondences between opposites
such as "clair" and "ombre" in those same lines.

While some of these effects may be found in Browning's dra-
matic monologues, they are certainly by no means so concentrated
and his poems do not depend on them for their unity but on the
chronological narration of events as recollected by their speaker.
His dramatic monologues tend, like novels, or autobiography, to
have a beginning, a middle and an end—albeit with variations, as

in the novel, such as "flashbacks" or beginnings *in medias res*—
which merely invite the reader to reconstruct the narrative's
chronology. In a word, Browning's poems have a much more defi-
nite plot than we find in the *Faune*, or in *Hérodiade*, *Igitur*, or *Un
coup de dés*, where "La scène n'illustre que l'idée, pas une action
effective." Davies notes that Mallarmé, having decided that *Hérodi-
ade* must be a poem rather than a play, "s'efforce d'affaiblir petit à
petit le récit, afin que les faits historiques restent de simples con-
tingences de son personnage." "J'ai laissé le nom d'Hérodiade," de-
clares Mallarmé, "pour bien la différencier de la Salomé je dirai
moderne ou exhumée avec son fait-divers archaïque—la danse,
etc.," and in his notes for a projected preface he writes of a "légende
dépouillée / de danse / et même de la / grossièreté— / de la tête /
sur le plat—."[23] This absence of *fait-divers* emphasizes the internal
nature of Hérodiade's drama, as of Igitur's and the Faun's. Conflicts
within the mind require little in the way of "story"—which would
also particularize the speaker too much, since each individual's
story is unique. As Block remarks concerning *Les Noces d'Hérodiade*,
"Linear anecdote is replaced by a wholly poetic evocation, not of
the adventure of Hérodiade, but of its inner consequences, rarefied
and abstracted through the poet's vision." Similarly, Dr. Bonniot
refers to Igitur as a "sorte d'Hamlet . . . dénué de toute anec-
dote";[24] and as for the Faun, hovering "entre le désir et l'accomplis-
sement, la perpétration et son souvenir," his playing with time, "ici
devançant, là remémorant," destroys normal chronology, and with
it, narrative.

## II. Drama and the dramatic monologue

Another figure who stands "entre le désir et l'accomplissement"
is Hamlet, prolonging, in Mallarmé's words, a "labyrinthe de trouble
et de griefs" with "le suspens d'un acte inachevé" (p. 300). All that
counts in *Hamlet*, according to Mallarmé, is the hero himself, "lisant
au livre de lui-même,"—hardly the type of action Aristotle would
have found suitable for a plot. And yet this play with its "suspens
d'un acte inachevé" is "la pièce que je crois celle par excellence"
(p. 299), and even "le spectacle même pourquoi [existe] la rampe."

As Kravis points out, Hamlet "is chiefly characterized by his delay-ing, and by his consequent filling of theatrical time with the quality of his delay." And his

> procrastination, his inability to become what he is, a man who must murder his uncle, constitutes to Mallarmé a realization of the essential qualities of the theatre. . . . For if a play is basi-cally concerned with an event which does not happen (or, as in *Hamlet*, only happens right at the end), then the substance of the play must create and sustain that sense of theatre which is pro-duced in too facile a fashion by an excess of action and event.[25]

An event (of uncertain nature) triggers off *L'Après-midi d'un faune* (and Hamlet), but the poem does not constitute simply the narra-tion of that event. Nevertheless, it is still a dramatic poem, enacting as it does the conflict between a man's dreams and his life; indeed, the *Faune* reflects very accurately its author's conception of drama. For him the "story," an "anecdote énorme et fruste" (p. 544), ap-pears both irrelevant and superfluous. Schérer exclaims, quoting Mallarmé's remark about "la pièce écrite au folio du ciel": "Le folio du ciel à déchiffrer . . . qu'importe après ces exigences le con-tenu de la pièce?"[26] Mallarmé states that "la Fable" should be "vierge de tout, lieu, temps et personne sus" (p. 544); he recommends for the theatre a hero, but devoid of personality, a "Signe" or "Type"; he would reduce the plot, in the sense of external action and events, to a minimum; and he would not seek to locate the play too precisely in time and space. What sort of drama, one might ask, could possi-bly survive such a stripping-down? One answer would of course be: a dramatic monologue. Mallarmé virtually says as much himself, speaking again of *Hamlet*:

> La pièce, un point culminant du théâtre, est, dans l'oeuvre de Shakespeare, transitoire entre la vieille action multiple et le Monologue ou drame avec Soi, futur. (p. 1564)

Langbaum would say that such an assessment summarizes a typi-cally nineteenth-century reinterpretation (or misinterpretation) of Shakespeare, one which he sees as directly relevant to the development of the dramatic monologue. Nineteenth-century readers, he suggests, read Shakespeare

> not as drama in the traditional Aristotelian sense, not in other words as a literature of external action in which the events derive meaning from their relation to a publicly acknowledged morality, but as literature of experience, in which the events have meaning inasmuch as they provide the central character with an occasion for experience—for self-expression and self-discovery. What such a reading suggests is that drama depends for its structure on belief in a single objective moral system, and dissolves without that belief into monodrama—into the nineteenth century's substitute for poetic drama, the dramatic monologue.

Such a "relativist" reading, he says, "gives great weight to the soliloquies" (c.f. "le Monologue, ou drame avec Soi") "which are just the moments when the point of view of the central character seems to obliterate the general perspective of the play." Hamlet's soliloquies "become self-deceiving pretexts for inaction"; rather than believing, for example, that he fails to kill the king at prayer because that would send the latter straight to heaven, we "understand him to be rationalizing his reluctance to act." Once we stop judging the central character by an external standard and "start understanding him from inside  .  .  .  the central character is no longer the Aristotelian 'agent' of the action but the creator of its meaning. Drama, in other words, gives way to monodrama, to the dramatic monologue,"[27] to the kind of work which does not require the benefit of a stage performance.

*Hamlet*, says Mallarmé, "s'accommode de la mise en scène de maintenant, ou s'en passe, avec indifférence," because the play is "si bien façonnée selon le seul théâtre de notre esprit" (p. 300). "Le seul théâtre de notre esprit": this is the theatre for which Mallarmé elected to write, for which he wrote *Igitur*, addressed to "l'Intelligence du lecteur qui met les choses en scène, elle-même." Not that Mallarmé was the only writer, in late nineteenth-century France, to envisage a type of theatre which should dispense with elaborate staging and leave as much as possible to the imagination of the audience. "Ce qu'on demandait au décor désormais et aussi aux costumes, c'était d'être aussi vagues, aussi imprécis que possible," states Jacques Robichez in *Le Symbolisme au théâtre*.[28] Indeed, many of Mallarmé's recommendations for the theatre were adopted, to a greater or lesser degree, by the early Maeterlinck, Vielé-Griffin, Henri de Régnier and others. Block declares that *Hérodiade* and the *Faune* "may be viewed in retrospect as important experiments in the creation of a symbolist drama, a drama of suggestion rather than statement, of inner rather than external movement, of mystery and spirituality, directly opposed to the reproduction of literal reality."[29] In a drama of this type, as Robichez notes, the actor himself can become an encumbrance, "l'intrus qui rompt le charme dans l'âme du spectateur, l'empêche de communier intimement avec le poète, interpose une réalité gênante entre deux rêves." The logical outcome of this viewpoint is expressed by Teodor de Wyzewa (in 1886):

> Un drame, lu, paraîtra aux âmes délicates plus vivant que le même drame joué sur un théâtre par des acteurs vivants[30]

as well as by Mallarmé (in 1887):

> un livre, dans notre main . . . supplée à tous les théâtres, non par l'oubli qu'il en cause mais les rappelant impérieusement, au contraire.(p. 334)[31]

Having renounced his original ambition to have *Hérodiade* staged, Mallarmé congratulates himself on the decision, "parce que j'y gagne ainsi toute l'attitude, les vêtements, le décor et l'ameublement, sans parler du mystère" (p. 1442). He prefers to suggest these elements of the poem himself, in words, and let the reader imagine them in a theatre "inhérent à l'esprit" (p. 328), rather than have them visible, solid and irrevocable, on the stage, We can suppose that he experienced a similar pleasure in re-writing the *Faune* as a poem after its rejection by Banville and Coquelin; though he was apparently still considering a staged version of the work as late as 1891 (p. 1463).

Bearing in mind Mallarmé's preference for suggestion over statement, it is interesting to compare *L'Apres-midi d'un faune* with its original version, entitled "Monologue d'un faune" and intended for stage production. The latter starts off from a much more definite situation as regards the Nymphs: the spectator sees them in the act of escaping from the Faun's arms, which immediately establishes their reality—whose uncertainty in the final version provokes all the Faun's self-questioning as well as the play with fictionality. The "Monologue d'un faune" also contains various stage directions, pinning the Faun down to specific actions rather than allowing the reader to imagine them. At times his gestures demonstrate a certain peremptory petulance tending to define this Faun more closely than his successor, e.g., *"Frappant du pied: / Où sont-elles?"* and *"A grands pas: / Je les veux!"* (pp. 1450–51). The necessary presence of an actor, for the "Monologue d'un faune," could only be an embarrassment. Either he had to dress up as a faun, half-man, half-beast, exposing himself to possible ridicule, or he had to remain himself—patently not a faun. With the poem as it stands, however, the reader can, of course, create his own image of the Faun, in which either man or beast may predominate.

Many of the textual changes between the first and final versions of the poem reveal a move away from the concrete and particular towards allusiveness and delicate suggestion. Thus the "clair / Rubis des seins levés" of the nymphs becomes "Leur incarnat léger"; the "rameaux" and "roses" invoked in the first version are associated in the second, in a totally transformed and much more suggestive context, with the adjectives "subtil" and "idéale," "leur ôtant ainsi leur peu de pesanteur," as E. Noulet points out.[32] The reeds, "domptés / Par ma lèvre" are tamed less concretely "Par le talent" in the final poem, and the line "La troupe par ma flûte effarouchée" becomes "Trop d'hymen souhaité de qui cherche le *la*," which alludes without naming and plays suggestively with the different meanings of "hymen" and "la." The bite inflicted by the teeth of a real nymph in the "Monologue" becomes an invisible "morsure / Mystérieuse, due à quelque auguste dent" in the finished poem. The gesture of the Faun throwing stones at the water-lilies (apparently in spite because they helped to hide the nymphs) is omitted in the *Faune*. Finally, the phrase which ends the original poem, "duo de vierges quand je vins," explicitly establishes the reality of the nymphs and of their defloration by the Faun, while "je vais voir l'ombre que tu devins" maintains the ambiguity as to the nymphs' status characteristic of *L'Après-midi d'un faune*. The move away from the concrete towards suggestiveness reflects not only the preferences of the mature Mallarmé but also the change from stage play to poem. The reader of a poem has time to work out the allusions contained in a line like "Trop d'hymen souhaité de qui cherche le *la*," whereas a spectator must catch the line as the actor pronounces it, and can hear it only once.

Nevertheless, the differences between the two versions of the poem remain only a question of degree. The "Monologue d'un faune" was clearly already more of a poem than a traditional stage drama: it offers no mimesis of man in action, as recommended by Aristotle, no depiction of character or conflict between characters; the time and place are largely immaterial, and the plot is minimal. These features of the "Monologue," corresponding to Mallarmé's aims for theatre in general, carry to an extreme similar tendencies within French classical theatre.[33] The characters of a Racinian play—Andromaque, Phèdre, Iphigénie—belong to the realm of myth, rather than reality; they undergo powerful, and universal, emotions but they do not possess character traits; that is why, as Barthes says, "il est absolument vain de disputer sur l'individualité des personnages, de se demander si Andromaque est coquette ou Bajazet viril."[34] Like the Faun, the *personnages* of classical French drama express themselves in an elevated language which makes no claim to reflect their individuality and no concessions to oral speech: it is the "noble" language of tragedy. By contrast, Shakespeare's characters often speak in the patterns of oral discourse; and they speak "in character," with language and mannerisms appropriate to their specific personality. Personality in Shakespeare can determine the course of events (Cordelia, the Macbeths), or it can be of interest in itself (Falstaff); Mallarmé himself notes that "Lear, Hamlet lui-même et Cordélie, Ophélie . . . agissent en toute vie, tangibles, intenses : lus, ils froissent la page, pour surgir, corporels" (p. 329). Furthermore, Shakespeare's plots are often quite complex and involve physical action, including fights and battles. Racine, on the other hand, would condemn with Mallarmé "l'anecdote énorme et fruste"; the ideal plot, he suggests, is "chargée de peu de matière"; external events are not shown but related in *récits*, while the main dramatic interest centres, as in the *Faune*, on movements within the psyche of the characters, expressed in *words*. Mallarmé, writing about classical tragedy, states that its "intention . . . ne fut pas l'antiquité ranimée dans sa cendre blanche mais de produire en un milieu nul ou à peu près les grandes poses humaines" (p. 319). Again, whereas Shakespeare's plays involve multiple changes of scene, a single empty room ("un milieu nul") suffices for all the scenes of a Racinian tragedy; the décor is unimportant. "La parole crée le décor comme le reste," wrote a contemporary of Mallarmé's who shared his vision of theatre,[35] and the words could be applied to classical théatre. Indeed we find Marc Fumaroli doing precisely that: the paradox of French classical theatre, he claims, is that it establishes "la visibilité théâtrale sur la seule magie du verbe oratoire." "Le dépouillement extérieur," he continues,

> crée les conditions favorables au déploiement somptueux du verbe rhétorique, dont la finalité est de créer dans l'esprit du spectateur auditeur *le relief de la vision intérieure.*[36]

The dramatic monologue could be said to push to the limits this emphasis on the "vision intérieure," since here all we have is words, without the props, physical actions, etc. of a stage play. Alexandre Lazaridès makes the same point about the dialogue genre: "le genre dialogique . . . ne possède, pour s'accomplir, que l'écriture; la représentation qu'il élabore ne s'adresse pas aux yeux de chair, mais à ce regard interne du lecteur qu'on peut appeler l'imagination."[37] Hence Mallarmé's choice of the monologue and dialogue forms for *L'Apres-midi d'un faune* and *Hérodiade*. True, Browning strives, unlike Mallarmé, to give his dramatic monologues a particular setting in time and space and to represent a concrete situation depending on external events, such as Fra Lippo Lippi's arrest, Porphyria's murder, the Bishop's imminent death; nevertheless, the action of a dramatic monologue must be essentially internal, reflecting the speaker's preoccupations, since all we have is his words, the "déploiement somptueux du verbe rhétorique." Indeed, Browning himself—whose stage plays, it may be remembered, were not a success—claimed that his "stress lay on the incidents in the development of a soul."[38] But whereas the internal action of a Browning monologue consists in revelation of character, that of a monologue by Mallarmé, Laforgue, Valéry (or Racine) concerns a conflict within a speaker devoid of character. Their speakers are less self-confident and more introspective, each one "lisant au livre de lui-même," as Mallarmé says of Hamlet, aware of a plurality of selves within themselves and unsure which mask to adopt. Again they resemble in this the characters of classical tragedy: "le personnage classique," according to Fumaroli, is "un visage à la recherche de son masque définitif." The conflict within the character hesitating over the choice of his "masque définitif" provides the dramatic action. "Bien des monoloques de tragédies," says Fumaroli, "ne sont que des délibérations où les différentes *personae* possibles du même personnage sont tour à tour évoquées," and "ce qu'on appelle sa psychologie est la vibration même des *personae* possibles qui s'offrent à lui en cours de route, jusqu'à ce qu'il trouve celle qu'appelait sa vocation."[39] We have seen Laforgue's speakers trying out different roles, and revealing that a persona is only a mask made of words; Valéry's Parque, too, chooses between the roles of the "Harmonieuse Moi" and the "Mystérieuse." Hérodiade, apparently so sure of her own purity and self-sufficiency, confesses at the end of the "Scène" that ". . . Vous mentez, ô fleur nue / De mes lèvres." As for the Faun, we saw that his identity depends to a large extent on the ontological status of the nymphs: if they were real he is one kind of person, if not, then he may be another. The story he tells to establish his identity as a raper of nymphs is, as he himself points out, a fiction; the persona he adopts therein is a mere system of discourse.

Browning's characters, also, can only be masks made of words, but, being composed in the mode of mimesis, they speak as if both they and their creator were unaware of this; and they reflect a certain belief in the possibility both of preserving a central essence or personality and of expressing it in words. The personalities of Browning's speakers are fixed from the outset; they have no need to try out different roles and are not engaged in internal debate, but in attempting to impose their viewpoint on others—specifically, on their interlocutors, since Browning's dramatic monologues actually represent one side of a dialogue. Although *Hérodiade* is written in dialogue form, her essential conflict is an inner one, proper to monologue, as she struggles with her own sensuality. The Faun, too, is engaged in an inner drama; indeed, the speaker of a French dramatic monologue is usually groping his way towards a decision, towards the assumption of a certain role or attitude, and this represents a dynamic, dramatic process quite different from the dramatic situation obtaining in Browning's dramatic monologues, but no less marked.

With respect to this dramatic element, a contrast may be drawn between *L'Après-midi d'un faune* (or *Hérodiade*, or *Igitur*) and another group of monologues in Mallarmé's output, namely the early prose poems, contemporary with the *Faune* (1864). They are written in prose, but by an author who was later to maintain that "en vérité, il n'y a pas de prose : il y a l'alphabet et puis des vers plus ou moins serrés" (p. 867), so that this difference is actually much less significant than the relative dramatic impact of the two groups of monologues.

Like the *Faune*, the prose poems present first-person utterance (except in "Le Phénomène futur"), and many of them deal with a theatrical space: "La Pipe" and "Frisson d'hiver" set a very precise scene like a conventional stage setting; popular theatre is evoked by the "orgue de Barbarie" of "Plainte d'automne," by the "pauvre enfant pâle" who sings for his living, and by the "tentes de fête" of "Réminiscence" (or "baraques de foire" in the poem's original version, entitled "L'Orphelin"). According to Noulet, "Réminiscence" "décrit la baraque bariolée d'où le pitre s'est évadé,"[40] "le pitre" being the clown speaker of "Le Pitre châtié." Despite their theatrical setting, however, the prose poems (unlike "Le Pitre châtié") are not dramatic. They do not stage a persona engaged in conflict; the "I" of these poems simply describes something he has seen or heard, and can easily be identified with the poet.

Barbara Johnson comments on a similar difference in the status of the "I" in Baudelaire's prose poems, compared to his poems in verse:

> La plupart des *Fleurs du mal* mettent en scène une apostrophe directe et spéculaire de la deuxième personne par la première personne. Mais dans la vaste majorité des *Petits Poèmes en prose*, le "je" est devenu un observateur-narrateur, rapportant à un "vous" lecteur quelque anecdote qui le met en scène en tant que spectateur et non en tant que spectacle.[41]

The same phenomenon is noticeable in certain of Mallarmé's prose poems, particularly "Le Démon de l'analogie," which begins with a direct address to the reader: "Des paroles inconnues chantèrent-elles sur vos lèvres, lambeaux maudits d'une phrase absurde?" In "Pauvre enfant pâle" the addressee, "tu," is the child himself, but again the "je" is an "observateur-narrateur" rather than an actor; the same is largely true in "Réminiscence," "La Pipe," and "Un spectacle interrompu" (which dates from somewhat later, 1875). "Frisson d'hiver" comes close to being "une apostrophe directe et spéculaire de la deuxième personne par la première personne" with the "je" being an actor rather than a mere spectator, but even here the speaker seems to discard his role for a moment when he comments "N'as-tu pas désiré . . . qu'en *un de mes poëmes* apparussent ces mots 'la grâce des choses fanées'?" (emphasis added). The speaker's status as an "observateur-narrateur" in poems like "Le Démon de l'analogie," "Pauvre enfant pâle," "La Pipe," "Réminiscence," "Plainte d'automne" and "Un spectacle interrompu" gives them a narrative, even at times a didactic, flavour, rather than a dramatic one. They present no internal debate, as in the *Faune*, no persona, and little or no sense of distance between speaker and poet.

## III. Distance

The suspense created in *L'Apres-midi d'un faune* by the Faun's debate as to the reality or otherwise of the nymphs helps to distance the speaker—an important characteristic, as we have seen, of the dramatic monologue; for our doubt as to the nymphs' physical reality makes it impossible to identify with the Faun's pursuit of them, since we retain an awareness that they may be merely figments of his imagination. Distance is also created between reader and speaker by the fact that the latter is a faun, especially as he keeps reminding us of this, addressing himself as "Faune . . ." or referring to his "toison," his flute, and his horns. The question of distance is central to Mallarmé's poetic doctrine in general, which favours a wide gap not only between speaker and reader but also, most emphatically, between speaker and poet; the latter should keep himself, his personality, views and emotions, out of poetry altogether. It was one of the points that preoccupied Mallarmé during the crisis year (1865-66) at Tournon; whereas at the beginning of this period we find him describing himself to Cazalis as "un pauvre poète, qui n'est que poète, c'est-à-dire un instrument qui résonne sous les doigts des diverses sensations," later (May 1867) he was able to write to the same correspondent "je suis maintenant impersonnel, et non plus Stéphane que tu as connu,—mais une aptitude qu'a l'Univers Spirituel à se voir et à se développer, à travers ce qui fut moi." The author of his poems in future, then, will be "l'Univers Spirituel," expressing itself through him. Mallarmé formed this notion during his early work on *Hérodiade*, and he dismisses his previous work—poems like "Les Fenêtres" and "L'Azur," "Brise marine," "Don du poème"—as being too personal, too close to himself: "autant d'intuitives révélations de mon tempérament, et de la note qu'il donnerait."[42]

In his later theoretical writings about poetry, collected in "Variations sur un sujet," Mallarmé continues to stress the fundamental importance of impersonality. The work of the poet who keeps his distance, remaining "multiple, impersonnel pourquoi pas anonyme" (p. 407), can stand on its own: "Impersonnifié, le volume, autant qu'on s'en sépare comme auteur, ne réclame approche de lecteur. Tel . . . il a lieu tout seul : fait, étant" (p. 372). What survives the author's disappearance is the words themselves in all their glory:

> L'oeuvre pure implique la disparition élocutoire du poète, qui cède l'initiative aux mots, par le heurt de leur inégalité mobilisés; ils s'allument de reflets réciproques comme une virtuelle traînée de feux sur des pierreries, remplaçant la respiration perceptible en l'ancien souffle lyrique ou la direction personnelle enthousiaste de la phrase. (p. 366)

Independently of the poet, words gesture to one another ("s'allument de reflets réciproques"), creating unexpected patterns of meaning and sound, by a process which is specifically poetic. Julia Kristeva uses Mallarmé's *Un coup de dés* in illustration of this point:

> L'énoncé poétique n'est lisible dans sa totalité signifiante que comme une mise en espace des unités signifiantes. Chaque unité a sa place nettement définie et inaltérable dans le *tout*. Ce principe, latent et à l'oeuvre dans chaque texte poétique, est mis

à jour lorsque la littérature prend conscience de son ir-
réductibilité au langage parlé, et Mallarmé en donne le premier
exemple frappant. La disposition spatiale d'*Un coupe de dés* vise à
traduire sur une page le fait que le langage poétique est un *volume*
dans lequel s'établissent des rapports inattendus (illogiques,
méconnus par le discours); ou même une *scène de théâtre*
"exigeant l'accord fidèle du geste extérieur au geste mental."[43]

An element of drama of another type can be perceived in this sur-
face play of words; they beckon to one another like notes in music
or actors on a stage, and in this sense the poem represents an event
or performance, like a theatrical or musical performance, whether
on the page or in the theatre of the mind. Divorced from their
normal contexts and placed in an unusual order, the words of po-
etry assume a life of their own:

Les mots, d'eux-mêmes, s'exaltent à mainte facette reconnue la
plus rare ou valant pour l'esprit, centre de suspens vibratoire; qui
les perçoit indépendamment de la suite ordinaire, projetés, en
parois de grotte. . . . (p. 386)

As we have seen, the structural basis of a poem like the *Faune* de-
pends on the "reflets réciproques" between words, rather than on a
chronological progression as in Browning's dramatic monologues.
Moreover, for Mallarmé, the magical medium of language can bring
about a metamorphosis, the "absente de tous bouquets" represent-
ing something *other* than "les calices sus" (p. 368). This emphasis
on the power of language to transform reality sets Mallarmé—and
Valéry—apart from Browning or Laforgue who are still basically
intent on mimesis, with whatever degree of involuntary or deliber-
ate stylization. For Mallarmé the "jeu de la parole" which is the
poem should not aim to represent reality but to transpose "un fait
de nature en sa presque disparition vibratoire" (p. 368); nor does it
depend on an author's "direction personnelle enthousiaste"; it is a
performance in its own right, a celebration of its own "reflets réci-
proques." The statements of poetry therefore share with Austin's
"performative utterances" the quality of being neither true nor false;
every reading of a poem is a performance, like every utterance of
sentences such as "I promise" or "I bet."[44] Johnson, however, in an

article relating the concept of the performative utterance to Mallarmé's prose poem "La Déclaration foraine," points out a significant discrepancy between the former and Mallarmé's theory of impersonality in poetry. In order for a performative utterance to be "felicitous," as Austin terms it, some sign "of the speaker's presence to his utterance is indispensable. . . . But in this prose poem, it is precisely the intentional continuity between the speaker and the utterance which is being questioned by the poet and his lady, for the 'rêverie' which has been proclaimed to the crowd 's'*ignore* et se lance nue de peur. . . .' " The sonnet "jaillit, forcé, sous le coup de poing brutal à l'estomac" (i.e., the demands of an expectant audience), which specifically denies the speaker's presence to his utterance, in accordance, as Johnson points out, with Mallarmé's theory of impersonality. "Indeed," she concludes, "the active production of this discontinuity between the speaker and his words, far from eliminating the performative dimension in Mallarmé's poetry, may itself constitute that poetry's truly revolutionary performativity."[45] In other words, ideally, for Mallarmé, poetry performs itself, without any reference to the poet's subjectivity, the performative utterance which is the poem being made by a speaker who is not the poet but, in Mallarmé's words, "l'Univers Spirituel."

Even more than performative utterances like "I promise" or "I bet," since it does not depend on the intentionality of a speaker (poet), the poem is *self*-referential. Mallarmé seems to be proclaiming the self-referentiality of poetry in his comments on the sonnet "Ses purs ongles":

> J'extrais ce sonnet . . . d'une étude projetée sur la parole : il est inverse, je veux dire que le sens, s'il en a un (mais je me consolerais du contraire grâce à la dose de poésie qu'il renferme, ce me semble) est évoqué par un mirage interne des mots mêmes. (p. 1489)

However, Mallarmé was acutely aware that referentiality could not be totally abolished in poetry; reality is subject to but a "*presque disparition vibratoire*" (emphasis added). "Quasi affranchis," points out John Jackson,

> de leur vection référentielle, [les mots] se redistribuent selon la

logique poétique virtuelle de leur autonomie. Certes. Mais non
sans continuer, dans le même temps, à fonder un ordre dont la
rigueur et la cohérence, pour être de nature purement notion-
nelle, n'en vient pas moins redoubler, comme analogiquement,
l'ordre du monde. "Aboli", celui-ci se retrouve, dans le poème,
transfiguré, dans ces "notions pures" qui, privées d'assise onto-
logique directe, existent d'une existence à la fois véridique et
feinte.

Since the world can never disappear altogether, pursues Jackson,
"la non-référentialité rêvée du langage est autant une *dénégation*
qu'une réalité." The subject of the Faun's preoccupations is, indeed,
precisely "la non-référentialité *rêvée* du langage." For, as Jackson
says, the solution to the problem of staging the " 'glorieux men-
songe' d'un rêve qui sait sa nature fictive" (like the Faun's),
"ou . . . d'un langage épuré de toute attache référentielle . . .
consistera à faire du poème son propre objet, autrement dit à faire
du texte l'espace de son propre réfléchissement."[46]
   Jackson sees Hérodiade as a symbol of this "réflexivité poétique."
Her virginity "exprime le rêve de parthénogenèse que 'Don du
poème' avait formulé dès 1865, rêve d'une parole née d'elle-même,
sans contact avec le sol des intérêts humains."[47] However, the proof
of the impossibility of this dream lies in Hérodiade's last-minute
admission of deceit:

> . . . . . . . . Vous mentez, ô fleur nue
> De mes lèvres.
> J'attends une chose inconnue. . . .

The "chose inconnue," according to Jackson's interpretation of
Hérodiade as a symbol of poetic reflexivity, must be "l'intrusion,
incarnée dans la figure d'un homme, du réel." This opposite prin-
ciple, that of the real which breaks through the illusory autonomy of
poetic language is, Jackson continues, the underlying theme of the
*Faune* (which Mallarmé certainly opposes, in his correspondence,
to *Hérodiade*): the Faun attempts to embrace reality, in the shape of
the nymphs, but it escapes his grasp. The reason for this, Jackson
suggests, may be found in the Faun's impression that "Mon crime,
c'est d'avoir, gai de vaincre ces peurs / Traîtresses, divisé la touffe

échevelée / De baisers que les dieux gardaient si bien mêlée." If the Faun symbolizes the poet, then this division "figure, sur le plan érotique, la fatalité d'un esprit d'analyse sur le plan de la conscience," says Jackson. For the Faun-poet has at his disposal only language, "dont l'essence analytique ne peut que briser l'intégrité, et la présence, du réel. . . . Le langage ne saisit pas la réalité dans sa plénitude, il la décompose selon l'ordre de la raison." Language is guilty, in Mallarmé's eyes, of two cardinal sins: firstly it tends to forget itself, subordinating itself to the interests of communication, and secondly it fails to express reality "dans sa plénitude." Only verse can compensate for the inadequacies of language: "lui, philosophiquement rénumère le défaut des langues, complément supérieur" (p. 364); nevertheless, even the "Glorieux Mensonge" of verse cannot reproduce reality, it can only create fictions.[48]

## IV. Language: monologue as dialogue

A fiction himself and a purveyor of fictions, the Faun constitutes a persona (without whom the poem would not be a dramatic monologue), a speaker whose "presence to his utterance" renders it, in Austin's term, "felicitous" as a performance, within the context of the fictional poetic world. (This does not, of course, guarantee its objective truth, but neither is the phrase "I promise" true or false.) Although determined to keep his poetry free from all trace of his own personality, Mallarmé still apparently felt inclined, at the time of writing the *Faune* and *Hérodiade*, to attribute speech to a particular speaker. (Similarly, according to Hugh Kenner, T.S. Eliot felt compelled to assign *The Waste Land* to the shadowy figure of Tiresias in order to "supply the poem with a nameable point of view.")[49] Yet a speaker can be as guilty as the poet himself of "direction personnelle enthousiaste de la phrase"; in order to "give the initiative to words" so that they seem to be writing themselves, the persona too must "disappear," as in *Un coup de dés* or, as far as can be judged from the evidence presented by Schérer, in Mallarmé's "Livre," the Reader of which Mallarmé designates by the impersonal term of "opérateur."

The Faun manages in a sense to disappear from his own speech in that he is, as we have seen, a persona devoid of personality. A symbol, as Mallarmé himself declares,[50] and a mythological figure, the Faun reveals certain universal human attributes but is not in any way particularized. His "direction personnelle . . . de la phrase" remains, therefore, minimal. Unlike Browning who deliberately aims to reflect the characters and preoccupations of his protagonists in their speech, Mallarmé avoids "oral realism." Some critics regard oral realism as an essential ingredient of the dramatic monologue but this is because they take Browning's poems as models for the whole genre. Tennyson's personae do not use a personal idiom, and as far as Mallarmé is concerned, any particularized or even simply colloquial speech would clearly be unsuitable for a persona representing an "haut et vivant Signe." The most he concedes to the Faun in the way of colloquial expressions is a "bast!" (1. 42), and a "Tant pis!" towards the end. The Faun's occasional self-interruptions (11. 14, 31, 104) convey a certain oral quality, but most of the writing in the poem's final version is far too complex syntactically to suggest speech. The original "Monologue," intended for stage performance, was somewhat more straightforward; Mallarmé explains in a letter to Cazalis that the verse of the "Monologue d'un faune" must be "plus rythmé encore que le vers lyrique parce qu'il doit ravir l'oreille au théâtre."[51] A glance at the original and final versions reveals in the former a larger proportion of short sentences and phrases, appropriate to oral speech and readily assimilated in passing by an audience, such as "J'avais des Nymphes!", "Est-ce un songe?", "Où sont-elles?", "Je les veux," "Tout ceci m'interdit" "Serais-je pur?", "Je ne sais pas, moi!" Moreover, the lines of the initial version are more broken up, at the beginning and the end of the poem, than in the final one; Mallarmé had boasted to Lefébure that he had discovered "un vers dramatique nouveau, en ce que les coupes sont servilement calquées sur le geste."[52] However, the main difference affecting the oral quality of the two versions overall lies in the number of questions and exclamations in each. Exclamations tend to be short and readily grasped, and the question-and-answer format is easy to follow in the theatre. The "Monologue d'un faune" contains no less than nineteen exclamations, as against twelve in the poem's final version; and eleven questions, compared with two overt questions plus one or two disguised ones in the

*Faune.* The presence of so many questions in the "Monologue" highlights the conflict within the Faun as he struggles to come to terms with his loss, e.g., ". . . . et je suis donc la proie / De mon désir torride, et si trouble qu'il croie / Aux ivresses de la Sève? Serais-je pur?" Though questioning is still present in *L'Après-midi d'un faune*, it is more subtle, involving fewer marks of punctuation: the phrase "ou si les femmes dont tu gloses / Figurent un souhait de tes sens fabuleux!" is undoubtedly interrogative, following "Aimai-je un rêve?", though marked only as an exclamation. Again, a question mark hangs over the disappearance of the flock of nymphs which fled ("par quel art . . . détala") at the Faun's approach, and the succeeding three lines beginning "Alors m'éveillerai-je à la ferveur première . . ." can certainly be read as a question. In *L'Après-midi d'un faune* self-interrogation is less often conveyed in the direct question-and-answer form more suitable for the theatre, but nevertheless, as in the so-called "Monologue," the Faun conducts a veritable dialogue with himself, attempting to establish what exactly happened to him and why.

Many writers on monologue stress its affinities with dialogue. Derrida quotes Plato, who says: "C'est ainsi . . . que je me figure l'âme en son acte de penser; ce n'est pas autre chose, pour elle, que dialoguer, s'adresser à elle-même les questions et les réponses, passant de l'affirmation à la négation." And Todorov, summarizing Bakhtin, states that "l'acte le plus personnel même, la prise de conscience de soi, implique toujours déjà un interlocuteur, un regard d'autrui qui se pose sur nous."[53] In the case of a monologue which, like Browning's, is really one half of a dialogue, the speaker aims to produce an effect on his interlocutor, to question him, impress him, or convince him. The solitary monologist, on the other hand, has no one to question, persuade or impress but himself—and this is precisely what we find him doing: attempting to convince himself of some truth, or exhorting himself to adopt a particular attitude or course of action. In other words, Browning's monologues fulfil the normal rhetorical aim of persuading or in some way affecting the listener, whereas Mallarmé's conception of the monologue involves, in the words of Michel Beaujour, "la négation d'autrui" and therefore "la subjectivisation de la rhétorique." Engrossed in his "Monologue ou drame avec Soi," Hamlet, the hero par excellence, "nie du regard les autres," who are "tous comparses"; he is engaged not in persuasion, but in "autopersuasion":

> Il transcende le multiple pour s'affirmer l'Un dans le soliloque, la méditation, l'autodramatisation, l'auto-persuasion. Le héros hamlétien opère en somme la subjectivisation de la rhétorique, ce qui entraîne, dans un premier mouvement, la négation d'autrui.[54]

Like Hamlet, Hérodiade negates "autrui," or attempts to, though the last lines of the "Scène" suggest that she may not be succeeding. In spite of the dialogue form of the poem, she is not really trying to impress or persuade the Nurse, but herself. The Faun, too, thinks only of reliving his own experience; the nymphs, "comparses" to such an extent that he remains unsure of their very existence, are simply the occasion of his desire.

Benveniste defines *discours* as "every utterance assuming a speaker and a hearer, and in the speaker, the intention of influencing the other in some way"[55]—a definition that applies to the type of dramatic monologue we are considering only if we accept that speaker and hearer are identical, and that the speaker, engaged like Hamlet in "autodramatisation," is trying to convince himself (the "hearer") of something, or to resolve a conflict between his two selves. "Le monologue," claims Barthes, "est l'expression propre de la division"[56]—hence its tendency to adopt the structure of dialogue. Todorov, in an article entitled "Les Registres de la parole," observes that "la plupart des monologues d'une tragédie sont des paroles ou le 'je' se dédouble et devient son propre récepteur, ou bien des paroles adressées très directement à quelqu'un absent en ce moment."[57] It follows that, linguistically, monologue and dialogue should resemble each other, and Todorov concedes this initially: "dans les monologues et dialogues réels que nous trouvons, par exemple, dans la tragédie classique, les mêmes traits se rencontrent indifféremment dans les deux." Subsequently, however, he tries to oppose monologue and dialogue, claiming that monologue represents "une projection, au niveau de l'énoncé, de la forme syntaxique exclamative," whereas dialogue basically has an interrogative format: quoting some lines of dialogue from Molière, he comments that "On est tout de suite frappé, à la lecture d'un tel dialogue,

du nombre de questions qu'il comporte." Yet the five lines of mono-
logue Todorov quotes from *Bérénice* contain as many questions
(four) as the much longer dialogue extract from *Le Bourgeois gentil-
homme*. Since, as Todorov himself pointed out "le 'je' se dédouble et
devient son propre récepteur," questions are as common in mono-
logue as in dialogue.

Nor is it only the interrogative forms which monologue "bor-
rows" from dialogue. According to Lazaridès, the following linguis-
tic elements are typical of dialogue: "pronoms personnels de la
première et de la deuxième personne, apostrophes, exhortations,
interrogations, exclamations," and all of them feature equally prom-
inently in monologues. "Contre toute attente," claims Pierre Lar-
thomas, "la figure la plus utilisée dans le monologue est, sans nul
doute, l'apostrophe qui, par nature, appartient au dialogue."[58] He
cites as an example Emilie's monologue at the beginning of *Cinna*,
where she addresses first her feelings ("impatients désirs . . . en-
fants impétueux de mon ressentiment"), then Cinna, and again her
feelings ("vaines frayeurs," "lâches tendresses," "Amour"). Apos-
trophe is not typical of Browning's dramatic monologues, in which
second-person address is occasioned by the presence of an audi-
tor, but in monologues with no auditor it is indeed very common.
We have seen Lord Pierrot indulging in apostrophe:

> Inconscient, descendez en nous par réflexes;
> Brouillez les cartes, les dictionnaires, les sexes.
> . . . . . . . . . . . . . . . . . . . . . . .
> Après nous le Déluge, ô ma Léda!
> ("Complainte de Lord Pierrot")

In the majority of cases, instances of apostrophe in Laforgue's
poems constitute address to an absent lady, as in "O vaillante oisive
femme" ("Locutions des Pierrots," I), "Coeur de profit, petite âme
douillette" ("Locutions des Pierrots," VII), or to the moon, e.g. "O
Lune, *Ave Paris stella!*" ("Locutions des Pierrots," XI). The Faun, on
the other hand, addresses not only the Nymphs ("Couple, adieu,"
"O nymphes, regonflons des SOUVENIRS divers"), but the scenery
("O bords siciliens . . ." "Lys!" "Etna!"), and his flute ("instrument
des fuites, ô maligne / Syrinx"). Hérodiade, too, apostrophizes in-

animate objects, as in her speech to the mirror ("O miroir! / Eau froide par l'ennui dans ton cadre gelée . . .") and in her long address to precious stones and metals beginning "Vous le savez, jardins d'améthyste . . ."; she also addresses the "Nuit blanche de glaçons et de neige cruelle" as "Toi qui te meurs, toi qui brûles de chasteté," and, in the final lines, when she is alone, declares "Vous mentez, ô fleur nue / De mes lèvres." Such a frequent use of apostrophe is unusual in dialogue, where the recipient of second-person address is normally the interlocutor, and it shows to what extent Hérodiade's speeches are in fact monologues; totally bound up in herself, she tends to forget the Nurse's presence.[59] The same phenomenon occurs in classical French tragedy when the main characters ignore their confidants and talk to themselves, as in the second scene of *Cinna* where Emilie no longer speaks directly to Fulvie but to her own passion: "Tout beau, ma passion, deviens un peu moins forte." Very often in classical tragedy, as in this example or in Emilie's opening monologue quoted earlier, the addressee of apostrophe proves to be an abstraction, such as the speaker's own feelings ("ma passion," "vaines frayeurs," etc.). The Faun, too, addresses his passion ("Tu sais, ma passion, que, pourpre et déjà mûre . . .") and the "wrath of virgins" ("Je t'adore, courroux des vierges").

Larthomas comments that the degree of artificiality inherent in apostrophe varies according to the nature of the *apostrophé*: "on distinguera ainsi l'apostrophe à Dieu dans la prière . . . de l'apostrophe à un personnage invisible . . . puis à soi-même, à ses sentiments, aux objets inanimés."[60] This progression represents an increasingly more pronounced departure from the usage of normal spoken language. Since monologue itself constitutes "par rapport au langage ordinaire, un écart," Larthomas suggests that apostrophe is used so frequently because it helps to realign the language of monologue with normal speech, by reintroducing "l'opposition entre les deux premières personnes, opposition qui est le caractère fondamental du dialogue." In other words, the "artificial" device of apostrophe is used in order to reduce the artificiality inevitably associated with the monologue form. Quoting Andromaque's line: "Non, vous n'espérez pas de nous revoir encore, / Sacrés murs que n'a pu conserver mon Hector," Larthomas points out that "Rien n'est plus artificiel en un sens que cette apostrophe à des objets inanimés; mais en même temps le langage tend à redevenir ce qu'il est dans la vie, instrument de communication." As well as supplying an illusion of communication, the use of apostrophe introduces a certain dramatic element: Schérer, noting that apostrophe, in classical tragedy, commonly addresses an abstraction, in particular personified feelings, comments that "grâce à cette sorte de dialogue qui s'établit entre l'abstraction ou le sentiment personnifié et le héros solitaire, le mouvement s'introduit dans la scène qui risquait d'en manquer."[61] Apostrophe can inject dramatic movement into an otherwise static speech by reintroducing the "opposition entre les deux premières personnes" typical of dialogue, the textual essence of drama.

A paradoxical inter-relationship between dialogue and monologue can be perceived on a totally different level in the circumstances of Mallarmé's poetic composition. The vast majority of his poems were written on and for specific occasions: toasts, *tombeaux*, dedications, birthday greetings; poems inscribed in albums, on fans and photographs, even on Easter eggs. Their quantity in relation to his whole output betrays his fascination with ritualized, public utterance (reflected also in a different way in his admiration for the Mass, pp. 395–96), and his preoccupation with the poem as act or performance, or gift (cf. "Don du poème"); with the poem, in other words, as apostrophe of another. This "transitive" gesture is remarkable on the part of a notoriously difficult poet who always insisted on the intransitive nature of poetic language itself and refused to compromise his own poetic ideals for the sake of "des contemporains [qui] ne savent pas lire" (p. 386), and it implies a fine balance between dialogue and monologue. Again, the various contemporary accounts of Mallarmé's "Mardis" suggest that they provided an opportunity not so much for dialogue or discussion as for listening, enraptured, to Mallarmé's at times incomprehensible but compelling, low-voiced monologue.[62] As he held forth, pipe in hand and surrounded by a haze of tobacco smoke, he was simultaneously apostrophizing his guests and voicing his own private soliloquy.

Not only apostrophe serves the dual purpose of providing an element of drama and an illusion of communication through dia-

logue: self-address, a common feature of the dramatic monologue
with no auditor, fulfils the same functions. When the " 'je' se
dédouble et devient son propre récepteur," as Todorov says, it leads
to self-address in the second person, which frequently appears
both in stage monologues and dramatic monologues. It constitutes
a highly dramatic procedure since, as well as reintroducing dia-
logue, it emphasizes the split within the character, torn in two di-
rections at once. Thus Titus: "Eh bien! Titus, que viens-tu faire? /
Bérénice t'attend. Où viens-tu, téméraire? / Tes adieux sont-ils
prêts? T'es-tu bien consulté?" At the beginning of *L'Après-midi d'un
faune* the sudden transition from the first to the second person
clearly illustrates the Faun's bewilderment:

> . . . . . . . . . Aimai-je un rêve?
> . . . . . . . . . . . . . . . . . . . . . . . . . . .
> . . . ou si les femmes dont tu gloses
> Figurent un souhait de tes sens fabuleux!
> Faune, l'illusion s'échappe des yeux bleus
> Et froids, comme une source en pleurs, de la plus chaste:
> Mais, l'autre tout soupirs, dis-tu qu'elle contraste
> Comme brise du jour chaude dans ta toison?

Similarly, some of Laforgue's monologues express the "dédouble-
ment" of the speaker through self-address in the second person, as
when the "paria" in "Simple agonie" (*Derniers vers*, VI) declares
". . . tu ne peux que te répéter, ô honte!" or the "pauvre, pâle et
piètre individu" of "Dimanches" tells himself that

> Toujours enfermé tu te rendras malade!
> Vois, il fait beau temps tout le monde est dehors,
> Va donc acheter deux sous d'ellébore,
> Ça te fera une petite promenade.
>
> (*Derniers vers*, III)

Such commands to the self are common in monologues with no
auditor, as the character urges himself to adopt some course of
action. Sometimes they appear in the first person plural, again re-
flecting a split within the speaker. Examples abound in Racine's
monologues; Laforgue's Lord Pierrot says to himself "Tournons

d'abord sur nous-même, comme un fakir" ("Complainte de Lord Pierrot"), and the Faun muses "Réfléchissons. . . ."

Like the use of questions and apostrophe, self-address in the second person provides an element of drama both by reintroducing into monologues the linguistic forms of dialogue and because it highlights the character's inner conflict.

## V. Performance as *Ecriture. Le Poème dramatique.*

However, the dramatic elements that can be detected in the *Faune* do not make it suitable for stage production; as Lazaridès says of the dialogue genre (such as Valéry's *Eupalinos*): "La force dramatique d'un dialogue ne réside pas tant en sa possibilitié d'être representé que dans sa capacité de suggérer le jaillissement toujours imprévu de la parole vive." The same can be said of dramatic monologues in general, and of Mallarmé's *Faune* in particular, despite the poet's intention—revived in 1891—to have it staged. The dramatic monologue achieves its full effect only when considered, like the dialogue genre, as "une substitution hallucinatoire de la parole par l'écriture."[63] Mallarmé envisages even certain types of performance as a form of *écriture*; he regards ballet as an "hiéroglyphe" (p. 312), or a "poème dégagé de tout appareil du scribe" (p. 304). What takes place, he would suggest, is "une substitution hallucinatoire de la [danse] par l'écriture," for the dancer "*ne danse pas*, suggérant, par le prodige de raccourcis ou d'élans, avec une écriture corporelle ce qu'il faudrait des paragraphes en prose dialoguée autant que descriptive, pour exprimer, dans la rédaction" (p. 304). The dancer "*écrira* ta vision à la façon d'un Signe, qu'elle est" (p. 307). Signs of another kind—the silent gestures of mime—can also effect a "substitution hallucinatoire de la parole," or a "notation de sentiments par phrases point proférées" (p. 310). The "pitre châtié" says: ". . . . du geste évoquais / Comme plume la suie ignoble des quinquets," and Lucette Finas comments as follows on these lines: "Evoquer du geste brise la dualité 'de la voix et du geste'," introducing "un autre ordre où la voix (vox) est geste: l'ordre silencieux de la mimique."[64] Significantly, the piece entitled "Mimique" in *Crayonné au théâtre* begins "Le silence, seul luxe après les rimes . . ."; and the importance to Mallarmé of silence in poetry, marked by the typographical layout of the page, is well-known. The writing thus achieves what the voice usually does, creating on the page the pauses, emphases and the suspense which the voice normally provides.

The poet's task, according to "Mimique," is to transcribe the silence of "une ode tue." In his later writing Mallarmé frequently refers to the great poem of the future as "l'Ode" (originally a poem set to music):

> J'imagine que la cause de s'assembler, dorénavant, en vue de fêtes inscrites au programme humain, ne sera pas le théâtre . . . ni la musique . . . mais à soi fondant ce que ces deux isolent de vague et de brutal, l'Ode, dramatisée ou coupée savamment; ces scènes héroïques une ode à plusieurs voix (p. 335).

The *ode* was to achieve nothing less than "l'explication orphique de la Terre" (p. 663) and was to retain the features of impersonality and universality we have noted in Mallarmé's earlier writings. Mallarmé clearly intended it to display a dramatic element: "dramatisée ou coupée savamment," it could even take the form of a dialogue ("une ode à plusieurs voix"). Yet he had earlier expressed reservations about the *poème dramatique* as such; in a letter of 1876 to Anatole France concerning the latter's *Noces corinthiennes* he writes:

> Avant de parler des *Noces*, je tiens à exprimer à leur endroit une opinion qui fait loi pour moi, relativement au moule où vous les avez jetées : le poëme dramatique me désespère, car si j'ai un principe quelconque en critique, c'est qu'il faut, avant tout, rechercher la pureté des genres. Théâtre d'un côté ou poëme de l'autre. . . . [65]

Strange words coming from the author of the "Monologue d'un faune" (although by *poème dramatique* Mallarmé certainly understood, in 1876, not a monologue but a poem like the *Noces corinthiennes*, divided into scenes and engaging several characters in dialogue), and from the pen of one who later freely interchanges the words "poem," "Book" and "drama" in the fragments of the "Livre." Indeed, far from the "séparation des genres" recommended in Mallarmé's letter to France, most of his later writings strive for a fusion of literary genres. As Schérer points out, "Le Livre est théâtre, il est poésie, il est prose, il est même journal, rien de ce qui est littéraire ne peut lui être étranger, rien ne peut rester en dehors de lui, puisque, par définition, le monde aboutit à lui. Il est donc normal que le Livre intègre tous les genres littéraires."[66] As far as drama is concerned, Mallarmé's conception of theatre renders its integration with other genres very easy; stripped of conventional décor, costumes, and allusions to period, presenting not characters but figures devoid of personality, and involving little external action, the type of drama envisaged by Mallarmé lends itself more readily to book form than to stage production. Block points out that the

> problem of Mallarmé's effort in the theater is essentially the problem of a symbolist drama: in what way can the poetics issuing from Poe and Baudelaire be brought into harmony with the art of the drama? The values of suggestiveness, musicality, mystery, reverie, and dream all point to an indifference to character and to human relationships, which have been a central part of the drama from ancient times to the present.[67]

Paul Valéry, whose dramatic monologues we shall consider next, was well aware of this conflict: his (and Mallarmé's) "conception *liturgique*" of drama, he declared, "excluait méthodiquement l'imitation directe de la vie sur la scène."[68]

Mallarmé's attitude towards the *poème dramatique* became more positive than in the letter to France quoted above: a letter of 1888 to Vielé-Griffin expresses his admiration for the latter's *Ancaeus*, a *poème dramatique* consisting, again, of dialogue between several characters:

> Je suis enchanté de votre *Ancaeus*. . . . Tout ce qu'un esprit pénétré de futur comme le vôtre devait ajouter à cette forme, envers quoi j'ai été jusqu'ici injuste mais elle s'était mal produite, du *poëme dramatique*, vous l'avez fait. . . . [T]ant qu'il n'y aura pas un théâtre pour les pompes secrètes, outre la Musique, je crois qu'il faut s'en tenir au genre par vous excellemment rénové.[69]

A fascination with the dramatic poem seems inevitable in a poet who implies that the very act of reading should evoke a kind of mental theatre: "Le Poëte," Mallarmé claims, "éveille, par l'écrit, l'ordonnateur de fêtes en chacun" (p. 330). In *L'Après-midi d'un faune* he has created a dramatic monologue which, though totally unlike Browning's in its depreciation of character and deliberate eschewal of the realistic and particular in favour of the universal quality of myth and the poetics of suggestion, nevertheless remains dramatic in its portrayal of the "antagonisme" between dream and reality and in adopting the forms of dramatic dialogue in the Faun's self-address. It also establishes the distance we have found crucial to the dramatic monoloque: by the use of a persona, by the play with fictionality which makes it impossible to know exactly what has occurred, and by the very method of suggesting rather than naming, which keeps us constantly at one remove from the object. Moreover, the poem manages, without impairing its dramatic qualities, to illustrate some of Mallarmé's most cherished theories about poetry, such as the relation between reality, poetry and fiction.

# CHAPTER FIVE

# Self-consciousness: Valéry

The attraction of theatre for Valéry, especially in the latter phases of his career, is obvious from his output and has often been mentioned by critics. His whole *oeuvre*, beginning with the poems, of which many contain a dramatic element and some may be termed dramatic monologues, continuing with the Dialogues and libretti, and concluding with *Mon Faust*, can be seen as a gradual evolution towards more specifically dramatic forms. With respect to the monologues, Francis Scarfe, in his book *The Art of Paul Valéry: A Study in Dramatic Monologue*, examines them all, discovering varying degrees of drama in them. He classes "L'Ebauche d'un serpent" and "La Pythie" as dramatic monologues, as well as "Le Cimetière marin" and "Fragments du Narcisse," but justifiably tends to see *La Jeune Parque* as the most consummate example of the genre.[1] This chapter will concentrate on the latter poem, without being restricted to Scarfe's view of it or repeating his analysis; reference will also be made to the "Fragments du Narcisse" and "La Pythie," as well as to relevant passages in Valéry's *Cahiers*. In discussing *La Jeune Parque* as a dramatic monologue we shall again encounter several issues broached in our study of Laforgue and Mallarmé (and with which Scarfe was not specifically concerned), such as the rejection of mimesis in literature; the questions of personality, of the poetic "I," of Voice, and of "distance"; but again we shall find that the essential elements of a dramatic monologue are present: the speaker is identified and distanced from the reader, and she is involved in a drama.

# I. Mimesis and Myth

Despite his fascination with theatre, Valéry, like Mallarmé, was prevented by his very conception of theatre—a conception he termed "liturgique"[2]—from completing a play that could be successfully performed or attract wide audiences. He spurned the idea that a stage play should deliberately seek to produce effects on an audience; instead, a liturgical play should resemble the Catholic mass in which "*rien au fond n'est pour le public*"; it can be said "*avec ou sans public.*"[3] Valéry further notes that the mass is nobler than theatre since it avoids "la grossièreté du simulacre." A liturgical conception of theatre suggests elements of ceremony, mystery, musicality and symbolism foreign to the "simulacre" of realist drama, and Valéry frankly declares that his notion "excluait méthodiquement l'imitation de la vie sur la scène."[4]

Valéry's views on mimetic literature, whether on the stage or in novels, are categorical: to write in imitation of life is to write "La Marquise sortit à cinq heures," a totally arbitrary sentence. When the author puts pen to paper is he free—too free—to write what he likes, as Valéry himself has found when describing real events:

> . . . Je sens que je puis,—une fois la plume intervenue, faire ce que je veux de ce qui fut. . . .
> Le roman est possible à cause de ce fait que le *vrai* ne coûte rien et ne se distingue en rien de l'invention gratuite que fournit la mémoire à peine déguisée. (PC, 1, 275)

This awareness of the arbitrary nature of anecdote drives him, as a reader, to propose his own equally arbitrary alternatives: "Il m'est presque impossible de lire un roman sans me sentir . . . substituer aux phrases données d'autres phrases que l'auteur aurait pu écrire tout aussi bien, sans grand dommage pour ses effets." Unfortunately, the realist novel relies for its *effet de réel* on precisely the details Valéry is tempted to alter: "Par malheur, toute l'apparence de réalité que veut produire le roman moderne réside dans ces déterminations si fragiles et ces précisions insignifiantes."[5] Valéry therefore concludes: "Je ne suis fait pour les romans ni pour les drames" (PC, 1, 45). Poetry, on the other hand, does not aim to imitate reality, for the poet knows that "le réel d'un discours, ce sont les mots seulement et les formes" (PC, 2, 1099). However, even in poetry referentiality cannot be totally ignored, and Valéry confides that, for this reason, he would have preferred—given the talent and technical expertise—to be a musician, for example, rather than a poet:

> bien plutôt que dans les Lettres, j'aurais placé mes complaisances dans les arts qui ne reproduisent rien, qui ne feignent pas. . . . Ces modes "purs" ne s'embarrassent pas de personnages et d'événements qui empruntent de la réalité observable tout ce qu'elle offre d'arbitraire et de superficiel, car il n'y a que cela qui soit imitable. (*O*, I, 1472)

Valéry here specifically mentions events and characters as contributing to the arbitrary and superficial mimetic effect. At least in poetry it is possible to reduce the emphasis on these elements to a minimum. Nothing "happens" in *La Jeune Parque* other than the initial—and probably figurative—serpent's bite; in the "Fragments du Narcisse" the only "events" are Narcisse's gaze at his reflection and the fall of darkness. Like Mallarmé, Valéry felt that the poem should make no attempt to imitate reality or narrate real events, but aim to transform reality through the medium of language, to evoke "l'absente de tous bouquets"; or, as Valéry asserts, to *create* rain, rather than state that it is raining (PC, 2, 1120).

As for characters, Valéry marvels at the novelist's capacity to take them seriously:

> Un Romancier me disait qu'à peine ses personnages nés et nommés dans son esprit, ils vivaient en lui à leur guise; ils le réduisaient à subir leurs desseins et à considérer leurs actes. . . .
> J'en ai conclu . . . que la sensation de l'arbitraire n'était pas une sensation de romancier. . . . (*O*, II, 675)

Again, of his own creations, he states: "Il m'est difficile de vouloir *créer* des personnages, trop certain que je suis de l'absence de rigueur et de sanction dans ces créations: je me dis: quelqu'un d'habile verrait que ce sont d'impossibles fantoches" (PC, 1, 236). Accordingly, Valéry does not, like Browning, create as speakers of his poems fictional reconstructions of realistic or historical characters but chooses mythical figures such as Sémiramis, Narcissus, the Parque, the pythoness, etc., for whom the question of realism does not arise. The adventures of mythical beings are not totally arbitrary, but deeply symbolical of some universal aspect of human existence, and the mythical hero, though he may be exemplary, is not life-like, so that the reader is less inclined to identify with him.

The mythical status of the Parque and many other Valéryan speakers (Sémiramis, Narcisse, the Serpent, the pythoness, Amphion, Faust and others) sets them apart from ordinary men, thus creating the distance between speaker and reader which we have come to associate with dramatic monologues. They are also named, or given an identifying title such as "la jeune Parque," which again helps to prevent a close association of the poem's "I" with that of the poet, or of the reader. (Though the Parque may forget her name— "Quelle conque a redit le nom que j'ai perdu?"—the reader does not.) The sense of distance between speaker and reader is further enhanced by the diction of Valéry's speakers, confined almost entirely to a noble, poetic style and bound within strict formal conventions of rhyme and rhythm. If the rhyming couplets of "My Last Duchess" remind us that the Duke's speech is also Browning's, the same is even more true in Valéry. As Christine Crow says, "there is always a deliberately stylised element in Valéry's poetry which prevents us from identifying with the voice of the speaker."[6] To some extent the "Ebauche d'un serpent" represents an exception, with its use of irony, interjections and word-play, as in:

> Sitôt pétris, sitôt soufflés,
> Maître Serpent les a sifflés,
> Les beaux enfants que Vous créâtes!
> Holà! dit-il, nouveaux venus! . . .

Scarfe analyzes these effects and suggests that, in this poem, a "somewhat colloquial turn of expression . . . constantly threatens poetic tone in such a way as to draw the reader's attention towards the speaker, the Serpent."[7] In other words, like Browning's characters, the serpent is particularized through his speech, but this is very rare in the work of the poet who declares: "Plus un personnage est *important*, moins il doit être particulier" (*C*, VII, 185). For the same reason, Valéry makes no attempt to endow his speakers with a personality; indeed, in his *Cahiers* and elsewhere he continually discredits the notion of a central, fixed personality. His ideas on this subject are so relevant to *La Jeune Parque* that we must examine them in some detail.

## II. Personality and *le moi*

In the "Note et Digression" of 1919 to the "Introduction à la Méthode de Léonard de Vinci," Valéry states: "notre *person-nalité* . . . n'est qu'une *chose*, et muable et accidentelle"; "acciden-telle" because "elle a commencé par une chance séminale, et . . . elle a couru des milliards de risques" (*O*, I, 1226–27); "mu-able" because people's characteristics can change, voluntarily or otherwise: we can forget certain facts about ourselves, our tastes can change, our energy and knowledge fluctuate (PC, 1, 305); madness can alter the whole personality (PC, 2, 292) or, to take a less extreme case, if we become conscious of certain "singularités" we can mod-ify them at will, "preuve qu'elles ne sont pas essentielles mais tien-nent à un autrui que tout le monde et moi-même peuvent prendre pour moi, mais grossement et faussement" (PC, 2, 282). Not only does one's character slowly evolve; it also reveals different facets of itself from one day to the next, or indeed one hour to the next, in that it changes according to circumstances: "Je puis être 'bon' ou 'mauvais'; délicat ou brutal—etc. Je puis l'être suivant les circon-stances immédiates, l'humeur etc. Je puis aussi, sous l'empire d'idées, d'attentions, surveiller ces alternances; vouloir supprimer tout l'un ou tout l'autre" (PC, 1, 338). Different companions or inter-locutors elicit different versions of the *moi* (PC, 1, 180), which in-deed has the potential to be all things: ". . . *Un individu est un ESPACE de possibilités*" (PC, 2, 277). Nevertheless, life requires the individual to choose between these possibilities, to speak or act in one way or another, and the sum of his acts tends, eventually, to define him, which he finds enormously distressing ("Notre histoire fait de nous *un TEL*—et c'est une injure" (PC, 2, 333)), because being "plus général que sa vie et ses actes," man is "comme *prévu* pour plus d'éventualités qu'il n'en peut connaître" (PC, 2, 305). To Valéry, his own life-story seems no more essentially "his" than other possible versions it might have assumed: "tant d'autres vies imaginables ne me sont ni plus ni moins étrangères que la mienne" (PC, 2, 330–31). This feeling of "strangeness" increases with the lucidity of the observer: "Plus une personne est 'consciente' plus son personnage, plus ses opinions, ses actes, ses caractéristiques, ses sentiments propres lui paraissent particuliers et *étranges*,— étrangers" (PC, 2, 303). For Valéry, self-awareness leads to deliber- ate role-playing; as he says, "Se connaître n'est que se prévoir; se prévoir aboutit à jouer un rôle" (*O*, I, 558), a formula that at once evokes Laforgue's personae. All in all, our personality, far from be- ing "notre plus intime et plus profonde propriété," "n'est pas sûre d'être positivement *quelqu'un*; elle se déguise. . . . Elle vit de ro- mans, elle épouse sérieusement mille personnages" (*O*, I, 1226–27). The Self is a constantly-changing process rather than an object.

Despite the changeability of the personality, however, each indi- vidual, Valéry acknowledges, has a continuous awareness of his own identity—an awareness which he can only label "I" but which must nevertheless be distinct from the "I" of his so-called personal- ity with its constantly-changing characteristics, since it is con- scious of the latter: "La conscience consciente . . . introduit la relativité de la situation du *moi/non-moi*; montre le *moi* immédi- atement précédent—comme un *non-moi*" (PC, 2, 240). Valéry calls the second "I" *le Moi, le MOI*, or *le moi pur* in order to distinguish it from the ephemeral *je*, the "shifter." The "Moi" does not possess character traits and is therefore unchanging:

> Le Moi—que j'appelle le Moi pur . . . ne peut qu'être ou ne pas être—Il ne subit aucun changement. Démence, âge, rien ne l'altère—En revanche, il ne peut rien—ne sait rien.
> Il est identité pure—Pas de qualités, pas d'attributs.
> (PC, 2, 317)

"Identité pure," this *Moi* is "une *propriété fonctionnelle de la con- science*"—"Pas de conscience sans M[oi]," declares Valéry (PC, 2,

315)—and it is totally impersonal: "La seule chose qui subsiste dans la conscience—ce qui demeure malgré les temps est de la nature d'une pure forme—et juste le contraire d'une personnalité. Le moi le plus éternel est le plus impersonnel" (PC, 2, 281). The impersonal, universal, quality of this *Moi* causes the surprise "de qui se regarde dans un miroir et s'étonne de *se voir particulier, se sentant universel*" (PC, 2, 280). His reflection in a mirror reduces man's "I," with its vast potential, to the image of a specific person, at which he protests vigorously," for "le possible ne peut avoir *un seul* objet pour image" (PC, 2, 319). This thought recurs in several *Cahiers* entries relating to Narcisse, e.g., "la Pensée trouve un Monsieur dans le miroir" (PC, 2, 308). In the Narcisse poems the "confrontation du Moi et de la Personnalité" (PC, 2, 284) is in a sense externalized, since the fountain-mirror provides Narcisse with a reflection of one of his selves, of the "quelque chose de particulier" which is "étroitement . . . lié à quelque chose d'universel, ou qui se croit telle" (PC, 2, 302), i.e., his "Moi pur." Thus in "Fragments du Narcisse" he addresses his body's reflection as "temple qui me sépares / De ma divinité."

In *La Jeune Parque*, on the other hand, the whole struggle is internalized: particular and universal are both contained within one being. The Parque knows that she is "un ESPACE de possibilitiés" for, on awakening, she is prepared to wait until "de mes destins lentement divisé / Le plus pur en silence éclaire un coeur brisé," and she affirms that "Tout peut naître ici-bas d'une attente infinie," echoing Valéry's suggestion in the *Cahiers* that each individual is "comme *prévu* pour plus d'éventualités qu'il n'en peut connaître" (PC, 2, 305), and that only chance circumstances—of which death is one (PC, 2, 290)—prevent us from fulfilling our entire potential. The Parque spends the whole night, or the whole poem, reviewing different roles or versions of herself, the "Harmonieuse Moi" and the "Mystérieuse." Like the speakers of Mallarmé and Laforgue, and like the dramatis personae of a French classical tragedy, the Parque is "un visage à la recherche de son masque définitif."[8] Coming close at one point to suicide, she finally opts for Life, although this acceptance can hardly be seen as an affirmation of unity, in answer to the initial question "Qui pleure?", since she adopts this attitude, as she herself explicitly states, "malgré moi-même"; perhaps it implies, rather, a willingness to accept disunity, i.e., multiplicity.

Having roused herself from sleep and dismissed the Serpent, the Parque remembers herself in the role of "Harmonieuse MOI," "Femme flexible et ferme aux silences suivis / D'actes purs! . . . / . . . l'égale et l'épouse du jour," untainted as yet by thoughts of her own mortality or by a longing for death. This all seems strange to her now ("Je ne rends plus au jour qu'un regard étranger")—and we have seen Valéry, in the *Cahiers*, emphasizing that, from the stand-point of our universal "Moi pur," our past life seems no more "ours" than that of a stranger. "En quoi es-tu le *Même* que *celui* qui eut 10 ans, 15 ans—etc.?" asks Valéry (PC, 2, 321); and the Parque, evoking her own childhood, barely recognizes herself: "Fut-ce bien moi, grands cils, qui crus m'ensevelir / Dans l'arrière-douceur riant à vos menaces. . . ." She dislikes the signs of awakening sensuality connected with this image ("la voix / Que j'ignorais si rauque et d'amour si voilée . . ."), yet is forced (in the passage beginning "Quelle résisterait, mortelle, à ces remous?") to recognize the strength of that element in her present make-up.

Rejecting the idea of suicide as pointless ("Hélas! de mes pieds nus qui trouvera la trace / Cessera-t-il longtemps de ne songer qu'à soi?"), the Parque falls asleep; and sleep, in Valéry, is a metaphor for death: both form a descent into "le néant," but after sleep comes a "resurrection": thus the Parque, describing herself asleep, says "elle imitait la mort" and asks "par quelle sourde suite / La nuit, d'entre les morts, au jour t'a reconduite?" The moment of waking is one when consciousness returns and the "Moi pur" is faced again with its contingent self, or selves: "Réveil," states Valéry in the *Cahiers*, "—Dialogue du Moi et du moi. Le *se réveillant* plus *universel*—trouve comme *cas particulier* ce qu'il (le moi) est, ses projets—etc." (PC, 2, 315).[9] Hence the Parque's gradual, groping re-discovery of her own body and her own thoughts on awakening at the beginning of the poem. She refers to her hand initially as "Cette main," as if she did not recognize it, and to her heart as "un coeur" (1. 8); but the latter soon becomes "mon coeur" ("J'interroge mon coeur quelle douleur l'éveille") and her hand "ma main" ("Je baisais sur ma main cette morsure fine"), as though she were now acknowledging these physical entities as her own.[10] She also begins, after her initial bemused question: "Qui pleure là?" to rediscover the various particular manifestations of her inner self: "Dans me lourde plaie une secrète soeur / Brûle," she declares, "qui se préfère à l'extrême attentive." Here already are two versions of the *moi*, and these lines also posit a third one, aware of the others and of their rivalry. A similar triad emerges from the Parque's expression "Je me voyais me voir," which recalls M. Teste's "Je suis étant, et me voyant; me voyant me voir, et ainsi de suite." The mirror of the fountain in which Narcisse surveys his image is replaced for the Parque by the internal mirror of consciousness itself. Valéry has described *La Jeune Parque* as "une rêverie dont le personnage en même temps que l'objet est la *conscience consciente*" (*O*, I, 1626).

Clearly, a figure representing "la conscience consciente" cannot be a "character" of the type found in Browning's dramatic monologues. We have already seen that one feature of the universal, unchanging "Moi pur" is its impersonal quality, its lack of attributes. The Parque is indeed even more devoid than Hérodiade of attributes, or character traits (except for the sensuality of the "secrète soeur" which at once distinguishes her from Mallarmé's heroine). And as with Mallarmé, the omission of a context—details of time and place—helps to reinforce the impression of universality and prevents the reader from attempting to turn the mythical figure into a "whole" character. *La Jeune Parque* provides no context other than the sea-shore in the hours leading up to dawn; and the sea represents a symbol, precisely, of timelessness (as well as of life and death, important themes in the poem). The Narcissus myth, too, requires as props only a pool at dusk. The Parque and Narcisse are "Sans lieu ni date," as Valéry felt himself to be (PC, 1, 184).

"Ni un temps daté, ni un lieu défini, mais tous les temps, tous les lieux," comments Jean Levaillant, referring to *La Jeune Parque*. For him, the Parque is so lacking in definition that " 'la jeune Parque' ne désigne pas un 'personnage', un hors-texte; elle est écrite et, fictivement, parlée par l'écriture; nous indiquerons ainsi par 'la jeune Parque' un parcours, un discours. . . . La jeune Parque n'est donc en rien différente ici de *La Jeune Parque*."[11] It seems difficult, however, to reduce to "un parcours" the speech of one who addresses the "îles de mon sein nu" and in general takes her physical being so emphatically into account.[12] Moreover, to suggest that the poem is totally lacking in a centre, as Levaillant does, is to ignore the unifying effect of the Parque's voice. Although her question "Qui pleure là?" may never be fully answered, in view of the "impossibilité de connaître . . . le fondement de la conscience" on which Levaillant rightly insists, there can be no doubt of the central presence of the consciousness asking the question and of the voice putting it into words.

# III. Voice

Valéry everywhere stresses the importance of voice to his conception of poetry: "Le point délicat de la poésie est l'obtention de la voix," he declares (PC, 2, 1077). He makes an important distinction between his own notion of poetic voice and that of Mallarmé:

> Mais, *au fait, qui* parle dans un poème? Mallarmé voulait que ce fût le Langage lui-même.
> Pour moi—ce serait—l'Etre *vivant* ET *pensant* (*contraste, ceci*). . . . En somme, le *Langage* issu de la voix, plutôt que la voix du *Langage*.[13]

The voice in question, then, is not simply that of Language—of that poetic language which Mallarmé terms "essentiel" in contrast with everyday language, "brut ou immédiat";[14] it is the recognizably human voice of an "Etre vivant et pensant." Far from representing a personal voice, however, reflecting a specific character and speaking in realistic inflections like that of a Browning persona, the voice of the poem should, according to Valéry, be as impersonal as the "Moi pur" from which it emanates: "cette voix ne doit faire imaginer quelque homme qui parle. Si elle le fait, ce n'est pas elle" (PC, 2, 1077). Simultaneously intimate and impersonal, the voice of the poem should have "une sorte de vie propre, autonome, intime, impersonnelle—c'est-à-dire personnelle-universelle (par opposition avec personnelle-accidentelle)" (PC, 2, 1090). Here we see again Valéry's preference for the universal over the "accidentel" or contingent. Also, the impersonal quality of this voice helps to create distance between the speaker and reader of a poem like *La Jeune Parque*. Indeed it would be difficult to relate closely to something as abstract as "la conscience consciente"; the reader may share the Parque's problem (that of self-knowledge), but the very nature of that problem must prevent his identifying with her.

Valéry's profound concern with the question of voice explains
the frequency in his poetry of first-person utterance, whether of an
unidentified "I" or of Sémiramis, Narcisse, the Parque, the Serpent,
the pythoness, etc. "La plus belle poésie a toujours la forme d'un
monologue," declares Valéry (PC, 1, 285) and, even more categori-
cally, "Le discours (en littérature) est un monologue" (C, XIII, 117)
and "La littérature commence et finit et finira par des monologues"
(C, XII, 384). Thus, in a play like Phèdre, the minor characters fade
into the background, leaving the impression of a monologue
spoken by the heroine (a comment recalling those of Mallarmé
concerning the "comparses" of Hamlet): "Ils ne survivent pas, mais
Elle survit. L'oeuvre se réduit dans le souvenir à un mono-
logue . . ." (O, I, 500). A different type of work which Valéry also
regards as a monologue is the Discours de la Méthode, whose main
attraction, for Valéry, is Descartes' voice (O, I, 818 and 806). No
doubt Valéry's preoccupation with monologue partially explains
his difficulty with stage drama, in which "le dialogue est condition
immédiate" (C, XXIV, 624), as Nicole Celeyrette-Pietri suggests:
"Qu'est-ce, en vérité, que son théâtre, sinon, très consciemment, un
'monologue à plusieurs Moi'?"[15]

Voice is more crucial to a poem than the thought it expresses: "la
poésie n'est pas la pensée; elle est la divinisation de la Voix" (O, I,
597). Indeed, says Valéry, "la seule voix dit bien des choses, avant
d'agir comme porteuse de messages particuliers" (C, XXVIII, 866).
The reader, once acquainted with the voice, comes to recognize
and love it, and wants to hear more of it;[16] in this way his relation-
ship with the poem resembles that of the lover, who cries: "ta voix
veut en moi, veut encore ta voix!" (C, XXVI, 203). The tone of the
voice can—and should—change from poem to poem, or within
one long poem: E. Noulet demonstrates in Le Ton poétique how two
poems with the same metre, "Le Sylphe" and "L'Insinuant," never-
theless present quite different tonalities, and illustrates some of the
changes in tone within La Jeune Parque. She concludes that "Le ton
change, chez Valéry, avec chaque poème, chaque vers, chaque
parole, toujours chargée de son idée."[17] Valéry himself has stated
that the writing of La Jeune Parque constituted an inquiry into "ce
qu'on pourrait tenter en poésie qui fût analogue à ce qu'on nomme
'modulation', en musique" (O, I, 1473); these modulations permit

smooth transitions in tone between different parts of the poem, from the muted hesitancy of the opening to the declamatory fervour of the conclusion, via the many shifts and oppositions reflecting the changing moods of the Parque. Meanwhile, the Parque's voice remains the same even though her tone alters: it retains its intensity of expression and nobility of diction; its musicality (though the effects of the music vary); its fondness for certain stylistic features such as apposition, inversion, apostrophe, alliteration, periphrasis, allusion; and a preference for certain words and motifs, repeated in different sections of the poem (to be examined later in connection with the poem's structure).

At times there seems to be little difference between Valéry's idea of voice and the normal concept of style. In "Poésie et pensée abstraite" he refers to voice as "la forme, les caractères sensibles du langage, le son, le rythme, les accents, le timbre, le mouvement" as opposed to "toutes les valeurs significatives, les images, les idées . . ." (O, I, 1332). His definition of style, however, is: "Notre 'style' c'est notre voix, altérée par notre travail, complétée" (C, X, 498). The poet should listen to his own voice and work on it to achieve a finished "style." He should be faithful to this voice: Valéry affirms in the Cahiers that "Langage vrai est celui dont nous reconnaissons tous les termes comme nôtres. . . . Ils sont de notre voix" (C, XXIII, 526). And the voice to which the poet must listen is the inner monologue, in whose value for poetry Valéry had great faith: "Fais que . . . mon ouïe intime écoute avec ravissement ma voix intime" (C, XXIV, 283); "J'écoute quelqu'un qui parle—Et quand il parle bien—j'écris" (C, X, 308).

Not only in the area of poetic technique does the question of voice in Valéry assume such importance; it also guarantees, as was suggested above in relation to the Parque, the central presence of the "I" to whom the voice belongs: "La Voix . . . est l'unité" writes Valéry (C, XII, 806), and there are two reasons for this. Firstly, the physiological dimension of voice links it to the body, which is unique: hence Valéry's claim that the speaker of a poem is the living as well as the thinking being ("l'Etre vivant ET pensant"). Secondly, Valéry sees a close connection between voice, the Moi and consciousness. "Le Moi, c'est la Voix," he declares (C, XIV, 390), and "Pas de conscience sans M[oi]" (PC, 2, 315).[18] The "I" 's consciousness of self ("self-consciousness" as Valéry terms it, in English) depends on its awareness of the inner monologue constantly unfolding within consciousness; the individual's very acknowledgement of his existence relies therefore on his perception of a voice, for, asks Valéry, "Qu'est le moi dans son silence?" (*C*, IV, 313).[19] The inner voice supplies the essential transition from being to knowing: "L'espirt se parle ou va se parler; et ce n'est que par là qu'il se distingue de l'être" (*C*, XII, 896). The Parque's self-awareness, and the beginning of her quest for self-knowledge, are precipitated by an auditory perception, as she asks "Qui pleure?"

While the inner voice provides consciousness of self at any given moment, a sense of continuity depends on memory: "C'est la mémoire qui fait de l'homme une entité," declares Valéry, and "Le problème de la mémoire contient celui de l'identité" (PC, 1, 1215 and 1219). We have seen the Parque trying to relate her present self to past images of self; she uses these versions of herself to help solve her present dilemma; for past events can, as memories, instantaneously become part of the present: "le passé oublie qu'il est passé; et à ce prix, joue dans le présent" (PC, 1, 1244).

## IV. Drama

Memory and the inner voice, then, confer on the subject an identity and a sense of continuity, and this is crucial, since *La Jeune Parque* could not be considered a dramatic monologue if the speaker were not perceived as a distinct entity. The Parque may not be an individual with specific characteristics, but her central presence pervades the poem. However, although awareness of the inner monologue provides a sense of identity and unity, it also represents, paradoxically, a source of *disunity*, and therefore of dramatic conflict, another prerequisite of the dramatic monologue. For if "Le Moi, c'est la Voix," the question at once arises: which *Moi*, the speaker or the listener? Indeed, "La personne qui parle est déjà autre que moi—et je suis fait autre qu'elle, par cela seul que cette *personne qui parle* m'engendre *personne qui entend*" (*C*, XX, 15). "Qui est MOI, du parleur ou de l'auditeur?" asks Valéry (PC, 1, 463); he opts for the latter, since the speaker can take the listener by surprise: "Ma parole intérieure peut me surprendre et je ne puis la prévoir. Quand elle parle, j'appelle moi non ce qui parle (le tiers inconnu) mais l'auditeur" (PC, 2, 282).[20] In any case, the inner monologue reveals the fundamental duality of the *moi:* "Si je pense, si je m'entretiens avec moi, si je m'apprends quelque chose, si je m'interroge etc.—c'est que je suis composé—c'est que je *donne* à quelqu'un *qui n'a pas,*—c'est que je *reçois* de quelqu'un *qui a*" (C, IX, 434). Valéry calls the "I" a "*Binité* en deux personnes" (C, XXVII, 393).

"L'existence de cette parole de soi à soi," says Valéry, "est signe d'une *coupure*" (PC, 1, 407), and this dichotomy within consciousness constitutes a source of tension which largely accounts for the dramatic features of his monologues. An entry in the *Cahiers* confirms this with respect to the Narcisse poems:

> *Narcisse*—La confrontation du Moi et de la Personnalité. Le conflit du souvenir, du *nom*, des habitudes, des penchants, de la forme mirée, de l'être arrêté, fixé, inscrit—de l'histoire, du *particulier* avec—le centre universel, la capacité de changement. (PC, 2, 284)

The externalized confrontation between Narcisse as "centre universel" or "Moi pur" and his personality or accidental self mirrored in the water illustrates a conflict intrinsic to the life of the consciousness. Reunification of the two elements would mean death for Narcisse, and the end of all monologue/dialogue, for there can be no conscious existence without duality: "En dernière analyse, c'est le *Dédoublement* qui est le fait essentiel psychique. . . . C'est lui qu'on appelle 'conscience" ' (PC, 2, 224).

Valéry's interest in the processes of consciousness led him to value the effort of composition over the finished work—an attitude which, as he himself points out, distinguishes him from Mallarmé for whom "le suprême objet au monde . . . était, ne pouvait être qu'un *Livre*" (O, I, 637). He recognizes that his own tendency to consider the "calculs de l'agent" more important than the finished work "s'opposait curieusement à mon admiration pour un homme qui n'allait . . . à rien de moins qu'à diviniser la chose écrite" (O, I, 641). Valéry's greater concern with the mind's activities is reflected in the complexity of the Parque's own mental world, which is explored in far greater depth than that of Hérodiade, both as regards the scope of her meditation and the extent to which the mechanisms of thought itself are revealed, involving processes of repetition, analogy, and contradiction. "Le sujet véritable du poème," declares Valéry, "est la peinture d'une suite de substitutions psychologiques, et en somme le changement d'une conscience pendant la durée d'une nuit" (*O*, I, 1613); and elsewhere he describes the poem as "une rêverie dont le personnage en même temps que l'objet est la *conscience consciente*" (*O*, I, 1636). Again, Valéry himself points out the differences between his poem and Mallarmé's *Hérodiade* and *Faune*:

> Tandis que—les 2 poèmes de M[allarmé] sont faits par un *tramé* sur la forme, avec un sujet dont le dessin n'est assujetti qu'à se faire reconnaître,—le poème ne conduisant pas à approfondir le sujet, mais le traitant en prétexte . . . la *J[eune] Parque* qui n'a, à proprement parler, de sujet, dérive de l'intention de définir ou désigner une connaissance de l'être vivant, qu'il ne suffit pas de—reconnaître, mais qu'il faut apprendre (PC, 1, 297).

Nevertheless, as Valéry acknowledges in the same *Cahiers* entry, *La Jeune Parque* would never have existed without *Hérodiade*. And although this remark certainly refers to more than the similarities between the two heroines, the latter do resemble each other closely in many ways: in their narcissism, their urge towards self-sufficiency, their sterility, their defensive preoccupation with virginity and simultaneously with the possibility of its violation (a theme both authors would extend to the act of writing, of marking the blank page "que la blancheur défend"). Less vain than Hérodiade, perhaps, and less petulant, the Parque also differs in another, more important respect: in her sensuality. A repressed sensuality is barely hinted at in the last lines of *Hérodiade*, whereas in *La Jeune Parque* is it blatant, even though the passages in which it expresses itself were, according to Valéry, "non prévus et faits après coup" (*O*, I, 1621). Apart from the *dédoublement* discerned by Valéry in the very act of conscious thought, the Parque thus embodies another conflict which preoccupied the poet all his life, as evidenced by hundreds of *Cahiers* entries—that between mind and body. The Parque is shocked to discover the duality of her own nature: "Dieux! Dans ma lourde plaie une secrète soeur / Brûle, qui se préfère à l'extrême attentive," and half regrets the time of a more united, though less lucid, former self, of the "Harmonieuse Moi . . . / Femme flexible et ferme aux silences suivis / D'actes purs!" Erotic memories of a still earlier time, in her childhood, make her feel she should blush with shame (11. 190–203); but she is forced, during her celebration of spring, to recognize the power of the sexual instinct (11. 243–257), and seems at the end of the poem to have come to terms with it ("Tu viens! . . . Je suis toujours celle que tu respires"). The poem's final lines combine the themes of consciousness ("pensées," "âpre éveil," "connaître") and of sensuality:

> et si l'onde
> Au cap tonne, immolant un monstre de candeur,
> Et vient des hautes mers vomir la profondeur
> Sur ce roc, d'où jaillit jusque vers mes pensées
> Un éblouissement d'étincelles glacées,
> Et sur toute ma peau que morde l'âpre éveil,
> Alors, malgré moi-même, il le faut, ô Soleil,
> Que j'adore mon coeur où tu te viens connaître,
> Doux et puissant retour du délice de naître. . . .

Many other contradictory urges and emotions illustrate the speaker's inner conflict in the course of the poem, and the constant shifts in register between despair and optimistic affirmation, timidity and indignation, uncertainty and confidence, serenity and agitation, contribute to the poem's dramatic effect.

The very expression "la conscience consciente" which Valéry uses to summarize La Jeune Parque implies a doubling within consciousness, a "split" involving great dramatic potential. Indeed, Valéry's fascination with the drama inherent in the workings of the conscious mind no doubt largely accounts for the constant pull he felt towards drama as a means of artistic expression—and towards the dramatic monologue in particular since a mental drama can only be played out within the mind of one individual. Valéry even compares consciousness to a theatre: "La conscience de Beyle est un théâtre" (O, I, 558); and the narrator of "La Soirée avec M. Teste" tells the latter: "Je voudrais voir un théâtre inspiré de vos méditations." La Jeune Parque is described by Valéry as a "drame lyrique"

(*C*, XXVI, 706), its two parts being "actes" (*O*, I, 1626); and the Parque herself declares "Ma lassitude est parfois un théâtre." The Parque's anguished introspection and her distress at the discovery of her inner disunity lead her to the brink of suicide—a supremely dramatic moment for any individual:

> Que si ma tendre odeur grise ta tête creuse,
> O Mort, respire enfin cette esclave de roi:
> Appelle-moi, délie! . . . Et désespère-moi,
> De moi-même si lasse . . .

As we saw with the "Fragments du Narcisse," the only solution to the problem of *dédoublement* within consciousness, apart from acceptance, is death. The question is resolved as the Parque exclaims "Mystérieuse MOI, pourtant, tu vis encore!"—attributing the adjective "Mystérieuse" to that multiple being which she has now come to recognize as herself, and which she must accept if she is to live. Yet part of her wonders whether she has taken the right decision:

> O n'aurait-il fallu, folle, que j'accomplisse
> Ma merveilleuse fin de choisir pour supplice
> Ce lucide dédain des nuances du sort?

and how she reached it:

> Cherche, du moins, dis-toi, par quelle sourde suite
> La nuit, d'entre les morts, au jour t'a reconduite?

Though she still insists on the need to know oneself ("Souviens-toi de toi-même"), the memory of the previous night and of her own sensuality again produces an unwelcome sense of "otherness": "Au milieu de mes bras, je me suis faite une autre . . . / Qui s'aliène? . . . Qui s'envole? . . . Qui se vautre? . . .", questions which recall the opening one, "Qui pleure?" In other words, the search for an identity continues and must indeed be unending in one whose consciousness of self is as acute as the Parque's.

"The function of consciousness is to explore, that of character to conserve and to habituate";[21] and we see the Parque—like the

Faun—exploring, questioning, examining different roles or options, and developing; whereas Browning's speakers, with their well-defined characters, are static and do not change. And while the drama in Browning's monologues hinges largely on the discrepancy between the speaker's view of himself and the reader's, in Valéry, as in Mallarmé's *Faune* or *Hérodiade*, it stems from the conflict within the self and the incessant self-questioning to which this leads ("J'interroge mon coeur quelle douleur m'éveille"). The dramatic element in Mallarmé or Valéry, very different from the drama of Browning's poems, is nevertheless central, as of course it must be in a dramatic monologue. The totally internalized kind of drama typical of the *Faune* and *La Jeune Parque* resembles that of French classical tragedy (particularly that of Racine, whom Valéry greatly admired) with its emphasis on movements within the psyche, expressed in words, rather than on external events. Valéry comments frequently on this aspect of classical tragedy: "Le théâtre classique est fait de discours—qui posent, préparent, définissent, déclarent,—des *actes*" (*C*, VIII, 853). The Parque's origin in myth, her lack of character traits and her preoccupation with thoughts and emotions of a universal nature also link her, like the Faun, with classical theatre.

Valéry himself had lived through a night of internal crisis similar to that of the Parque in that it involved the *dédoublement* of "la conscience consciente." He refers to it in the *Cahiers* as "Mon analytique 1892, produit de la 'conscience de soi' " (*C*, XXIII, 757), and elsewhere he states "J'essayai . . . d'opposer la conscience de mon état à cet état même," and concludes "Je devins alors un drame singulier."[22] "Singulier" can no doubt be taken here in both senses of the word; as with the Parque, the drama was enacted within one consciousness.

The drama of the "split" within the *moi* is heightened by the fact that the inner "monologue," with its symptomatic division into "parleur" and "auditeur," employs the dramatic form of *dialogue*. "L'individu est un dialogue," claims Valéry (PC, 1, 440), and "Tout monologue est un dialogue" (*C*, XI, 230). To replace the term "monologue," therefore, Valéry coins "mono-dialogue" (*C*, XIII, 147), or speaks of the "monologue à deux voix" (*C*, XXII, 125) or "monologue à plusieurs Moi" (*C*, XXI, 709). Dramatic monologues, as we saw in connection with Mallarmé, also tend to appropriate various dialogue forms, including apostrophe, questions, commands, and all types of second-person address. By a process which Beaujour terms the "subjectivisation de la rhétorique,"[23] the solitary monologist adopts the linguistic forms of dialogue and directs them, very often, to himself. The most obvious example is the question, which normally implies the presence of an interlocuter. *La Jeune Parque* opens with a question, and they continue to proliferate throughout the poem, the final one appearing in the last section. Questions have a dramatic quality all their own, for, as Scarfe points out, the "state of doubt . . . is the most fertile source of drama," and "certainty is the end of dramatic tension."[24] The Parque interrogates the Serpent ("Qu'es-tu, près de ma nuit d'éternelle longueur?") and occasionally the subjects of her apostrophe ("D'où nais-tu? Quel travail toujours triste et nouveau / Te tire avec retard, larme, de l'ombre amère?"). More frequently, however, her questions are addressed to herself; this is the most dramatic form of questioning, since it emphasizes the conflict within the Self, as in:

> O n'aurait-il pas fallu, folle, que j'accomplisse
> Ma merveilleuse fin de choisir pour supplice
> Ce lucide dédain des nuances du sort?

Inner conflict is also signalled by the Parque's creation in the third person of "other selves" (the "secrète soeur," "l'extrême attentive," "mortelle soeur," "Harmonieuse Moi," etc.) which, as Scarfe comments, make possible a "more truly dramatic diction,"[25] provoking in particular the phenomenon most typical of dialogue, namely second-person address, but in the form of self-address, which illustrates the dramatic *dédoublement* of the consciousness. Valéry sometimes uses it himself in his explorations of the inner monologue: "qui parle intérieurement? *qui es-tu*? quel est le sujet parlant" (*C*, X, 547; emphasis added; "Ce que tu dis, ô Moi,—cela se dit comme de soi-même entre soi et soi" (PC, 2, 234); the direct address to the "Moi" in the second person in the latter example reproduces the structure of the Parque's phrase "Mystérieuse Moi, pourtant, tu vis encore!" The height of the dramatic potential of self-address, "the very summit of . . . self-exacerbation," as Scarfe puts it, is reached in Section XIV ("O n'aurait-il fallu, folle . . ."). Significantly, notes Scarfe, this passage, where "the use of the second-person form of address is most sustained," satisfied Valéry himself better than any other.[26] The Parque actually manages here to speak of herself in the second, first and third persons in the space of four lines:

> Trouveras-tu jamais plus transparente mort
> Ni de pente plus pure où je rampe à ma perte
> Que sur ce long regard de victime entrouverte,
> Pâle, qui se résigne et saigne sans regret?

A few lines later begin the commands to the self which again reveal the dramatic split in the speaker's psyche:

> Non, non! . . . N'irrite plus cette réminiscence!
> . . . . . . . . . . . . . . . . . . . . . . . . . . . . . . . .
> Cherche, du moins, dis-toi, par quelle sourde suite
> La nuit, d'entre les morts, au jour t'a reconduite?
> Souviens-toi de toi-même . . . . . . . .
> Sois subtile . . . cruelle . . . ou plus subtile! . . . Mens
> Mais sache! . . .

This section represents the climax of the Parque's tormented self-address; in the final part (XVI) we again find a progression through the different persons, from third to second to first ("Lasse femme absolue, et les yeux dans ses larmes . . . / Mes transports, cette nuit, pensaient briser ta chaîne; / Je n'ai fait que bercer de lamentations / Tes flancs chargés de jour et de créations!" Subsequently, i.e., in the poem's closing lines, the Parque refers to herself only in the first person, which might suggest that she has finally achieved a sense of identity were it not for the ominous "malgré moi-même" of the fifth line from the end implying that this neat impression of unity may be illusory.

Second-person address is by no means restricted, in *La Jeune Parque*, to self-address: the Parque makes frequent use of apostrophe and, like the Faun, she directs it not only to "animate" beings such as the real or imaginary Serpent and the hypothetical "fantômes naissants" but, most frequently, to inanimate objects and abstractions: the stars (11. 18-25), her own tear (280-98), the islands (348-60), her resting-place (465-74); Memory (190-99), Death (217-42), her "sagesse" (457-60) and her "divins dégoûts" (362-65). The use of apostrophe, and of questions, evokes the presence of a listener, implying therefore a real speaking situation aimed at communication. Thus we hear the impersonal voice of the poem, never sounding like the voice of a real person, and yet engaged in the normal activity of speech.

As with the *Faune*, the artificial device of apostrophe paradoxically counterbalances the artificiality inherent in monologue by reintroducing "l'opposition entre les deux premières personnes, opposition qui est le caractère fondamental du dialogue," i.e., of language in its "normal," communicative, function.[27] Most of the Parque's apostrophes are quite long (around ten lines or more), which means that, given also her second-person self-address, large portions of the poem are written in the second person. This, together with the numerous questions and exclamations, injects movement into what could have been a static, totally non-dramatic speech.

For Valéry, then, the inner monologue of "la conscience consciente"—his source for the dramatic monologue of *La Jeune Parque*—tends spontaneously to assume a dramatic character, partly because of the split it entails between *l'auditeur* and *le parleur* and the anguished sense of division this involves; and partly because it automatically takes the form of dialogue, or "monodialogue." Laurenti suggests that, for Valéry, the "monologue intérieur porte en lui son pouvoir dramatique";[28] Valéry himself calls the interior monologue a "monodrame" (*C*, XX, 278) and declares that "Nous sommes habités par un effet de théâtre . . . qui est pensée, et qui est moi" (*C*, X, 626). His dramatic conception of the interior monologue at once distinguishes it from the type of inner monologue presented by James Joyce, or by Dujardin before him. The Joycean monologue rambles from one subject to another; as Dujardin says, the thought "court d'un plan à l'autre," reproducing as closely as possible the "course 'à bâtons rompus'" of the so-called stream of consciousness, i.e., of the *pre*-conscious flow of thought. Dujardin is quite aware that the latter cannot be reproduced exactly: "Le monologue intérieur ne doit pas donner la pensée 'tout venant', mais en donner l'impression"[29]—the reason being that once the writer begins to note down the ramblings of the "stream of consciousness" he tends to organize and so distort them. In fact, the "stream of consciousness" ceases as soon as one becomes aware of it, long before any attempt to set it down on paper: we cannot deliberately think such a monologue, only realize that we have thought it. "Parler intérieurement n'est pas *se* parler," says Valéry (*C*, III, 698). The intervention of consciousness represents the crucial difference between the dramatic monologue which is *La Jeune Parque* and the interior monologue as "invented" by Dujardin and developed by Joyce. Joyce offers, according to a literary convention which assumes such things are possible, an imitation of the inner flow of thought *before* the intervention of consciousness, even though the process of imitation itself clearly must be conscious, on the part of the author. Valéry's own, much more dramatic, monologues present the utterance of a divided *moi*, aware of its own duality, with the dramatic consequences this split entails.

Dorrit Cohn, in *Transparent Minds*, makes the interesting observation that the discourse of a monologue "no longer conforms to Benveniste's definition of *discours* as 'every utterance assuming a speaker and a hearer' unless we extend this definition to include a hearer who is identical to the speaker."[30] We can make such an extension in the case of the dramatic monologue, where the character does use language to communicate with his "other self," but the situation as regards interior monologue is more ambiguous, because the speaker is not even addressing himself. This language does not consciously attempt to say anything to anyone, it "drops its communicative dimension"; it simply *is*. Benveniste's definition of *discours* reads in full: "every utterance assuming a speaker and a hearer, and in the speaker, the intention of influencing the other in some way."[31] Even this latter clause can be said to apply to the dramatic monologue if we accept that the speaker is usually trying to convince himself, to resolve conflicts between his two selves, just as the Parque struggles, in the course of her inner dialogue, to reconcile her own contradictory attitudes to such issues as motherhood, sexuality, suicide.

Valéry declares that "Monologue n'existe pas—si ce n'est peut-être comme activité toute inconsciente—celle du dormeur parlant" (whereas when consciousness intervenes a split takes place and dialogue begins) (*C*, XXIV, 624). Significantly, a passage does occur in *La Jeune Parque* where, on the verge of sleep, the Parque's mind wanders and she produces some barely coherent, disjointed phrases (centering, however, on the love of the "Cygne-Dieu"), which she is clearly not fully conscious of uttering. This withdrawal of consciousness sets these lines apart from the rest of the poem, a fact which is marked by their being placed in parentheses and in italics. They are lines of so-called "interior," pre-conscious monologue within the conscious discourse of a dramatic monologue.

The mental flow known as the stream of consciousness has a random, arbitrary, and inconclusive quality which can only have repulsed Valéry: he condemns it as "*désordonné* en tant . . . qu'il est *non-choix*" (*C*, XXIII, 106). The contrast between deliberate choice and arbitrariness can be illustrated with reference to descriptions: in a Joycean interior monologue the character's surroundings are often mentioned, in a random way, as they happen to impinge on his consciousness. The Parque's evocations of scenery, however, are not accidental but closely linked to her own moods and deliberations: thoughts of death lead her to describe "L'insensible rocher, glissant d'algues, propice / A fuir," which lies nearby. Similarly, her most buoyant mood in section XII causes her to imagine the imminent spectacle of dawn rising over the islands—a speech far removed from the random, fragmented ramblings of interior monologue. For Valéry, the inner voice serves as a check or guideline (*C*, VI, 170), not as a model. He describes the "langage intérieur" of the stream of consciousness as "cet égout, ce désordre, ce chemin brisé," noting that it is "fait d'images, de bouts de phrases . . . de coq-à-l'âne, de brusques rappels et de diverticules, fuites, pertes distraites etc." (*C*, V, 895). He chooses to *select* material from this *égout*, whereas Joyce's monologues, since they aim to imitate as closely as possible the pre-conscious musings of a given individual, must include *all* the material his mind supposedly surveys, irrespective of its intrinsic interest, its decency or its relevance to the work as a whole. They therefore tend to include a great deal of banal, trivial matter whose significance is restricted to what it reveals about a given character and which must be expressed in a language appropriate to the individual in question. To Valéry, all these features are anathema: he is not interested in the portrayal of character or therefore in particularizing his speakers through their language; and he considers that the material of interior monologue, belonging to the abhorrent, "accidental" side of everyday life, should be banished from poetry with its accent on the essential and the universal. Laurenti makes this point in *Paul Valéry et le théâtre*: "Il est bien certain qu'aux yeux d'un artiste tel que Valéry le monologue spontané se réduirait à l'expression de banalités sans intérêt, ou à l'extériorisation des instincts les plus communs."[32]

Presumably, then, Valéry would not approve of the assimilation of *La Jeune Parque* to interior monologue in the manner of Joyce or his successors. Cohn draws a close parallel between the Parque's monologue and Molly's at the end of *Ulysses*.[33] Although both works may present intimate "night-thoughts," however, the dramatic monologue links them together logically, whereas the interior monologue strives to reproduce the random, fragmentary nature of thought as it is formed in Molly's mind. Cohn comments on Valéry's "high poetic diction" which, she says, "loses the essential intent of interior monologue in fiction: to present a mind in unhampered motion, speaking without intent or purpose, as it never was meant to speak in the strait jacket of regular versification, much less in the rhymed alexandrine." This illustrates clearly enough that Valéry did not in fact aim to produce an interior monologue of this type, or to "present a mind in unhampered motion." "La conscience consciente" cannot speak "without intent or purpose."

# V. Roles and scripts

"La 'vie consciente' est théâtre," declares Valéry (*C*, XVIII, 708)— a statement which has its negative side, implying that role-playing begins within the mind itself, as another entry in the *Cahiers* demonstrates:

> Tout ce qui est de l'esprit est comédie.
> Ceci n'est pas une remarque morale, mais descriptive.
> Connaître = n'être pas ce que l'on est.
> Et *n'être pas ce que l'on est* est possible, est réalisable par

des actes et des attitudes.
L'image de quoi est une comédie. (IX, 907)

The mind is the scene of a "comédie intérieure" that can be ex-
teriorized (C, III, 183), and Valéry defines comédie as "le fait d'im-
primer aux actes et attitudes même intérieurs . . . des impulsions
. . . conformes à quelque idée de soi que l'on espère produire dans
les autres ou dans soi. Tout homme dont l'idée de soi à produire ou à
suggérer est l'objet, joue la comédie" (C, XIV, 601). The intervention
of an "I," or a conscious awareness, into the disorderly ramblings of
the stream of consciousness at once provokes mental role-playing
(C, V, 895). In his essay on Stendhal, Valéry suggests that self-
awareness leads directly to a sense of diversity and to the deliberate
adoption of a role: "Peut-être l'accroissement de la conscience de
soi, l'observation constante de soi-même conduisent-elles à se
trouver, à se rendre divers? . . . Se connaître n'est que se prévoir;
se prévoir aboutit à jouer un rôle" (O, I, 558).

"Se connaître n'est que se prévoir": the Parque, too, complains
that hyper-lucidity leads to an unwelcome prescience resulting in
mental and spiritual atrophy:

> O dangereusement de son regard la proie!
>
> Car l'oeil spirituel sur les plages de soie
> Avait déjà vu luire et pâlir trop de jours
> Dont je m'étais prédit les couleurs et le cours.
> L'ennui, le clair ennui de mirer leur nuance
> Me donnait sur ma vie une funeste avance:
> L'aube me dévoilait tout le jour ennemi.

She also dislikes the predictability of repetitive and cyclical
phenomena, the "éternels retours" of "La semence, le lait, le sang."
Judith Robinson suggests that the reason she tries to deny her own
sexuality and rejects the idea of maternity—of her "destinée pro-
prement féminine"—is that "être femme, c'est presque inévitable-
ment sacrifier une partie de sa nature 'unique' pour devenir
'semblable' á toutes les autres femmes, pour être englobée dans
l'immense courant vital où 'La semence, le lait, le sang coulent tou-
jours.' "[34] Valéry himself actively sought to be different from other

people in order to avoid repeating their lives (*C*, XXIV, 374), and, like the Parque, expresses resentment at the predictable and repetitious side of life: "Je suis né, à vingt ans, exaspéré par la répétition—c'est-à-dire contre la vie. Se lever, se rhabiller, manger, éliminer, se coucher—et toujours ces saisons, ces astres . . ." (PC, 1, 175). This irritation has a Laforguian ring; and later in the same fragment we read "L'amour me paraissait redites," which neatly summarizes the most constant preoccupation of Laforgue's poetry. " 'Je t'aime' impossible à dire," continues Valéry, "sans que l'on perdît sa raison d'être, d'*Etre d'une seule fois*. Comment s'entendre murmurer cela sans entendre un *autre*, et tout le monde?"

For if the conscious "I" inevitably finds itself playing another's part, this is because the only medium in which it can express itself, that of language, comes to it, like an actor's script, from outside:

> Le langage constitue un *autre* en toi et cet *autre* est "conscience",—comédie, peut-être! (*C*, XVIII, 708).

> Société, tas d'autruis inconnus ou connus, ceux qui nous ont communiqué le virus du discours qu'ils tenaient d'autres autruis, et, en deçà de ces porteurs de mots, une quantité immense de disparus, dont . . . les échanges entre eux ou avec eux-mêmes, ont forgé ce Langage, actuellement comme vivant en nous, et plus fort que nous . . qui nous impose ce qu'il est (PC, 1, 471).

Many of Valéry's *Cahiers* entries touching on this aspect of language recall passages from Bakhtin concerning the impossibility of original discourse in a language that inevitably carries the meanings and intentions of others: "Le langage donné," writes Valéry, ". . . m'est étranger, n'est pas fait sur ma mesure . . . me fait me satisfaire de réponses qui ne viennent pas de moi" (PC, 1, 446).

Again, if the individual is "un ESPACE de possibilités," this is largely because, while using language to express himself, he simultaneously *creates* himself—in the eyes of others, and even in his own eyes—through his speech, through the limitless potential of language. The poem "La Pythie"—as well as *La Jeune Parque*—explores this question of whether we contain language or are contained by it; the pythoness both engenders language, after a painful and exhausting labour, and is engendered by it, since she could not be known or know herself without it. Similarly, the Parque, another female figure who devotes some time to the theme of birth, creates language, since she speaks the poem, or "thinks" it; and at the same time she is formed by language, because it is through language that she analyses her inner being and, incidentally, makes it known to the reader. Even as she asks "Who am I?" and struggles with words to piece together the evidence, so the reader, saying "Who is she?", confronts her language and tries to identify her from it.

Simultaneously creating language and created by it, the Parque is both speaking and spoken, active and passive—which coincides with the image Valéry evokes of the *Moi* as incorporating both a *parleur*, who speaks, and an *écouteur* who is spoken to, or for. The *Moi* (the conscious "I") is thus created by language. The Parque can know herself only through language because thought—conscious thought at least—is impossible without it (c.f. PC, 1, 394); and yet language comes to us from outside, from others. Part of the Parque's difficulty in attaining self-knowledge stems from this battle with language: apart from her struggle towards unity via the dialogue with the self inevitably associated with consciousness, and which implies duality, she is striving to achieve a lucid view of herself in a medium clouded by the ambiguities and opacities accumulated by others: "Ce qui obscurcit presque tout c'est le langage" (*C*, I, 491). Valéry complains vigorously that "Nous recevons notre *Moi* connaissable et reconnaissable *de la bouche d'autrui*" (PC, 1, 467); and exclaims: "—Eh quoi! vous êtes l'unique, ô Moi, et vous n'avez, jusqu'au plus intime de votre pensée, que des voix statistiques. Vous vous éveillez, pensée, toute préformée par je ne sais qui ou quels! *Et dans mon sein je ne trouve que d'autres!*" (PC, 1, 453).

This aspect of language entails important consequences for poetry, which has to use the same devalued currency as everyday language, namely words. In fact, words acquire a new importance for the poet, who knows that "le réel d'un discours, ce sont les mots seulement et les formes" (PC, 2, 1099). He must strive to deploy words and forms in an original manner, and one way of achieving this is by being faithful to the inner voice for, as Socrates says in *Eupalinos*, "Le réel d'un discours, c'est après tout cette chanson, et cette couleur d'une voix, que nous traitons à tort comme détails et accidents" (*O*, II, 85). Indeed, if the content of speech can only be a repetition of what others have said, then little remains beyond "la couleur d'une voix." Hence the importance we have seen Valéry accord to the notion of voice. As he explains in "Poésie et pensée abstraite," prose achieves its aim by communicating a message as quickly as possible. The tone and individual words of the speech are forgotten once the message has been understood, whereas the form of poetry remains constant every time it is repeated.[35] The poem draws attention not only to the ideas and images it contains but also to "les caractères sensibles du langage, le son, le rythme, les accents, le timbre, le mouvement—en un mot, la *Voix* en action" (*O*, I, 1331–32). Like prose, then, poetry must use "ce moyen essentiellement pratique, perpétuellement altéré, souillé, faisant tous les métiers, le *langage commun*"; but from it the poet strives to "tirer une Voix pure, idéale, capable de communiquer sans faiblesses, sans effort apparent . . . une idée de quelque *moi* merveilleusement supérieur à Moi" (*O*, I, 1339). This is "la voix de personne" celebrated at the end of "La Pythie"—not the voice of the poet's *moi*, or of any individual, but of a generalized, universal "I" "merveilleusement supérieur à Moi," of the "Moi pur" which, in its limitless potential to be all things, belongs therefore to everyone—and to no one.

# VI. Wholeness and fragmentation

Valéry states in the *Cahiers* that if he were to write his Memoirs they would be "ceux d'un esprit sans mémoire" (PC, 1, 177), i.e., not the story of a remembered life, but that of "le moi pur"—a purely spiritual autobiography (or, as he describes *La Jeune Parque* in a letter to Gide, an "intellectual" one (*O*, I, 1624)), dealing with a universal present rather than an individual past. Valéry says of *La Jeune Parque* "Tandis que l'élément *historique* d'un MOI joue en général le rôle principal, j'ai—ici comme ailleurs—préféré son sentiment d'actuel éternel" (PC, 1, 285). The time of *La Jeune Parque* is the eternal present of the mind; as Valéry says, "Le passé *oublie* qu'il est passé; et à ce prix, joue dans le présent" (PC, 1, 1244). The scenes from the Parque's past, in the passages beginning "Harmonieuse MOI" and "Souvenir, ô bûcher . . ." are introduced not as part of a chronological narration of her past life, but in order to throw light on her present dilemma summarized in the initial question "Qui pleure là," i.e., "Qui suis-je?" Her past is not presented as a narrative with specific events and dates in the manner of a Browningesque monologue, for Valéry disliked reminiscences about the past: "Je ne puis souffrir le passé—/ J'entends le passé au sens 'historique,' celui qui se présente comme scènes, situations,—récits de moments à action,—et à paroles" (PC, 1, 164). There is no recollection of the past in this sense in *La Jeune Parque*, and no events other than the original snake-bite (itself probably a figurative allusion to a mental or physiological act, since the Parque is equated with the snake at various points in the poem).[36] "J'ai une sorte d'ennui des 'événements,' " writes Valéry (PC, 1, 214).

A poem eschewing the relation of events foregoes the element of narrative chronology that normally provides the structural basis of an autobiography, a novel, or a dramatic monologue à la Browning. However, in his commentary on the process of composition of *La Jeune Parque*, Valéry explicitly rejects the chronology of events or emotions along with passion and logic, as solutions to the "problème d'organisation complète" in a poem (O, I, 1483). Chronology should be replaced by composition:

> En tant qu'écrivain, je n'ai rêvé que *constructions* et j'ai abhorré l'impulsion qui couvre le papier d'une production successive.
> Si pressante et riche et heureuse soit-elle, cette foison ne m'intéresse pas. J'y vois une génération "linéaire" qui exclut toute composition. (PC, 1, 285)

As a reader, Valéry was always very sensitive to the arbitrary nature of events described in literary works, and to the possibility of altering them without significantly affecting the work as a whole; this, he says, no doubt explains why he sought to give his own works an inner coherence independent of events or chronology: "C'est sans doute pourquoi j'ai toujours songé à des restrictions, conventions qui donnassent artificiellement aux fictions des relations internes" (PC, 1, 270).

*La Jeune Parque* forms a complex web of "relations internes," on both the thematic and the formal levels. Many images and themes are repeated at intervals throughout the poem, forming a network of interconnected elements. For example, the theme of tears with which it opens is taken up again in lines 21, 91 and 380 as well as in the long invocation to the "imminente larme" of 11. 280-98 (and within this latter passage, various phrases evoke the theme of birth which the Parque has just been exploring). The link between the stars and human tears established in 11. 21-22 is repeated in the mention of "joyaux cruels" (1.300) immediately after the invocation to the tear, and the stars themselves are alluded to again in 11. 329 and 486. The Parque's reference to her heartbeart ("Et quel frémissement d'une feuille effacée / Persiste parmi vous, îles de mon sein nu? . . .") is echoed in 11. 376-78, "Un frémissement fin de feuille," and later in 1. 467. "Frémir" and "feuilles" are linked again in 11. 334-35. Examples of alliteration as in the above quotations form another instance of "relations internes" and are too numerous to mention. Allusions to shivering and trembling, as above, occur throughout the poem; death is another recurrent theme. The sea and shore are evoked at the beginning and end of the poem's two parts, or "acts" as Valéry called them, and within each act a distinct tonal pattern emerges of laughter and tears, joy and apprehension, light and darkness, constituting, according to one critic, a "schéma . . . de forme ABA.BAB."[37] The image of the serpent, apostrophized by the Parque in lines 50-96, recurs frequently in phrases referring to the Parque herself; and other images re-appear in different forms more than once in the course of the poem: swan, sea, mirror, dawn. These various cross-references bind the poem together, requiring that it be read as a whole, like the *Faune*, rather than as a narrative with a beginning, a middle and an end, like many of Browning's poems.

Paradoxically, although Valéry declares he was born "exaspéré par la répétition," all the above effects depend on some form of repetition. The paradox is inevitable since poetry, by its very nature, always involves repetition, whether of rhythms, of sounds or of images; so Jakobson suggests, in asserting that, in poetry, "one syllable is equalized with any other syllable of the same sequence; word stress is assumed to equal word stress, as unstress equals unstress; prosodic long is matched with long, and short with short . . ." etc. Poetry supposes the "regular reiteration of equivalent units, and the *"poetic function projects the principle of equivalence from the axis of selection into the axis of combination."*[38] If processes of repetition and substitution are characteristic of metaphor and poetry, as opposed to the juxtaposition typical of metonymy and prose, it is worth noting Valéry's abhorrence of "l'impulsion qui couvre le papier d'une production successive" (PC, 1, 285) and his tendency when reading prose to "*substituer* aux phrases données d'autres phrases que l'auteur aurait pu écrire tout aussi bien" (O, I, 1468; my emphasis). As a poet, he automatically inclines towards substitutions (metaphor) rather than accepting the linearity of narrative (metonymy). Efforts have been made to read *La Jeune Parque* as a narrative—to establish exactly when she left her bed (ll. 24–25), how many times she fell asleep and at what points in time; and to realign the sections of the poem into a chronological order; but such attempts remain inadequate, as Crow points out.[39] Whereas Browning positively invites the reader to move from the parts given in his poems to an implied whole, to reconstruct a complete sequence of events, indeed a whole life and a whole personality, in Valéry there is no guarantee that such a whole exists. True, the Parque engages in a struggle for self-discovery but, as has been suggested, it is by no means certain that she achieves total unity, or wholeness, at the end (cf. "malgré moi-même"), in spite of her enthusiasm. Nevertheless, there is a certain play with metonymy in her attempt at the beginning to assemble a total physical image out of the various parts she hesitantly perceives: "mains," "traits," "coeur," "îles de mon sein nu"; these apparently come together in "Je scintille"—yet in the rest of the poem also she refers metonymically to parts of herself, e.g. "bras," "tempes" (l. 30), "cils," "paupières" (110–11), "épaule," "gorge" (118–19), "front" (452), "flancs" (484), "yeux" (485). Laurenti remarks that the Parque sees herself as it were from outside, "soit par les yeux, soit par le regard '*spirituel*,' " which emphasizes her *dédoublement*: the outer self, like the inner one, is "un Moi *vu* . . . et par conséquent *séparé*. Le Moi n'apparaît ainsi que comme une suite de pointillés, un assemblage de fragments."[40] The poem represents her search for a feeling of wholeness, in the course of which she tries out different masks or versions of herself.

While the parts of the Parque's outer and inner life may not add up to any whole, the poet can attempt, in the poem, to fashion a whole, interconnected by multiple allusions of sound and sense. Thus Valéry aims to give "des liaisons et des correspondances d'un bout à l'autre" (PC, 1, 285–86). No number of beautiful, but isolated, lines, can, in his estimation, save a work which does not, solely by virtue of its "relations internes," form a whole: "ce *tout* était tout pour moi," he declares in the "Fragments des mémoires d'un poème" (O, I, 1484). The ideal poem should not need to rely on an arbitrary, logical or chronological narrative for its coherence, but should have its own inner structure of "liaisons" and "correspondances," forming a closed system, a "*monde* fermé" (C, XVI, 138).

Nevertheless, this concept of the poem as a totally unified whole remains unrealisable in practice; it is the ideal towards which Valéry strives, and which he envies the musician "pouvant véritablement *composer*, concevoir et mener l'ensemble avec le détail de son entreprise, voler de l'un à l'autre, et observer leur dépendence réciproque" (O, I, 1483). Whereas the musician distributes notes, bearing no referential relation to the world of people and things, (O, I, 1473), the poet must use language, whose inevitably referential nature precludes for him such absolute perfection of form. Language is also inadequate as a means of self-expression, for "La parole ne signifie ce qu'elle prétend signifier qu'ex-cep-tion-nel-le-ment" (PC, 1, 395). "Si le moi pouvait parler," writes M. Teste (O, II, 42). . . . Crow suggests that the reason M. Teste does not compose literary works may be his "discovery of the nature of words": "When Teste's silence is approached as a frustration with certain aspects of language, it becomes surprisingly plausible to imagine that it is caused not by indifference to expression, but, on the contrary, by an intense need to express in a way which language cannot provide." Given Teste's all-embracing mind, his aim would have to be "a kind of universal work or discourse by which the limitations of the perceiving self in its creative relationship with reality, together with the limitations of all individual works of art and scientific discoveries, could be permanently overcome." Crow comments on the similarity between this ideal and that of Mallarmé's "Grand Oeuvre," but also points out "one major difference between the aesthetics of Mallarmé and Valéry. . . . Where in Mallarmé's symbolism such a total discourse *could* exist (individual works being the mere intimations of its perfection), for Valéry no such work could actually be possible, for it would involve the disruption of the very conditions responsible for the ambition in the first place."[41]

For Valéry, total integration and unity are as impossible for a poem as for the individual *Moi*, and in both cases language is responsible. The individual "I," as soon as it becomes conscious of itself, is split in two: monologue becomes dialogue, and the very form of dialogue suggests the impossibility of achieving one total discourse or meaning. The duality, indeed multiplicity, of the "I" leads inevitably to the fragmentation of its language: "comment lier le pluriel et l'écriture; multiplier la langue comme mimésis du sujet éclaté?" asks Daniel Oster, with respect to Valéry. "Plus que la tentation ou la tentative poétique (*la Jeune Parque*, par exemple), c'est le fragment, la graphie au jour le jour des *Cahiers* . . . qui vont lui permettre de répondre à la question, intimement."[42] From his origins in the nineteenth century dedicated to "une certaine représentation totalitaire du sens," Valéry "se retrouve, non sans effroi ni réticences, dans l'espace de la perdition, du hasard, du monstrueux et de l'inimaginaire,"[43] i.e., in the world of the twentieth century.

# CHAPTER SIX

# Conclusion

## I. Two types of dramatic monologue

There are, according to Valéry, two kinds of art: one aiming to give an imitation of life ("l'*impression* de la vie"); the other preferring to reconstruct life itself ("reconstruire la *vie*") (*C*, XXIV, 599).[1] Commenting on this idea, Huguette Laurenti asserts that the first, essentially representational, aesthetic "est bien celle de Shakespeare," whereas Racine attempts to "reconstruire la vie."[2] The oft-noted opposition between Racine and Shakespeare clearly has some bearing on the present analysis of two different types of dramatic monologue. On the "Shakespeare" side we have the Browningesque monologues with their tendency towards mimesis, their three-dimensional, "life-like" characters placed in "exciting" situations, given plenty of historical context and speaking, very often, with the accents and rhythms of a recognizably oral discourse. With Mallarmé and Valéry, on the other hand, we move in a more Racinian universe, in an ahistorical world of myth, where fully-rounded characters are replaced by universal figures speaking, like Racine's dramatis personae, in a stylized language of their own. The drama in Browning stems, typically, from the protagonist's struggle with others or from a discrepancy between his own view of himself and the reader's; whereas in Mallarmé and Valéry, as in Racine, it arises from an inner conflict raging within the speaker himself.

Francis Scarfe goes so far as to suggest that only a monologue involving "a dramatic situation of an internal nature" (i.e., within the psyche) can be termed a "dramatic monologue proper." He is somewhat unfair to Browning, whose poems he regards merely as examples of "a monologue which is dramatic by its situation, i.e., a speech related under pressure from some person present, such as whoever was threatening *Sludge the Medium* while he spoke." He omits any reference to the tension created by dramatic irony: by that discrepancy between what the speakers of Browning's poems understand about themselves and what they unwittingly reveal, which constitutes one of the chief interests of his poems and is certainly a dramatic feature, involving a conflict between two viewpoints, the character's and the reader's. It seems more appropriate to agree that Browning's monologues are of a different type from the French ones, without trying to decide which type represents the "dramatic monologue proper."[3]

## II. Late Browning

For the purposes of comparison, I have been using, as examples of the Browningesque monologue, only poems from the three collections *Dramatic Lyrics* (1842), *Dramatic Romances* (1845) and *Men and Women* (1855)—poems like "My Last Duchess, "Fra Lippo Lippi," "The Laboratory," "Soliloquy of the Spanish Cloister," "Porphyria's Lover," "The Bishop of St. Praxed's," "Andrea del Sarto," on which Browning's reputation today largely rests. It must be pointed out, however, that some of his later works, such as "Rabbi Ben Ezra" and "Abt Vogler" in *Dramatis Personae* (1864) and certain longer poems like *Prince Hohenstiel-Schwangau* (1871) and *Fifine at the Fair* (1872), move away from the representational mold. In such poems Browning no longer seems concerned simply with the portrayal of characters, so much as with the discussion of various universal human experiences or problems: the effect of music on the soul in "Abt Vogler," old age in "Rabbi Ben Ezra," political expediency versus idealism in *Prince Hohenstiel-Schwangau*, love and fidelity in *Fifine at the Fair*. Roma King notes this tendency beginning in *Dramatis Personae* where "Browning exhibits a growing concern with ideas" (rather than characters); he wonders whether Browning was "seeking to discover some means of bringing his isolated men and women together in a relation that would transform their private visions into universal truths." Concerning *Prince Hohenstiel-Schwangau*, King comments that

> Browning remains interested in the "soul," but, increasingly impatient with external manifestations of character, he seems determined to seize directly the inner life. He moves, consequently, toward a poetry of abstraction—dialectical, complex, subtle. When he fails in these poems it is less because he violates the monologue form, as many of his critics have assumed, than because he does not always achieve a new structure capable of expressing his poetic intention.[4]

This quotation suggests that Browning was moving towards the type of monologue loosely termed "Racinian" above. A "poetry of abstraction—dialectial, complex, subtle" evokes the work of Mallarmé and Valéry; a desire to "seize directly the inner life" represents Valéry's chief concern in *La Jeune Parque*, and no one was more "impatient with external manifestations of character" than he. Reduced interest in characterization does not, however, in either Valéry or Browning, preclude a search for self-knowledge on the part of the speaker himself: like the Parque, if less exclusively, Prince Hohenstiel-Schwangau, that "multiple Prince," is engrossed in the effort of trying to know and understand himself: " 'Who's who?' was aptly asked," he exclaims, "Since certainly I am not I!" (11. 2078–79). In *Fifine at the Fair*, too, "the action is internalized," representing "the dialogue of a soul with itself," the speaker being "more an abstracted soul than a complete character" and unconnected with a specific place and time.[5] This speaker, like the Parque and the Faun, and like Prince Hohenstiel, is engaged in a conflict with himself—whereas most of the characters in Browning's earlier monologues exhibit a certain degree of complacency. In order to qualify as dramatic, however, such a conflict must be structured, not confused and verbose as is the case in the overlong *Prince Hohenstiel-Schwangau*. As King says, Browning fails in this poem, as in *Fifine at the Fair*, "because he does not . . . achieve a new structure capable of expressing his poetic intention"—a structure which both Mallarmé and Valéry were eminently capable of providing.

King suggests that, in *Prince Hohenstiel-Schwangau*, Browning "pushes his skepticism further than in any previous poem to question the reality not merely of the act but of the actor."[6] Certainly Browning's lessening interest in character-portrayal in monologues of his later period may have derived from a growing awareness of the "indeterminacy of selfhood," as J. Hillis Miller terms it. Miller ascribes this awareness to uncertainty on Browning's part about his own "character," and to a need "to enact, in imagination, the roles of the most diverse people."[7] Already in *Pauline*, an early poem, Browning envisages the self not in terms of character traits but as pure self-consciousness:

> I am made up of an intensest life,
> Of a most clear idea of consciousness
> Of self, distinct from all its qualities,
> From all affections, passions, feelings, powers.
>
> (I, 268–71)

Valéry says no less: "[Le Moi] est identité pure. Pas de qualités, pas d'attributs" (PC, 2, 317). And the speakers of Browning's "Abt Vogler" and "Rabbi Ben Ezra," for example, exhibit no particular qualities or attributes but act as spokesmen for universal human experiences: Abt Vogler is a musician but is not characterized beyond that; he discusses the nature of music, human reactions to it, and its possible connections with the divine. Ben Ezra muses on the human condition in general and in particular on the advantages old age can bring.

Doubts about the existence of, and about the possibility of portraying in poetry, an " 'I' who is a *whole* subject . . . conscious, knowable"[8] must have been linked for Browning with the problem of such a character's self-expression, of language. Language cannot express "wholes" for, as Browning specifically states, in *Sordello*, words are merely the presentation "of the whole / By parts, the simultaneous and the sole / By the successive and the many" (Book II, 593–95). Elsewhere, too, Browning implies that language is incapable of containing some of the concepts or "Fancies" formed by the brain: he refers, in "Rabbi Ben Ezra," to "Thoughts hardly to be packed / Into a narrow act, / Fancies that broke through language and escaped"; and he tells us that Sordello

> . . . left imagining, to try the stuff
> That held the imaged thing, and, let it writhe
> Never so fiercely, scarce allowed a tithe
> To reach the light—his language.
>
> (*Sordello*, Book II, 570–73)

Despite this awareness of the inadequacy of language to deal with "wholes," Browning seems determined, during his "middle" period, to manipulate language in such a way as to create whole characters: expressions, vocabulary and syntactical constructions help to characterize a given speaker; and the flavour of oral speech is achieved by colloquial turns of phrase, interjections, interruptions, repetitions and a loose syntax. However, loosely-constructed, overlong sentences, involving many interruptions and changes of direction, can become very difficult to follow if not supported by the intonations and gestures of oral discourse. An example of this can be seen in a passage from "Andrea del Sarto" in which Lucrezia, and the reader, lose the thread of Andrea's argument:

> For, do you know, Lucrezia, as God lives,
> Said one day Agnolo, his very self,
> To Rafael . . . I have known it all these years . . .
> (When the young man was flaming out his thoughts
> Upon a palace-wall for Rome to see,
> Too lifted up in heart because of it)
> "Friend, there's a certain sorry little scrub
> "Goes up and down our Florence, none cares how,
> "Who, were he set to plan and execute
> "As you are, pricked on by your popes and kings,
> "Would bring the sweat into that brow of yours!"
> To Rafael's!—And indeed the arm is wrong.
> I hardly dare . . . yet, only you to see,
> Give the chalk here—quick, thus the line should go!
>
> Ay, but the soul! he's Rafael! rub it out!
> Still, all I care for, if he spoke the truth,

(What he? why, who but Michel Agnolo?
Do you forget already words like those?)
If really there was such a chance, so lost,—
Is, whether you're—not grateful—but more pleased.

On the whole, however, the poems of the middle period remain fairly clear. It is in the notorious early *Sordello*, and in several late poems, such as the *Parleyings with Certain People of Importance in Their Day*, "La Saisiaz," or *Prince Hohenstiel-Schwangau*, that Browning indulges in lengthy, complex sentences, with excessively loose syntactical connections and multiple volte-face on the part of the speakers, as they attempt to express in language "Thoughts hardly to be packed / Into a narrow act." Such passages no longer sound convincing as oral speech; the reader finds it impossible to grasp their import immediately, needing to turn back and re-read them; this fact manifestly suggests a departure from oral discourse, which by its very nature tends to be readily comprehensible.

Many contemporaries complained about Browning's "hastily-scribbled poems as fuzzy and prickly and tangled as a furze-bush," as F.L. Lucas describes them. Curiously enough, a similar complaint was levelled at Mallarmé: Henri Cazalis protests at the "phrases beaucoup trop longues" and the "phrases incidentes, qui s'accrochent l'une à l'autre et font des broussailles obscures, épaisses, tellement enchevêtrées que l'on a peine à avancer."[9] The problems involved in understanding the work of both poets can often be traced to an unconventional syntax; but in the case of Mallarmé we have a tight, concise and compressed syntax rendering a multiplicity of meanings, whereas with Browning the difficulty lies more in the extreme looseness of the syntax which ceases to provide a continuous intelligible structure to the discourse. An identical aim can be claimed for both methods: that of restoring the instantaneous, many-facetted, and incoherent quality of the original perception. Hillis Miller refers to *Sordello* as an

> incoherent speech which goes on interminably and refuses to leap into any particular form of language. . . . The central bulk is potentially any form of language, and is therefore closer than any single statement to the whole perceptions Browning seeks to express. Browning's language is often close to the inarticulate

noise which is the source of all words. In that noise everything is
said simultaneously and so not said at all.

And King asserts that "Browning's attempt to communicate dramat-
ically the total experience of the speaker produces an unconven-
tional syntax." Similarly, with reference to Mallarmé, Charles Mau-
ron mentions his "tours singuliers du langage," and "bizarreries
grammaticales," but points out that "ces étrangetés ont une source
commune: la pensée qu'elles exprimaient exactement."[10]

A multiplicity of meanings, or the "totality" of an experience, can
be rendered, then, either by compressing syntax so much that it
allows for several possible extensions, or by expanding it so that
"everything is said simultaneously"; either method represents a de-
parture from normal speech. In some of his works, such as *Sordello*
and several of his later poems, Browning seems to move away from
oral discourse towards an *écriture* almost as radically divorced from
speech, in its way, as that of Mallarmé. His speakers become aware
both of the indeterminacy of selfhood (" . . . certainly I am not I")
and of the inadequacy of language, of the "stuff / That held the
imaged thing," as a means of self-expression.

On the whole, however, in his most successful and well-known
poems, the dramatic monologues of *Dramatic Lyrics, Dramatic
Romances* and *Men and Women*, Browning's speakers betray no sign
of impatience with language beyond the kind of groping for words
which occasionally afflicts all speakers. On the contrary, they usu-
ally say what they mean and mean what they say; it is the reader
(plus of course the poet) who construes another meaning from
their words and judges them in a totally different light from the one
in which they seek to present themselves. The accent is still on
character-portrayal—which, for the Browning of a later period, and
certainly for a Mallarmé or a Valéry, can no longer constitute an aim,
given the impossibility, in their view, of knowing someone's true
personality when the only way we have of expressing ourselves is
through language, which comes to us from outside.

Such doubts about both character and language can already be
detected in Laforgue, whose male speakers, at least, use clichés and
other stereotyped expressions in full cognizance of the fact that
they are merely repeating others' words and that, indeed, there is
no alternative. In other ways, too, Laforgue's dramatic monologues

constitute an intermediary stage between those of Browning and those of Mallarmé or Valéry. His speakers are less well-defined than Browning's, possessing only a limited range of character traits; and yet, within this range, certain characteristics can be ascribed to them far more readily than, say, to the Parque. They illustrate that break-up of the whole notion of a fixed personality which culminates in Valéry's replacement of it by, simply, consciousness. Accordingly, Laforgue's dramatic monologues exhibit a parallel internalization of the dramatic conflict. T.S. Eliot contrasts Laforgue and Browning precisely with regard to the internalization of the drama: he characterizes Browning, Donne, Corbière and Laforgue as writers of "either dramatic monologue or dramatic dialogue," and continues: "with Donne and the French poets, the pattern is given by what goes on within the mind, rather than by the exterior events which provoke the mental activity."[11] This interiorization of the dramatic conflict is even more pronounced in Mallarmé or Valéry: the tension in *La Jeune Parque* arises from the struggle between different elements of the Parque's own consciousness, not between her and the outside world.

The Parque, like Narcisse and many of Valéry's other personae, like the Faun and Hérodiade, is a universal figure, taken from myth; and again Laforgue's poetry suggests a step in this direction: his speakers are not individuals belonging to a specific time and place, but stereotypes embodying certain aspects of the human condition in general. In this respect, stock figures such as Pierrot and Hamlet may be said to approach the mythical status of the kind of personae favoured by Mallarmé and Valéry, with their concern for the universal over the particular (Hamlet having indeed become a quasi-mythical figure in late-nineteenth-century France, as Mallarmé himself indicates). Warren Ramsey, discussing Laforgue's "Persée et Andromède," speaks of the "step taken beyond realism, toward mythic structure," and the same movement can be detected in his poetry.[12]

# III. T.S. Eliot

A similar move away from "realism" towards myth, from the particular to the general, from character-portrayal to the exploration of consciousness, from colloquial speech to a more stylized language, may be detected within the work of a single poet, also well-known as a writer of dramatic monologues: T.S. Eliot, whose development from his early Laforguian poems to his *Four Quartets* involves similar changes to those between Laforgue and Valéry. Hugh Kenner asserts, somewhat surprisingly, that Prufrock is simply a "zone of consciousness" where the materials alluded to in the poem "can maintain a vague congruity; no more than that; certainly not a person." True, he is not "equipped with a history and little necessary context, like the speaker of a Browning monologue," or not to the same extent; but can we really say that we "have no information about him whatever"?[13] We know that he is thin and balding, and may assume that in general his looks are not particularly striking; he dresses conventionally, in a tasteful but unadventurous fashion ("My necktie rich and modest, but asserted by a simple pin"); he moves in fashionable circles, but is not at his ease there, being too overawed by other people. He describes himself as "Deferential, glad to be of use, / Poetic, cautious and meticulous"; and he is well-read but has no facility for displaying his culture, being inarticulate and diffident in the extreme—in fact, something of a coward in his relationships with other people ("And in short, I was afraid"). Robert Langbaum, indeed, goes so far as to say that "Compared to the characters in *The Waste Land*, Prufrock, for all his lack of vitality, has the sharp external delineation of a character in, say, Henry James. He has a name (a characterizing one), a social milieu to which he genuinely belongs, a face. . . . "[14] He is accorded, in fact, roughly the same amount of delineation, or context, as one of Laforgue's speakers; this may be less than we know about a Browning character, but it is a good deal more than we could say about the Parque, or Tiresias. Prufrock's personality exhibits similar traits to those of Pierrot and Hamlet: diffidence, lack of assertiveness, indecision. The resemblance is not, of course, fortuitous, given Eliot's early fascination with Laforgue.[15] Prufrock combines self-mockery with self-pity, and the Laforguian irony distances him, like Pierrot and Hamlet, from both poet and reader. Again, Prufrock, like most of Laforgue's male speakers, is paralyzed by self-consciousness: he watches himself constantly, seeing himself as he thinks others see him ("They will say . . ."), and can never act spontaneously ("Do I dare to eat a peach?"). The tension produced by this constant

awareness of self results, as in Laforgue, in the *dédoublement* sug-
gested by the poem's very first line, "Let us go then, you and I," and
by the pervasive tone of self-irony.

Like Pierrot, Prufrock hides behind a mask, preparing "a face to
meet the faces that you meet"; and like all Laforgue's male speakers,
Prufrock knows he is playing a role, whereas the women "come and
go / Talking of Michelangelo," just as unaware as their Laforguian
predecessors of their own banality. In "Prufrock," too, as in La-
forgue's poems, certain phrases are repeated till they begin to
sound like empty formulas, e.g., "there will be time" in lines 23–24,
and "would it have been worth it" in lines 87–100. "Ce à quoi le
langage échoue ici," affirms John E. Jackson, "coïncide avec l'échec
de Prufrock, qui est d'affirmer librement, au-delà du stéréotype, une
individualité propre."[16] The conventional social scene which
serves as background to the poem ("the taking of a toast and tea")
reflects a Laforguian emphasis on the stereotyped nature of human
intercourse in general, on the near-impossibility of acting, or
speaking, in an original manner, or of breaking down the barriers
between people. Kenner suggests that Eliot's preoccupation with
social behaviour

> is related to his early perception that social ritual, designed to
> permit human beings to associate without imposing on one
> another . . . may be actually the occasion of raising to nearly
> tragic intensity their longing to reach one another. The Eliot
> character feels that he needs to preseve the inviolacy of self and
> simultaneously feels that he needs sympathy from others whom
> he cannot reach and who cannot decorously reach him.

"Behind the décor of self-sufficiency," he continues, "—the ready
smile, the poised teacup, lies the Self; a mystery, sometimes an
illusion." An illusion: Eliot eventually went further than Laforgue in
questioning the whole notion of personality as a fixed, knowable
quantity—partly, perhaps, thanks to his study of F.C. Bradley,
which, according to Kenner, "freed him from the Laforguian pos-
ture of the ironist with his back to a wall, by affirming the artificial-
ity of *all* personality including the one we intimately suppose to be
our true one; not only the faces we prepare but the 'we' that pre-

pares."[17] Bradley rejected the concept of personality, insisting (like Valéry) that "the usual self of one period is not the usual self of another."[18]

"Eliot's nameless, faceless voices," in *The Waste Land*, says Langbaum, "express the sense—which by the twentieth century has come to prevail—that the self, if it exists at all, is changing and discontinuous." They also suggest a move from the particular to the general, from the delineation of individual character, as in "Prufrock," to an interest in archetypes and myths. Referring again to *The Waste Land*, Langbaum states that the

> protagonist has no character in the old-fashioned sense; for he acquires delineation or identity not through individualization, but through making connection with ancient archetypes. . . . [W]hen we delve deep into the psyche we find an archetypal self and a desire to repeat the patterns laid out in the sort of myths described by Frazer and Jessie Weston.[19]

A comparison with Ezra Pound's *Cantos* is instructive: Eliot, with the ladies in the pub, the typist, Mr. Eugenides, creates quasi-mythical figures, "*types* of modern decadence" whose "historical existence is irrelevant"; whereas Pound deals with historical figures giving voice to a multitude of *individuals*: politicians, scientists, artists, painters, etc.; his method is "narrative not mythical."[20] The links between *The Waste Land* and the Grail legend are well-known, having been pointed out by Eliot himself in his Notes to the poem. Also in those Notes, Eliot declares that the mythical figure of Tiresias, "although a mere spectator and not indeed a 'character', is yet the most important personage in the poem, uniting all the rest." Kenner implies that Eliot exaggerated the importance of Tiresias simply "in order to supply the poem with a nameable point of view," because, after it had been cut by Pound, the poem's "self-sufficient juxtaposition . . . had at first a novelty which troubled even the author." For no doubt Eliot, with Browning's example in mind, "conceived a long poem as somebody's spoken or unspoken monologue, its shifts of direction and transition from theme to theme psychologically justified by the workings of the speaker's brain." In other words, Tiresias simply serves as "a possible zone of consciousness where the materials with which he is credited with being aware can co-exist." "And what else, we seem to hear the author ask," he continues, "what else . . . can a developed human consciousness be said to be?"[21]

Yet character is still adumbrated, to a certain extent, in *The Waste Land*: we can imagine the personalities, and the stories, of Marie and of the lady whose "nerves are bad," of "Lil" and her friend, of the typist and her lover—even if they represent, as Langbaum suggests, archetypes. By the time we reach *Four Quartets*, however, there is no longer any trace of personality—either in the speaker or anyone else. Already Gerontion was "reduced to a voice"; like the Hollow Men, he embodies that "hollowness of personality which can express itself so admirably, and still express nothing but the bits of purely verbal intensity with which it has filled itself out of books."[22] In *Four Quartets*, too, we simply hear a voice, unlocated in time or space (except insofar as the poems' titles suggest places), meditating on a wide range of subjects: on Time, human behaviour, language, love, life. Like *La Jeune Parque, Four Quartets* presents the contents of a mind, but the mind itself is not attributed to anyone in particular. It is the "I" of a Bradleyan "finite centre."

A change in poetic diction accompanies this progressive depersonalization of the speaker in Eliot. Gone is the Laforguian tone of the early poems, the polite, cultured but conventional conversation of the upper class with its banalities about Michelangelo and Chopin:

> 'So intimate, this Chopin, that I think his soul
> Should be resurrected only among friends
> Some two or three . . .'

Gone, also, the artless tone of Marie:

> And when we were children, staying at the arch-duke's,
> My cousin's, he took me out on a sled,
> And I was frightened. He said, Marie,
> Marie, hold on tight. And down we went.
> In the mountains, there you feel free . . .

and the colloquial, working-class speech of Lil and her friend:

> It's them pills I took, to bring it off, she said.

Gone, too, is the Laforguian use of quotation marks attributing speech to given speakers. Closer to Valéry than to Laforgue, the tone of *Four Quartets* is totally impersonal; the Voice of the poem moves, as Kenner puts it, "from exposition through intimacy to reminiscence, passing through lyric, expending itself in overheard meditation, without ever allowing us to intuit the impurities of personal presence." The poem's "I" is not that of the poet ("The man holding the pen does not bare his soul," says Kenner); nor did Eliot any longer feel the need for a Tiresias to bind the poem together: "we feel no compulsion to posit or pry into some *persona*. The motifs of the poem simply declare themselves; and when we come upon the line,

> I can only say, *there* we have been: but I cannot say where

the first person pronoun prompts no curiosity." And lines like

> Footfalls echo in the memory
> Down the passage which we did not take
> Towards the door we never opened
> Into the rose-garden

"appear to be writing themselves."[23]

# IV. The spoken and the written; *la parole* and *l'écriture*

Here we come back to Valéry's insistence that the voice of the poem should be as impersonal as the "Moi pur" ("Cette voix ne doit faire imaginer quelque homme qui parle. Si elle le fait, ce n'est pas elle" (PC, 2, 1077)). Both poets stressed the importance of impersonality: in fact this aspect of Valéry's poetry was one of the first things Eliot found to praise in it.[24] Like Valéry in *La Jeune Parque*, Eliot presents, in *Four Quartets*, the speech of a totally impersonal voice, which speaks without evoking "quelque homme qui parle."

Indeed the speaker is not identified at all: no persona is offered for us to "posit or pry into"; and in this the *Four Quartets* differ from *La Jeune Parque*. Certainly the Parque does not constitute a specific individual or personality, but the very fact of naming her, of establishing her mythical persona with its context of sea, stars and sun, serves at once to distance her both from the reader and the author; this distance, crucial to the dramatic monologue, is missing from *Four Quartets*.[25] Moreover the latter poem is more meditative than dramatic: there is no fundamental inner conflict structuring it, as in *La Jeune Parque* or the *Faune* (though some of the issues raised reveal diverse inner tensions); nor does the poem suggest any basic conflict between the speaker and the outside world. In other words, while *La Jeune Parque* is a dramatic monologue, *Four Quartets*, unlike many of Eliot's earlier poems, is not.

Another crucial difference between the two poems relates to the question of voice, despite both poets' basic agreement on the need for its impersonality: whereas *La Jeune Parque* employs a stylized poetic diction based on the written language, the intonations of the speaker in *Four Quartets* are those of a speaking voice, or *parole*. Even when treating the most abstract or literary topics, this voice usually retains the rhythms and the syntactical constructions of oral speech:[26]

> Except for the point, the still point,
> There would be no dance, and there is only the dance.
> I can only say, there we have been: but I cannot say where.
> And I cannot say, how long, for that is to place it in time.

In *La Jeune Parque*, on the other hand, the frequent use of inversion alone suffices to distance this language from that of normal speech, likening it, in some degree, to the langauge of Racine:

> . . . Ou si le mal me suit d'un songe refermé,
> Quand (au velours du souffle envolé l'or des lampes)
> J'ai de mes bras épais environné mes tempes,
> Et longtemps de mon âme attendu les éclairs?

Such a "written" effect, produced not only by inversion but by many other aspects of the poem's syntax and vocabulary, stems from the strict distinction Valéry makes between the language of poetry and that of prose. In an otherwise laudatory article on Valéry, Eliot criticizes, precisely, such a division as leading ultimately to an undesirable artificiality of poetic language. "In assimilating poetry to music," he concludes, "Valéry has, it seems to me, failed to insist upon its relation to speech"[27]—a failure he attributes, significantly, to an excessive attachment to the poetics of Mallarmé at the expense of Laforgue and Corbière.

The voice Mallarmé wishes to resonate in his poetry is not that of a speaker but "la *Voix* du *Langage*," the voice of an essentially written poetic language. Valéry differentiates his own poetry from this attitude by affirming that it represents "la *Langage* issu de la *Voix*"; and yet his remains an essentially written language in that it deliberately avoids the vocabulary and, albeit less radically than Mallarmé's, the syntax, of everyday speech. The language issuing from the voice in a poem must be, for Valéry, an essentially poetic language, a "Discours prophétique et paré" ("La Pythie"), not that of everyday speech, of *parole*; everyday speech means prose, and Valéry's notion of pure poetry requires the elimination of prose elements as far as possible. Nicole Celeyrette-Pietri, in an article on, precisely, "L'Ecriture et la voix" in Valéry, notes that the written medium is in fact essential to Valéry's poetics, despite the importance he accords to voice, since, far more strongly than "l'inscription mnémonique," the sight of words on a page "entretient le besoin-phénix de l'infini esthétique et permet de l'imaginer comme un mouvement perpétuel."[28] Elsewhere she quotes Valéry's remark to poets: "Poète . . . tu peux considérer de haut . . . tous ceux . . . qui *doivent* croire que leur discours est *réel* par son contenu et signifie quelque réalité. Mais toi, tu sais que le réel d'un discours, ce sont les mots seulement et les formes" (PC, 2, 1098–99); and she remarks that if

> le réel d'un message n'est rien que la façon de dire et comme le timbre propre d'une pensée, le Scriptor doit rechercher le secours favorable des plus strictes contraintes. Les règles de la métrique et de la prosodie, qui interdisent d'omettre une syllabe et forcent l'oreille à compter, sont des auxiliaires de son dessein.[29]

Valéry's preference for the constraints of fixed poetic forms is well-known; thus he may be said to "intensify the specificity of the written," as Christine Crow asserts, despite his emphasis on the Voice of the poem.[30] In *La Jeune Parque*, which he terms "une autobiographie, dans la forme" (*O*, I, 1622), he unites voice ("autobiographie") and writing ("la forme"), or *parole* and *écriture*.

Gerald Bruns explores the difference between written and spoken language in the course of his discussion of "hermetic" and "Orphic" poetry. Speaking and writing, he affirms,

> emphasize the doubleness of language. Speaking magnifies the ontological dimension of language, together with the worldliness that makes linguistic meaning possible; writing, by contrast, magnifies the formal dimension of language and the logical requisites of intelligibility. Speaking testifies to the priority of being, writing to the priority of form.

And their respective emphasis on being and form distinguishes the Orphic from the hermetic poets. The opposition between speaking and writing, therefore, in his view,

> informs the opposition between Orphic and hermetic poetries: witness the contrast between Mallarmé's typographical efforts to escape the lyricism of the human voice . . . and Wallace Steven's conception of "speaking humanly":

> To say more than human things with human voice,
> That cannot be; to say human things with more
> Than human voice, that, also, cannot be;
> To speak humanly from the height or from the depth
> Of human things, that is acutest speech.[31]

The example Bruns chooses here to illustrate his point is significant, and reflects a certain divergence between French and Anglo-American poetry involving precisely this question of speaking and writing. For even those French poets placed by Robert Greene in the "Orphic" category—Reverdy, Char, Bonnefoy, Du Bouchet, Dupin,[32] a list that could also include Eluard, Saint-John Perse and Michaux—tend to use a language that could only be written, not spoken. Apart from a general avoidance of colloquialisms or conversational turns of speech, the cross-references, the sheer accumulation of images and, in some cases, the syntax, render this poetry too dense to represent anyone's spoken utterance. Orphic and hermetic poets alike tend to pursue the goal of pure poetry, as Greene remarks:

> Both . . . continue the progressive purification of poetry that began with Baudelaire, a process of ascesis whose goal has been to strip from poetry all that is non-poetic, such as conventional prosody, narrative development and moral or ideological concerns, so as to get at "la poésie pure."

Similarly, Michael Hamburger talks of a "line of development . . . towards 'pure' . . . poetry" and comments that

> in the Romance languages . . . that line of development has been much stronger than in the Anglo-Saxon, Slavic or Scandinavian language areas. In English poetry especially, every step forward in the direction of pure or hermetic verse has been followed by at least two paces backwards.[33]

"Pure" poetry, as defined by Valéry, strives to eliminate all elements of prose, including therefore everyday, conversational discourse, and we have noted Eliot's fear that such a differentiation between the idiom of prose and that of poetry could lead to a totally artificial poetic language. Nevertheless—despite a few exceptions such as Max Jacob, Prévert and Queneau, who use the diction of everyday speech in their poetry—most twentieth-century French poets, like Valéry and Mallarmé, regard the language of poetry as separate and different, and choose the "written" style over the spoken. English and American poets, on the other hand, tend to accept the language of normal speech as the language of poetry, which according to Pound should depart "in no way from speech save by heightened intensity."[34] Small wonder then that two late-nineteenth-century French poets picked out by Pound and Eliot at the time of their youthful enthusiasm for French verse wrote, exceptionally, in a conversational, even colloquial, idiom. Pound declared Corbière "the greatest poet of the period," and, like Eliot, had an immense admiration for that "exquisite poet," Laforgue.[35] Significantly, both poets have been less highly acclaimed in France.

Hamburger, commenting on Corbière's colloquialism, "an effective break with poetic conventions that retained a strong hold on Baudelaire," remarks that "the potentialities of his colloquial diction were to be appreciated outside France, even if later French poets, on the whole, preferred the example of Rimbaud's 'alchemy of the word' or of Mallarmé's hermetical symbolism."[36] Similarly, Francis Burch, investigating the reasons why Corbière is "quelque peu négligé dans son pays natal," notes that his work "est plus proche des traditions poétiques anglo-ameficaines que celle de n'importe quel poète français depuis Villon et ce dernier est, lui aussi, un favori des Anglo-Saxons." He mentions Marcel Raymond's well-known division of modern French poetry into two trends, that of the "artists," leading from Baudelaire through Mallarmé to Valéry, and that of the *voyants*, from Baudelaire through Rimbaud to the Surrealists, and asks: "Mais qu'en est-il de la filière qui va de Baudelaire à Corbière, puis à Laforgue, pour s'étendre ensuite à Apollinaire, à Ezra Pound et à T.S. Eliot?"[37] He would characterize this trend by a certain taste for realism ("Corbière partage avec les principaux poètes anglais . . . un réalisme dont les plus talentueux des romantiques n'ont pu faire passer le goût aux Anglo-Américains");[38] and also by its "harsh" style: "Corbière se rattache . . . en recourant à une prosodie quelque peu âpre, à un langage et à une imagerie qui fuient le 'précieux', à la tradition qu'illustre Shakespeare"; and he concludes:

> Peut-être, enfin, la renommée de Corbière chez les Anglo-Américains et le peu d'enthousiasme qu'il suscite chez les Francais, s'expliquent-ils par la profonde divergence d'orientation et de qualité des traditions poétiques les plus enracinées chez les uns et chez les autres. Villon n'est pas à la source du grand mouvement poétique français qui s'inspire bien davantage des poètes de la Pléiade, ne faisant ainsi que prolonger l'i'nfluence de la Renaissance. La tradition anglo-américaine descend, elle, en ligne directe, de Chaucer et de Shakespeare; elle est proche parente de la poésie de Villon et on y retrouve nombre d'éléments rabelaisiens. Ainsi, dans l'histoire de la littérature française, c'est la retour occasionnel et temporaire au lyrisme de Villon qui s'écarte du cours général de l'évolution, tandis qu'on observe le phénomène contraire en Angleterre, et aux Etats-Unis, c'est-a-dire que ce sont les poètes dont les vers se rapprochent de ceux

des Français, qui s'éloignent du cours général de cette même évolution.[39]

# V. The dramatic monologue: conclusion

The sweeping generalization made in the above quotation nevertheless seems valid and bears not a little relevance to the distinction we have noted between two types of dramatic monologue. The "Anglo-Saxon" or "Shakespearean" type favoured by Browning, early Eliot and, to a large extent, Laforgue and Pound, involves elements of mimesis or "realism" including colloquial diction, a certain amount of social, spatial and temporal context, and the adumbration of personality if not the portrayal of "whole" characters as in early Browning. The "Racinian" or "French" type, however, offers little or no context or mimesis, a purely "poetic" diction and, despite the presence of a speaker, a complete absence of characterization. It is still dramatic, still a monologue, still presents a persona distanced from the reader (by mythical perspective and linguistic effects), but it favours the universal, the mythical, and a drama which is totally internal in that it takes place within the psyche of the speakers, and simultaneously totally external in that tensions are established among the words themselves, in their interrelations, not just between their referents. For this type of dramatic monologue employs a language not of communication simply, but of exploration; a language, too, which draws attention to itself as much as to what it conveys. The tensions inherent in such a self-conscious use of language provide a further source of drama in these poems; and if the poetic diction of a Mallarmé or a Valéry appears dangerously artificial to Eliot, it is none the less dramatic, just as Racine's drama is not less dramatic than Shakespeare's, only dramatic in a different way.

The presence of Laforgue in the "Anglo-Saxon" camp (though in many respects he represents, as we have seen, a transitional figure) highlights the fact that, like Corbière, he has enjoyed a greater reputation with English and American poets and critics than in France. Ramsey notes that Laforgue is popular with Anglo-Saxons; Henri Peyre comments on the reluctance of French scholars to undertake a comprehensive study of Laforgue; and Michael Collie declares that Laforgue's importance as a poet was "more readily understood by English than by French critics."[40]

The preference for colloquial speech—often with an admixture of wit and irony—accompanying the tendency towards mimesis, or "realism," which characterizes the poetic trend represented by Browning, Laforgue, Pound and the early Eliot, helps to explain why they favour the dramatic monologue as a form, since the use of everyday language tends to suggest the presence of a speaker. Given, however, that it is perfectly possible to write dramatic monologues without using colloquial language, as evidenced by Mallarmé's *Faune* or Valéry's *Parque*, not to mention Tennyson's "Ulysses," some more fundamental reasons for the choice of this form must exist. We have seen that Browning and Laforgue, Mallarmé, Valéry and Eliot all expressed interest in drama, and all wrote works which were intended for the stage and in some cases—with varying degrees of success—actually performed. We have seen also the stress laid, around the middle of the nineteenth century in England, on "poeticity" in drama at the expense of action, and the tendency to replace the real stage by what an Englishman in 1846 called the "ideal stage which all men erect in their own minds" and Mallarmé referred to forty years later as "le seul théâtre de notre esprit."[41] A climate in which it is considered preferable to read a play, and visualize it in the imagination alone, rather than to watch it being performed, must be inherently conducive to the writing of dramatic monologues (instead of stage dramas), since they appeal solely to the "theatre of the mind," obviating the need for the props and physical actions of a stage play.

Looked at in another way, in its relation to lyric poetry rather than to drama, the popularity of the dramatic monologue with poets of the second half of the nineteenth century and later can be ascribed in part to the ambiguities which have come to surround the notion of self, and to the swing in fashion away from confessional poetry. The dramatic monologue, with its inevitable dichotomy between the voice of the speaker and that of the poet, provides one way of confronting the world, of analyzing some aspect of reality, of Life, while avoiding direct self-expression. Different poets use the inherent "split" in the voice of the dramatic monologue in different ways: it allows Browning to make apparent the discrepancy between his characters' view of themselves and his own judgement of them; Valéry takes advantage of it to write his "autobiographie intellectuelle" while maintaining total separation from his mythical, immortal, and female persona.

In the case of a Browningesque monologue, the reader can come to know the character from whose viewpoint the poem is spoken, empathize with him and, at the same time, judge him—processes which are impossible with "non-characters" like the Parque or the Faun. But if the persona set up in the dramatic monologue proves, paradoxically, to be devoid of "character," of personality, then it admirably illustrates the experience of modern man, throwing into relief the dubious validity of the whole notion of selfhood,[42] and suggesting that the self can be defined only by its very search for identity, by the questions it asks. The Parque does not succeed in establishing an identity, though the fact of her presence, asking the question "Who am I?" ("Qui pleure là?"), is keenly felt by the reader, who cannot fail also to recognize as his own the universal human problems explored in the poem—such as the search for identity. Valéry himself points to this link between the reader and the Parque in "Le Philosophe et la Jeune Parque":

> Mais je ne suis en moi pas plus mystérieuse
>     Que le plus simpe d'entre vous . . .
> Mortels, vous êtes chair, souvenance, présage;
> Vous fûtes; vous serez; vous portez tel visage:
>     Vous êtes tout; vous n'êtes rien
> . . . . . . . . . . . . . . . . . . . . . . . . .
>     Un mystère est tout votre bien,
> Et cet arcane en vous s'étonnerait du mien?

Although the Parque's mythical status distances her from the reader, at the same time it asserts her universality: her problems are those of every "conscience consciente." She is a contradictory figure, at once emphatically present, through her name, her physical being, her history, her thoughts and experiences as described in the poem; and yet curiously absent because she speaks not with the voice of an individual but with the impersonal voice of Poetry. Rather than the narration of a life or even the affirmation of a personality, the poem is an "autobiographie, dans la forme" in which it is precisely "la forme," the poetry, that matters, whereas "Le fond importe peu" (O, I, 1622).

Michael Hamburger points out that lyric poetry, being concerned with "epiphanies, moments in which experience or vision is concentrated and crystalized," was always "more dependent on the unity of inner experience—that is, of the experiencing consciousness—than on that sequence of outer events which provided a framework for verse or prose narrative"; doubts about the consistency of the self were therefore "bound to add to the lyrical poet's awareness of his peculiar freedom to escape from it altogether and 'fill some other body,' " a freedom, he says, of which "poets from Valéry to Pound and Pessoa made ample and various use," so that the "truth of poetry became inseparable from what Oscar Wilde called 'the truth of masks.' " To their doubts about the Self, such poets added "a profound scepticism about language and the power of words to render what only gesture or dance can convey—the self stripped of all its empirical accidents."[43]—a scepticism originating, like so much else in twentieth-century poetry, in Mallarmé:

> A savoir que la danseuse *n'est pas une femme qui danse*, pour ces motifs juxtaposés qu'elle *n'est pas une femme*, mais une métaphore résumant un des aspects élémentaires de notre forme, glaive, coupe, fleur, etc., et *qu'elle ne danse pas*, suggérant, par le prodige de raccourcis ou d'élans, avec une écriture corporelle ce qu'il faudrait des paragraphes en prose dialoguée autant que descriptive, pour exprimer, dans la rédaction: poème dégagé de tout appareil du scribe.[44]

The development of the dramatic monologue as we have traced it from Browning through Laforgue to early Eliot and Pound, and in its somewhat different treatment by Mallarmé and Valéry, reflects various stages in the evolution of the notion of selfhood: from the well-defined Browningesque character via the masks of Laforgue or Pound to the "essential" Self, "le Moi pur," which knows it is composed only of words and is condemned, ultimately, to silence.

# Notes

Chapter 1. GENERAL CHARACTERISTICS OF THE
                  DRAMATIC MONOLOGUE

[1]Benjamin Fuson, *Browning and His English Predecessors in the Dramatic Monolog* (Iowa City: State University of Iowa, 1948), pp. 9-10.

[2]Robert Langbaum, *The Poetry of Experience* (London: Chatto and Windus, 1957), pp. 75, 78 and 79.

[3]Philip Hobsbaum, "The Rise of the Dramatic Monologue," *Hudson Review*, 28 (1975-76), 229 and 232.

[4]A. Dwight Culler, "Monodrama and the Dramatic Monologue," *PMLA*, 90 (1975), 382.

[5]Culler, p. 366.

[6]This statement appears in the Advertisement to the first edition of the *Dramatic Lyrics* (1842).

[7]Fuson, pp. 10-11.

[8]Fuson, pp. 20-21.

[9]Ina B. Sessions, "The Dramatic Monologue," *PMLA* 62 (1947), 503-16.

[10]Langbaum, pp. 77, 73, 43.

[11]Hobsbaum, p. 228.

[12]Langbaum, p. 202.

[13]Wayne C. Booth, *The Rhetoric of Fiction* (Chicago: University of Chicago Press, 1961), p. 250, n. 6.

[14]Philip Drew, *The Poetry of Browning* (London: Methuen, 1970), p. 31, n. 2.

[15]Langbaum, p. 146.

[16]Langbaum, p. 85.

[17]Park Honan, *Browning's Characters* (New Haven: Yale University Press, 1961), p. 120. The phrase "tension between sympathy and moral judgment" occurs on p. 85 of Langbaum.

[18]Booth, p. 249.

[19]In the *Journal de la Cour et de Paris*. Quoted in Abbé Prévost, *Manon Lescaut*, ed. F. Deloffre and R. Picard (Paris: Garnier, 1965), p. clxi.

[20]Langbaum, pp. 146 and 190.

[21]Loy D. Martin, *Browning's Dramatic Monologues and the Post-Romantic Subject* (Baltimore: Johns Hopkins University Press, 1985), pp. 133 and 137.

[22]Frances Carleton, *The Dramatic Monologue: Vox Humana* (Salzburg: Salzburg University Press, 1977), p. 2; Roma A. King, Jr., *The Focusing Artifice* (Athens, Ohio: Ohio University Press, 1968), p. 65; Donald S. Hair, *Browning's Experiments with Genre* (Toronto University of Toronto Press, 1972), p. 100; Honan, p. 122.

[23]*Dictionary of World Literature*, ed. Joseph T. Shipley (New York: The Philosophical Library, 1943), pp. 615-16. The following references to this work in this paragraph are from p. 616.

[24] Honan, p. 123.

[25]Roman Jakobson, "Shifters, Verbal Categories, and the Russian Verb," in *Word and Language*, Vol. 2 of *Selected Writings* (Paris and The Hague: Mouton, 1971), 131-32.

[26]Emil Benveniste, "The Nature of Pronouns," in *Problems in General Linguistics*, trans. Mary Elizabeth Meek (Coral Gables: University of Miami Press, 1971), p. 218.

[27]Jean Cohen, *Structure du langage poétique* (Paris: Flammarion, 1966), pp. 157 and 159-60.

[28]Käte Hamburger, *The Logic of Literature*, trans. Marilynn J. Rose, 2nd rev. ed. (Bloomington: Indiana University Press, 1973), pp. 274-75.

[29]Cohen, p. 158.

[30]Jakobson, p. 131. (Quoted in Cohen, p. 162.)

[31]Cohen, p. 162.

[32]Cleanth Brooks and Robert Penn Warren, *Understanding Poetry*, rev. ed. (New York: Holt, 1950); p. liv; Reuben Brower, "The Speaking Voice,"

in *Approaches to the Poem*, ed. John O. Perry (San Francisco: Chandler, 1965), p. 259; John Crowe Ransom, *The World's Body* (New York: Scribner's, 1938), p. 250. The second quotation from Ransom in this paragraph also refers to p. 250.

33Philippe Hamon, "Pour un statut sémiologique du personnage," in *Poétique du récit* (Paris: Seuil, 1977), p. 128.

34Michel Foucault, *Les Mots et les choses* (Paris: Gallimard, 1966), p. 25.

35Wayne C. Booth, *A Rhetoric of Irony* (Chicago: University of Chicago Press, 1974), p. 151; George T. Wright, *The Poet in the Poem: the Personae of Eliot, Yeats and Pound* (Berkeley: California University Press, 1960), p. 7.

36See Ralph W. Rader, "Notes on some Structural Varieties and Variations in Dramatic 'I' Poems and Their Theoretical Implications," *Victorian Poetry*, 22 (Summer 1984), 105; and "The Dramatic Monologue and Related Lyric Forms," *Critical Inquiry*, 3 (1976), 140.

37Rader, "Notes on Some Structural Varieties," p. 106.

38Alan Sinfield, *Dramatic Monologue* (London: Methuen, 1977), pp. 65, 8, 23, 19-20.

39Hamburger, pp. 5, 13, 75, 292.

40Pierre Larthomas, *Le Langage dramatique* (Paris: Colin, 1972), pp. 372 and 21.

41Langbaum, p. 94.

42Rader, "The Dramatic Monologue and Related Lyric Forms," p. 133.

43Loy D. Martin, p. 112.

44Larthomas, p. 184.

45Alain, *Système des Beaux-Arts*, quoted in Larthomas, p. 42.

46 Alexandre Lazaridès, *Valéry: pour une poétique du dialogue* (Montréal: Presses de l'université de Montréal, 1978), p. 66.

## Chapter 2. SELF-ASSERTION: ROBERT BROWNING AND EZRA POUND

1Roma A. King, Jr., *The Bow and the Lyre: the Art of Robert Browning* (Ann Arbor: University of Michigan Press, 1964), p. 145; Edwin Muir, "Robert Browning," in *Robert Browning: a Collection of Essays*, ed. Philip Drew (London: Metheun, 1966), pp. 68-69.

2John Ruskin, *Works*, ed. E.T. Cook and Alexander Wedderburn (London: George Allen, 1905), VI, 449.

3Loy D. Martin, *Browning's Dramatic Monologues and the Post-Romantic Subject* (Baltimore: Johns Hopkins University Press, 1985), p. 95.

[4]J. Hillis Miller, *The Disappearance of God* (Cambridge, Mass: Harvard University Press, 1963), p. 127.

[5]King, pp. 25, 20-21, and 47.

[6]Martin, p. 124.

[7]Unpublished lecture quoted in F.O. Matthiessen, *The Achievement of T.S. Eliot*, 2nd ed. (New York and London: Oxford University Press, 1947), p. 74.

[8]K.W. Gransden, "The Uses of Personae," in *Browning's Mind and Art*, ed. Clarence Tracy (Edinburgh and London: Oliver and Boyd, 1968), p. 66; Douglas Bush, *Mythology and the Romantic Tradition in English Poetry* (New York: Pageant Books, 1957), p. 365.

[9]Dorothy Mermin, *The Audience in the Poem* (New Brunswick, N.J.: Rutgers University Press, 1983), p. 10.

[10]Mermin, p. 10. The following quotation from Mermin in this paragraph appears on p. 11.

[11]Robert Langbaum, *The Poetry of Experience* (London: Chatto and Windus, 1957), p. 85.

[12]Langbaum, p. 94.

[13]John Bayley, "Character and Consciousness," *New Literary History*, V. 1974, no. 2, 225-26 and 227.

[14]Clarence Tracy, "Browning Speaks Out," in *Browning's Mind and Art*, p. 4.

[15]T.S. Eliot, *The Three Voices of Poetry*, 2nd ed. (Cambridge: Cambridge University Press, 1955), pp. 4 and 14.

[16]Eliot, p. 13. The following quotation from Eliot also appears on p. 13.

[17]Langbaum, p. 146.

[18]Langbaum, p. 155.

[19]Cf. Herbert F. Tucker, "Dramatic Monologue and the Overhearing of Lyric," in *Lyric Poetry: Beyond New Criticism*, ed. Chavira Hosek and Patricia Parker (Ithaca: Cornell University Press, 1985), p. 229: "Tennyson . . . in effect relyricized the genre, running its contextualizing devices in reverse and stripping his speakers of personality in order to facilitate a lyric drive. Browning, on the other hand, moved his dramatic monologues in the direction of mimetic particularity. . . ."

[20]Fernando Ferrara, "Theory and Model for the Structural Analysis of Fiction," *New Literary History*, V, 1974, no. 2, p. 252.

[21]Hélène Cixous, "The Character of 'Character,' " *New Literary History*, V, 1974, no. 2, p. 386. All quotations from this article refer to pp. 383-86.

[22]Miller, p. 104. The following quotation from Miller appears on pp. 104-05.

[23]*The Letters of Ezra Pound 1907–1941*, ed. D.D. Paige (New York: Harcourt and Brace, 1950), p. 90.

[24]Thomas H. Jackson, *The Early Poetry of Ezra Pound* (Cambridge, Mass: Harvard University Press, 1968), p. 4.

[25]Ezra Pound, *Selected Prose 1909–1965*, ed. William Cookson (London: Faber and Faber, 1973), p. 432.

[26]Ezra Pound, "Vorticism," in *Gaudier-Brzeska: A Memoir* (New Directions, 1960), p. 85.

[27]N. Christoph de Nagy, "Pound and Browning," in *New Approaches to Ezra Pound*, ed. Eva Hesse (London: Faber and Faber, 1969), p. 124.

[28]Hugh Witemeyer, *The Poetry of Ezra Pound* (Berkeley: University of California Press, 1981), p. 62.

[29]Letters of Ezra Pound, pp. 3-4.

[30]Witemeyer, p. 68.

[31]Witemeyer, p. 75.

[32]Witemeyer, pp. 80-81.

[33]*Literary Essays of Ezra Pound*, ed. T.S. Eliot (London: Faber and Faber, 1954), p. 340. Similarly, Pound admires the "ubiquity of application" of Eliot's poetry. "Art does not avoid universals," he notes, "it strikes at them all the harder in that it strikes through particulars." See his essay on Eliot in *Literary Essays*, p. 420.

[34]*Literary Essays*, p. 340.

[35]Ronald Bush, *The Genesis of Ezra Pound's Cantos* (Princeton, N.J.: Princeton University Press, 1976), pp. 154, 159 and 175.

[36]Michael Bernstein, *The Tale of the Tribe* (Princeton, N.J.: Princeton University Press, 1980), pp. 164 and 7-9.

[37]*Literary Essays*, p. 86.

[38]Bernstein, pp. 30-31.

[39]Bernstein's definition of the epic appears on p. 14.

[40]Bernstein, pp. 171-72.

## Chapter 3. SELF-MOCKERY: LAFORGUE

[1]Emile Picot, *Le Monologue dramatique dans l'ancien théâtre français* (Mâcon, 1886-88; rpt. Genève: Slatkine Reprints, 1970).

²Jean-Claude Aubailly, *Le Monologue, le dialogue et la sotie* (Paris: Champion, 1976), p. 108.

³Charles d'Héricault, ed., *Oeuvres de Coquillart*, II (Paris: Jannet, 1857), 203. The following quotation from Héricault in this paragraph refers to p. 204.

⁴Jacques Schérer, *La Dramaturgie classique en France* (Paris: Nizet, n.d.), pp. 227–28.

⁵Alfred de Vigny, Preface (1837) to *Poèmes antiques et modernes*.

⁶Vigny, letter of 27 December 1838, quoted in *Poèmes antiques et modernes*, Collection Poésie, No. 89 (Paris: Gallimard, 1973), p. 274.

⁷From "Ballade" in *Des fleurs de bonne volonté*. See Jules Laforgue, *Poésies complètes*, ed. Pascal Pia (Paris: Gallimard, Livre de poche, 1970), p. 229. All quotations from Laforgue's poetry are taken from this edition.

⁸In the letter to Paul Demeny of May 15, 1871.

⁹Warren Ramsey, *Jules Laforgue and the Ironic Inheritance* (New York: Oxford University Press, 1953), p. 118.

¹⁰For a discussion of Schopenhauer's and Hartmann's influence on Laforgue see Ramsey, pp. 42–51 and 82–87 respectively.

¹¹Jules Laforgue, *Lettres à un ami 1880–1886*, ed. G. Jean-Aubry (Paris: Mercure de France, 1941), p. 37; *Oeuvres complètes*, IV (Paris: Mercure de France, 1925), 112.

¹²Ramsey, p. 119.

¹³David Arkell, *Looking for Laforgue* (Manchester: Carcanet, 1979), p. 151.

¹⁴Henri Davenson, *Le Livre des Chansons* (Neuchâtel: La Baconnière, 1946), p. 17.

¹⁵See François Ruchon, *Jules Laforgue: sa vie, son oeuvre* (Genève: Albert Ciana, 1924), p. 72.

¹⁶Davenson, p. 59.

¹⁷Haskell M. Block, "Laforgue and the Theatre," in *Jules Laforgue: Essays on a Poet's Life and Work*, ed. Warren Ramsey (Carbondale and Edwardsville: Southern Illinois University Press, 1969), p. 80. The following quotation from Block in this paragraph appears on p. 81.

¹⁸Block, pp. 85–86; Ramsey, *Ironic Inheritance*, pp. 118 and 119.

¹⁹John Porter Houston, *French Symbolism and the Modernist Movement* (Louisiana State University Press, 1980), p. 81. Cf. also Michael Collie, *Jules Laforgue* (London: Athlone Press, 1977), pp. 68–69.

[20]Edouard Dujardin, *Les Lauriers sont coupés suivi de Le Monologue intérieur* (Rome: Bulzoni, 1977), pp. 230, 233 and 232.

[21]Francis Scarfe, "Eliot and Nineteenth-Century French Poetry," in *Eliot in Perspective*, ed. Graham Martin (London: Macmillan, 1970), p. 53.

[22]Wayne C. Booth, *The Rhetoric of Fiction* (Chicago: University of Chicago Press, 1961), p. 163.

[23]See Robert Storey, *Pierrot: A Critical History of a Mask* (Princeton: Princeton University Press, 1978), chapters I and III.

[24]A.G. Lehmann, "Pierrot and fin de siècle," in *Romantic Mythologies*, ed. Ian Fletcher (London: Routledge and Kegan Paul, 1967), p. 210.

[25]Storey, p. 94.

[26]Quoted in Jean Starobinski, *Portrait de l'artiste en saltimbanque* (Geneva: Skira, 1970), p. 81. The following quotations from Starobinksi in this paragraph refer to pages 83-84.

[27]Starobinski, p. 77; Storey, p. xiv. Mallarmé's *pitre châtié* strives to free himself from a certain Hamlet image, "reniant le mauvais / Hamlet."

[28]Storey, p. 138.

[29]Mme. de Staël, "Des tragédies de Shakspeare," in *De la littérature* (Paris: Charpentier, 1872), p. 188.

[30]Paul Claudel, "La Catastrophe g'Igitur," in *Positions et Propositions*, (Paris: Gallimard, 1928), p. 198.

[31]Helen Phelps Bailey, *Hamlet in France from Voltaire to Laforgue* (Genève: Droz, 1964), pp. 137 and 141-42. Like Pierrot, Hamlet represents the artist in particular: Laforgue was the first to coin the word *hamlétisme* which, says Bailey, refers to the "spiritual sickness of the artist in the nineteenth century" (p. 60).

[32]Wayne C. Booth, *A Rhetoric of Irony* (Chicago: Chicago University Press, 1974), pp. 6 and 11.

[33]D.C. Muecke, *The Compass of Irony* (London: Methuen, 1969), p. 120. The following quotation from Muecke in this paragraph appears on p. 188.

[34]Charles Baudelaire, "Le Peintre de la vie moderne," in *Curiosités esthétiques* (Paris: Garnier, 1962), p. 483.

[35]Jules Laforgue, *Mélanges posthumes*, pp. 63-64.

[36]Albert Sonnenfeld, "Hamlet the German and Jules Laforgue," *Yale French Studies* 33 (1964), 97.

[37]Michael Riffaterre, *Essais de stylistique structurale* (Paris: Flammarion,

1971), p. 176; John E. Jackson, *La Question du moi* (Neuchâtel: La Bacon-nière, 1978), p. 58.

[38]Mikhaïl Bakhtine, *Esthétique et théorie du roman* (Paris: Gallimard, 1978), p. 115.

[39]Tzvetan Todorov, *Mikhail Bakhtine: La Principe dialogique* (Paris: Seuil, 1981), p. 77.

[40]Quoted in Todorov, p. 50.

[41]Quoted in Todorov, p. 51.

[42]Claude Bouché, *Lautréamont: du lieu commun à la parodie* (Paris: La-rousse, 1974), p. 32. The following quotations from Bouché in this para-graph refer to pages 41 and 44.

[43]For further discussion of these parodic procedures see Elisabeth A. Howe, "Repeated Forms in Laforgue," *Nottingham French Studies*, 24 (Oc-tober 1985), 49-53.

[44]Bouché, p. 44, n. 16; Riffaterre, p. 163.

[45]Ruth Amossy and Elisheva Rosen, *Les Discours du cliché* (Paris: SEDES, 1982), pp. 13-14 and p. 58.

[46]Riffaterre, pp. 180 and 176-77.

[47]Riffaterre, p. 178.

[48]Amossy and Rosen, p. 49. Further references to this work in this para-graph are from the same page.

[49]Anne Herschberg-Pierrot, "Problématiques du cliché," *Poétique*, 41-44 (1980), 340.

[50]Bouché, p. 17.

[51]Shoshana Felman, *La Folie et la chose littéraire* (Paris: Seuil, 1978), pp. 165 and 167.

[52]M. Bakhtin, *Problems of Dostoevsky's Poetics*, trans. R.W. Rotsel (n.p. Ardis, 1973), pp. 152-53.

[53]Bakhtine, *Esthétique et théorie*, p. 108.

[54]Quoted in Todorov, *Mikhaïl Bakhtine*, p. 103.

[55]*Esthétique et théorie*, p. 117.

[56]*Esthétique et théorie*, pp. 90 and 118.

[57]*Esthétique et théorie*, p. 101.

[58]Cf. the poem "Epicuréisme" in "Poèmes posthumes divers":
. . . . . . . . . . . . . . . Je prends
Sainte-Beuve et Théo, Banville et Baudelaire,
Leconte, Heine, enfin, qu'aux plus grands je préfère. . . .

[59]Bakhtin, *Dostoevsky's Poetics*, p. 165.

[60]Todorov, *Mikhaïl Bakhtine*, p. 102. Further references to this work in this paragraph are from pp. 101 and 102.

[61]Käte Hamburger, *The Logic of Literature*, trans. Marilynn J. Rose, 2nd rev. ed. (Bloomington: Indiana University Press, 1973), p. 271.

[62]Houston mentions Laforgue's "powerful ideas in fictional technique," referring principally to the use he makes of different voices. See *French Symbolism and the Modernist Movement*, p. 82.

[63]Jacques Derrida, *La Dissémination* (Paris: Seuil, 1972), p. 233.

[64]Stéphane Mallarmé, "Mimique," in *Crayonné au théâtre*, in *Oeuvres complètes* (Paris: Gallimard, Bibliothèque de la Pléïade, 1945), p. 310.

Chapter 4. SELF-QUESTIONING: MALLARMÉ

[1]In this I agree with John P. Houston; cf. his *French Symbolism and the Modernist Movement* (Louisiana State University Press, 1980), pp. 55-56.

[2]Stéphane Mallarmé, *Correspondance*, I, 1862-71, ed. Henri Mondor and Jean-Pierre Richard (Paris: Gallimard, 1959), 166 and 174.

[3]*Correspondance*, I, 25.

[4]Mallarmé, *Oeuvres complètes*, ed. Henri Mondor and G. Jean-Aubry, Bibliothèque de la Pléïade (Paris: Gallimard, 1945), p. 1411. Subsequent references to this edition will be given in parentheses in the text.

[5]Charles Chassé, "Le Thème de Hamlet chez Mallarmé," *Revue des sciences humaines*, January-March, 1955, p. 163; Paul Claudel, "La Catastrophe d'Igitur," *Positions et Propositions*, 6th ed. (Paris: Gallimard, 1928); Dr. Edmond Bonniot, Preface to *Igitur*, *O.c.*, p. 427.

[6]Haskell M. Block, *Mallarmé and the Symbolist Drama* (1963; rpt. Westport, Connecticut: Greenwood Press, 1977), pp. 45-48.

[7]Jacques Derrida, *La Dissémination* (Paris: Seuil, 1972), p. 233.

[8]Goethe, *Faust*, trans. Walter Arndt (New York: Norton, 1976), p. 184. (Part II, Act II).

[9]Cf. Hans-Jost Frey, "The Tree of Doubt," *Yale French Studies*, No. 54 (1977), p. 45. For an illuminating discussion of the interplay of reality and fiction in *L'Après-midi d'un faune* see Nathaniel Wing, *The Limits of Narrative: Essays on Baudelaire, Flaubert, Rimbaud and Mallarmé* (Cambridge: Cambridge University Press, 1986), pp. 96-113.

[10]Cf. Henri Mondor, *Historie d'un faune*, 9th ed. (Paris: Gallimard, 1948), pp. 257-58.

[11]Judy Kravis, *The Prose of Mallarmé* (Cambridge: Cambridge University Press, 1976), pp. 153-54.

[12]Kravis, p. 197. The notion of a "virtual, literary time" will be discussed presently.

[13]Jean-Pierre Richard, *L'Univers imaginaire de Mallarmé* (Paris: Seuil, 1962), pp. 295-96 and p. 345. James R. Lawler also discusses, with respect to the Faun, "the fullness we create to fill precisely a realized absence," in his *The Language of French Symbolism* (Princeton: Princeton University Press, 1969), p. 17.

[14]Richard, p. 405.

[15]Philippe Sollers, "Littérature et totalité," in *L'Ecriture et l'expérience des limites* (Paris: Seuil, 1968), p. 72.

[16]Cf. Mallarmé's admiring comment on Villiers de l'Isle-Adam's *Elën*: "c'est l'histoire éternelle de l'Homme et de la Femme," *Correspondance*, I, 153.

[17]Block, p. 30.

[18]Gardner Davies, *Mallarmé et le rêve d'Hérodiade* (Paris: Corti, 1978), p. 35.

[19]Block, p. 41.

[20]Jacques Schérer, *Le "Livre" de Mallarmé*, 2nd ed. (Paris: Gallimard, 1977), pp. 42 and 41.

[21]Cf. n. 12 above. The question of time specifically in the *Faune* is discussed by A.R. Chisholm in *Mallarmé's L'Après-midi d'un faune* (London: Cambridge University Press, 1958), pp. 9-10.

[22]Robert Greer Cohn, *Toward the Poems of Mallarmé* (Berkeley and Los Angeles: University of California Press, 1965), pp. 27, 31, and 264.

[23]Gardner Davies, *Stéphane Mallarmé, Les Noces d'Hérodiade: mystère* (Paris: Gallimard, 1959), p. 19, 51, and 93.

[24]Block, p. 19; Dr. Bonniot, Preface to *Igitur*, *O.c.*, p. 427.

[25]Kravis, pp. 153 and 149.

[26]Schérer, p. 26.

[27]Robert Langbaum, *The Poetry of Experience* (London: Chatto and Windus, 1957), pp. 160, 164, 167-68.

[28]Jacques Robichez, *Le Symbolisme au théâtre* (Paris: L'Arche, 1957), p. 187. The following quotation from Robichez in this paragraph also appears on p. 187.

[29]Block, p. 34.

[30]Quoted in Robichez, p. 37. Laforgue, too, expressed an interest in "le

théâtre injouable ou à jouer entre amis" in a letter of 1882. (*Oeuvres complètes* (Paris: Mercure de France, 1925), IV, 208.)

[31]Cf. also Mallarmé's comments on *Elën* by Villiers de l'Isle-Adam, in a letter of 1865: "je vous envoie un drame en prose pour lequel le théâtre serait trop banal, mais qui vous apparaîtra dans toute sa divine beauté, si vous le lisez, sous la clarté solitaire de votre lampe" (*Correspondance*, I, 153). A similar indifference towards the performative aspect of theatre had become prevalent in England earlier in the century; cf. Block, pp. 88-89, and Michael Mason, "Browning and the Dramatic Monologue," in *Robert Browning*, ed. Isobel Armstrong (London: Bell, 1974), pp. 244-45 and 249.

[32]E. Noulet, *L'Oeuvre poétique de Stéphane Mallarmé* (Paris: Droz, 1940), p. 230.

[33]Cf. Block, p. 55: "Both Hérodiade and the Faune 'Intermède' are close to the poetic tradition of French classical drama and its reinterpretation in the middle years of the nineteenth century by Banville and others who sought to bring poetry and the theater into nearer accord."

[34]Roland Barthes, *Sur Racine* (Paris: Seuil, 1963), p. 18.

[35]Quillard, quoted in Robichez, p. 188.

[36]Marc Fumaroli, "Rhétorique et dramaturgie: le statut du personnage dans la tragédie classique," *Revue d'histoire du théâtre*, 3, July-Sept. 1972, 231.

[37]Alexandre Lazaridès, *Valéry: Pour une poétique du dialogue* (Montréal: Presses de l'université de Montréal, 1978), p. 66.

[38]Preface to *Sordello*, (1863).

[39]Fumaroli, p. 241.

[40]Noulet, p. 72.

[41]Barbara Johnson, *Défigurations du langage poétique* (Paris: Flammarion, 1979), pp. 66-67.

[42]*Correspondance*, I, 151, 242 and 215.

[43]Julia Kristeva, *Semeiotike: Recherches pour une sémanalyse* (Paris: Seuil, 1969), p. 262.

[44]Cf. J.L. Austin, *How to Do Things with Words* (Oxford: Clarendon Press, 1962), pp. 4-11.

[45]Johnson, "Poetry and Performative Language," *Yale French Studies*, No. 54, 147-48.

[46]John E. Jackson, *La Question du moi* (Neuchâtel: La Baconnière, 1978), pp. 31-32.

[47]Jackson, p. 34. All quotations from Jackson in this paragraph appear on pp. 34–36.

[48]Concerning Mallarmé's unrealized project of entitling a volume of verse "Le Glorieux Mensonge" cf. *Correspondance*, I, 208.

[49]Hugh Kenner, *The Invisible Poet: T.S. Eliot* (New York: McDowell, 1959), p. 149.

[50]"Mon sujet est antique et un symbole." *Correspondance*, I, 169.

[51]*Correspondance*, I, 168.

[52]*Correspondance*, I, 169.

[53]Derrida, *La Dissémination*, p. 210; Tzvetan Todorov, *Mikhail Bakhtine: le principe dialogique* (Paris: Seuil, 1981), p. 50.

[54]Michel Beaujour, *Miroirs d'encre* (Paris: Seuil, 1980), p. 285.

[55]Emil Benveniste, "Tense in the French Verb," in *Problems in General Linguistics*, trans. Mary Elizabeth Meek (Coral Gables, Florida: University of Miami Press, 1971), p. 209.

[56]*Sur Racine*, p. 40. Cf. also Francis Scarfe, *The Art of Paul Valéry* (London: Heinemann, 1954), p. 136: "the dramatic monologue is constantly imitating dialogue, i.e., a dialogue in the self."

[57]Tzvetan Todorov, "Les Registres de la parole," in *Journal de Psychologie*, 1967, p. 276. All quotations from this article refer to pp. 276–78.

[58]Lazaridès, p. 68; Pierre Larthomas, *Le Langage dramatique* (Paris: Colin, 1972), p. 374.

[59]The Nurse, on the other hand, in her monoloque which constitutes the "Ouverture" of *Hérodiade*, shows anxiety not for herself but for Hérodiade; I cannot therefore agree with Block that the "Ouverture" is the "dramatic monolog" of "a character involved in an action" (Block, p. 12). The Nurse is not so much "involved in" as spectator of an action; whereas the speakers of dramatic monologues are always preoccupied with their own problems, the Nurse's incantation, creating as Block says "a mood of dread anticipation," concerns only Hérodiade.

[60]Larthomas, p. 375. The references to Larthomas in this paragraph are all from pp. 375–76.

[61]Jacques Schérer, *La Dramaturgie classique en France* (Paris: Nizet, n.d.), p. 251.

[62]Henri Mondor, *Vie de Mallarmé*, 10$^e$ ed. (Paris: Gallimard, 1941), pp. 476 and 477.

[63]Lazaridès, pp. 67 and 66.

[64]Lucette Finas, *Le Bruit d'Iris* (Paris: Flammarion, 1978), p. 148.

[65]*Correspondance*, II, 1871–85, ed. Henri Mondor and Lloyd James Austin (Paris: Gallimard, 1965), 116.

⁶⁶Schérer, Le "Livre", p. 79.

⁶⁷Block, p. 132.

⁶⁸Paul Valéry, "Histoire d'Amphion," in Variété III, 5th ed. (Paris: Gallimard, 1936), p. 94.

⁶⁹Correspondance, III, 1886-89, ed. Henri Mondor and Lloyd James Austin (Paris: Gallimard, 1969), 209.

## Chapter 5. SELF-CONSCIOUSNESS: VALÉRY

¹See Scarfe, The Art of Paul Valéry (London: Heinemann, 1954), pp. 235, 251, 266, 269, 271. John Porter Houston also terms La Jeune Parque a dramatic monologue (French Symbolism and the Modernist Movement (Louisiana State University Press, 1980), p. 154), and Kirsteen Anderson on p. 278 of her PhD thesis (see note 13 below) alludes to "Valéry's particular conception of poetry as dramatic monologue."

²See "Histoire d'Amphion," in Variété III (Paris: Gallimard, 1936), p. 94. For a discussion of Valéry's notion of liturgical drama see Huguette Laurenti, Paul Valéry et le théâtre (Paris: Gallimard, 1973), pp. 111-16.

³Paul Valéry, Cahiers, 29 vols. (Paris: C.N.R.S., 1957-61), VI, 508. Further references to this edition of the Cahiers will appear in parentheses in the text as C followed by a Roman numeral (vol. number) and by an Arabic numeral (page number). However, the two-volume Pléaïde edition of the Cahiers edited by Judith Robinson (Paris: Gallimard, 1973, 1974) will be cited in preference wherever possible, and will be referenced as PC followed by two Arabic numerals for volume and page number.

⁴"Histoire d'Amphion," p. 94.

⁵Valéry, Oeuvres, ed. Jean Hytier, 2 vols., Bibliothèque de la Pléïade (Paris: Gallimard, 1957 and 1960), I, 1468. The references to volume I are to the 1959 printing. Further references to Valéry's Oeuvres will appear in parentheses in the text as O followed by a Roman numeral (vol. number) and an Arabic number (page number).

⁶Christine M. Crow, Paul Valéry and the Poetry of Voice (Cambridge: Cambridge University Press, 1982), p. 39. Concerning the couplets of "My Last Duchess" see above, ch. 1, pp. 22-23.

⁷Scarfe, Art of Paul Valéry, p. 269.

⁸Marc Fumaroli, "Rhétorique et dramaturgie; le statut du personnage dans la tragédie classique," Revue d'histoire de théâtre, 3, July-Sept. 1972, 241. Cf. ch. 4, (p. 113) above.

⁹Cf., in Valéry's "Colloque dans un être" (which has as epigraph a line from La Jeune Parque), speaker B's reluctance to "redevenir UN TEL . . .

Celui qui porte mon nom, qui est barré de mes habitudes, de mes gênes, de mes opinions, chargé de tant de choses qui eussent pu être tout autres, que je sens tout accidentelles, et qui pourtant ME définissent" (O, I, 364).

[10]Cf. Scarfe, pp. 207-08.

[11]Jean Levaillant, "La jeune Parque en question," in *Paul Valéry contemporain* (Paris: Klincksieck, 1974), p. 137, n. 1. Further references to Levaillant in this paragraph appear on pages 138 and 141.

[12]Cf. Valéry's own preoccupation with man's physical nature as well as with mental phenomena, in the *Cahiers*, and also his stress, in the quotation cited at the beginning of the following paragraph, on "l'être *vivant* ET *pensant.*"

[13]A more complete version of this *Cahiers* entry with its revealing comparison to Mallarmé forms the epigraph of Crow's book *Paul Valéry and the Poetry of Voice*. This work, as well as other critical literature exploring the question of voice in Valéry, renders a lengthy examination of the subject superfluous here. I am grateful to Dr. Kirsteen Anderson of Queen Mary College London for permission to read her unpublished PhD thesis entitled "The Idea of Voice in the Work of Paul Valéry" (Cambridge, 1981), which covers many aspects of the question very thoroughly. Other articles on the subject of voice are: Nicole Celeyrette-Pietri, "L'Ecriture et la voix," in *Cahiers du 20e siècle*, No. 11, (Paris: Klincksieck, 1979), pp. 207-27, and the chapter "Je me parle" in her *Valéry et le Moi, des Cahiers à l'oeuvre* (Paris: Klincksieck, 1979); Walter Ince, "La Voix du Maître ou Moi et style selon Valéry," *Revue des Sciences Humaines*, 129 (jan.-mars 1968), 29-39; N. Bastet, "Valéry et la voix poétique," *Annales de la Faculté des Lettres et Sciences Humaines de Nice*, 15 (1971).

[14]Mallarmé, *Oeuvres complètes*, ed. Henri Mondor and G. Jean-Aubry, Bibliothèque de la Pléiade, (Paris: Gallimard, 1945), p. 368.

[15]Nicole Celeyrette-Pietri, "Deux font un," *Cahiers Paul Valéry*, 2 (Paris: Gallimard, 1977), p. 149.

[16]Cf. Valéry's theory of "l'infini esthétique" (O, II, 1342-44).

[17]E. Noulet, *Le Ton poétique* (Corti, 1971), p. 179. Cf. also Valéry's own affirmation that "le ton est en somme l'accommodation du parleur à sa pensée/parole" (C, VII, 21).

[18]Presumably, then, eliminating the common, middle term, "La voix est la conscience," as Jacques Derrida proclaims in *La Voix et le phénomène*, (Paris: Presses universitaires de France, 1967, p. 89), with reference, of course, not to Valéry but to Husserl. Despite radical differences in viewpoint, and despite Valéry's apparent ignorance of Husserl's work, certain spontaneous parallels in their thought can be detected, not least concerning the nature of the Self and its inner language. See Michel Lechantre, "L'Hiéroglyphe intérieur," *MLN*, 87 (1972), 630-43, and Hartmut Köhler,

"Valéry et Husserl: le Moi et son oeuvre," in *Cahiers du 20e siècle*, No. 11, pp. 191–206.

[19]Anderson deals at some length with the question of the role of voice in the acquisition of self-awareness in the first part of ch. 2 of her thesis. (See note 13 above.)

[20]In "La Pythie" the duality of the inner monologue is examined in relation to the question of inspiration. She asks, "Qui me parle, à ma place même? / Quel écho me répond: Tu mens!"; to which the answer might be: her own inner voice, or "Une intelligence adultère," a "Puissance Créatrice." Valéry himself did not believe in transcendental inspiration, and suggests that poets who consider themselves "inspired" simply do not recognize the promptings of their own internal monologue. Since "ma parole peut me surprendre," it can produce the effect of unsolicited inspiration: "L'inspiration étonne l'inspiré" (*C*, XIX, 755).

[21]John Bayley, "Character and Consciousness," *New Literary History*, V, No. 2 (1974), p. 225.

[22]Quoted in E. Noulet, *Les Cahiers de Paul Valéry Année 1934* (Jacques Antoine, 1973), p. 27.

[23]Michel Beaujour, *Miroirs d'encre* (Paris: Seuil, 1980), p. 285. See above, ch. 4, pp. 122–23.

[24]Scarfe, p. 207. The number of questions decreases somewhat in the second half of the poem, but it still contains over a dozen, so that one may not be inclined to agree with Scarfe that "the first half of the monologue is "concerned with a series of questions, while the second half gives a series of answers" (p. 207).

[25]Scarfe, p. 213. A detailed analysis of the dramatic effects engendered in many of Valéry's poems by linguistic forms, particularly self-address in the second person including questions and commands, forms the basis of Scarfe's definition of the poems as dramatic monologues.

[26]Scarfe, p. 223; Valéry, *O*, I, 1621.

[27]Pierre Larthomas, *Le Langage dramatique* (Paris: Colin, 1972), p. 376.

[28]Laurenti, p. 201.

[29]Edouard Dujardin, *Les Lauriers sont coupés suivi de Le Monologue intérieur* (Rome: Bulzoni, 1977), pp. 232–33. See above, ch. 3, p. 64.

[30]Dorrit Cohn, *Transparent Minds* (Princeton, N.J.: Princeton University Press, 1978), p. 189.

[31]Emil Benveniste, "The Correlations of Tense in the French Verb" in *Problems in General Linguistics*, trans. Mary Elizabeth Meek (Coral Gables, Florida: University of Miami Press, 1971), p. 209.

[32]Laurenti, p. 200.

³³Cohn, pp. 258-60.

³⁴Judith Robinson, "*La Jeune Parque*: poème de l'adolescence?" *RLM*, Nos. 498-503 (1977), pp. 48-49; see also p. 47. On the question of cyclical phenomena see Serge Bourjea, "Sang et soleil de la Parque: *La Jeune Parque* et l'éternel retour," *RLM*, Nos. 498-503 (1977), pp. 123-46.

³⁵These remarks (dating from 1939) may be compared with Jakobson's claim that "focus on the message for its own sake is the POETIC function of language." Cf. Roman Jakobson, "Linguistics and Poetics," in *Style in Language*, ed. Thomas A. Sebeok (Cambridge, Mass., M.I.T. Press, 1960), p. 356.

³⁶Cf. "sinueuse" (1. 35), "Je m'enlace" (1. 51) and also 11. 261, 423, 435, 472.

³⁷René Fromilhague, "La Jeune Parque et l'"autobiographie dans la forme,'" in *Paul Valéry contemporain* (Paris: Klincksieck, 1974), p. 223. His discussion of this overall pattern appears on pp. 215-24.

³⁸Jakobson, p. 358.

³⁹Crow, pp. 72 and 73-74.

⁴⁰Huguette Laurenti, "Les Langages de la jeune Parque," *Bulletin des études valéryennes*, No. 6 (juillet 1975), p. 29.

⁴¹Christine Crow, " 'Teste parle': the question of a potential artist in Valéry's M. Teste," *YFS*, 44 (1970), 163-64.

⁴²Daniel Oster, *Monsieur Valéry* (Paris: Seuil, 1981), p. 47.

⁴³Oster, pp. 9 and 155.

Chapter 6. CONCLUSION

¹Cf. also his statement, quoted in chapter 5, that for a poet "il ne s'agit jamais de dire qu'*il pleut. Il* s'agit . . . de créer la pluie" (PC, 2, 1120). For references to Valéry's *Cahiers* and *Oeuvres*, the same notation will be adopted in this chapter as in chapter 5 (see ch. 5, notes 4 and 6).

²Huguette Laurenti, *Paul Valéry et le théâtre* (Paris: Gallimard, 1973), p. 42.

³Francis Scarfe, *The Art of Paul Valéry* (London: Heinemann, 1954), p. 135.

⁴Roma A. King, Jr., *The Focusing Artifice* (Athens, Ohio: Ohio University Press, 1968), pp. 115 and 168.

⁵King, pp. 169 and 175. The following quotation from King in this paragraph appears on p. 168.

⁶King, p. 171.

7J. Hillis Miller, *The Disappearance of God* (Cambridge, Mass.: Harvard University Press, 1963), p. 105. The reference to the "indeterminacy of selfhood" appears on p. 104.

8Hélène Cixous, "The Character of 'Character,' " *New Literary History*, 5, No. 2 (1974), 385. Quoted more fully in chapter 2 above.

9F.L. Lucas, *Eight Victorian Poets* (Cambridge: Cambridge University Press, 1930), p. 23; letter from Henri Cazalis to Mallarmé dated March 1864, quoted in Mallarmé, *Oeuvres complètes*, ed. Henri Mondor and G. Jean-Aubry (Paris: Gallimard, 1945), p. 1427.

10Miller, pp. 89-90; Roma A. King, Jr., *The Bow and the Lyre* (Ann Arbor: University of Michigan Press, 1964), p. 147; Charles Mauron, *Mallarmé l'obscur* (Paris: Denoël, 1941), p. 75-76.

11T.S. Eliot, "Donne in Our Time," in *A Garland for John Donne*, ed. T. Spencer (Gloucester, Mass.: Peter Smith, 1958), pp. 15-16.

12Warren Ramsey, *Jules Laforgue and the Ironic Inheritance* (New York: Oxford University Press, 1953), p. 165.

13Hugh Kenner, *The Invisible Poet* (New York: McDowell, Obolensky, 1959), p. 40.

14Robert Langbaum, *The Mysteries of Identity* (New York: Oxford University Press, 1977), p. 92.

15Eliot was the first to acknowledge his debt to Laforgue who, he says, "together with the later Elizabethan drama," influenced his earliest poetic efforts (see his Introduction to Ezra Pound's *Selected Poems* (London: Faber and Faber, 1928), p. 8); he even called the relationship between Laforgue and himself at that time "a sort of possession by a stronger personality" (quoted in Ramsey, p. 199). The nature, extent and duration of this influence have already been well documented: cf. Ramsey, pp. 192-203; Kenner, pp. 13-39; Edward J.H. Greene, *T.S. Eliot et la France* (Paris: Boivin, 1951), pp. 17-68; Francis Scarfe, "Eliot and Nineteenth-century French Poetry" in *Eliot in Perspective* (New York: Humanities Press, 1970), pp. 52-61.

16John E. Jackson, *La Question du Moi* (Neuchâtel: La Baconnière, 1978), p. 49.

17Kenner, pp. 30, 31, and 55.

18Quoted in Kenner, p. 59.

19Langbaum, *Mysteries*, pp. 97 and 98.

20Michael Bernstein, *The Tale of the Tribe* (Princeton: Princeton University Press, 1980), pp. 31 and 76.

21Kenner, pp. 149, 148 and 41.

[22]Kenner, pp. 122 and 123.

[23]Kenner, pp. 294 and 293.

[24]In his Introduction to a translation of Valéry's "Ebauche d'un serpent" (1924). Cf. James Lawler, *The Poet as Analyst: Essays on Paul Valéry* (Berkeley: University of California Press, 1974), p. 292.

[25]It is missing, also, from another poem that might otherwise be considered a dramatic monologue, namely Rimbaud's *Une Saison en enfer*. In "A Stylistic Interpretation of Rimbaud" (*Archivum Linguisticum*, 3 (1951), 168–92), Scarfe describes this poem as a dramatic monologue portraying an inner conflict "not so very different from that conflict which forms the substance and dictates the organisation of the dramatic monologue of *La Jeune Parque*" (p. 187); he analyzes its forms of self-address, which represent a "dramatic conception and habit of speech" (p. 191). Nevertheless, as Scarfe himself points out, the conflict expressed in the poem arises from "a division . . . of the *poet's* personality" (p. 187; my emphasis); in other words, no persona is set up, no distance created between poet and speaker.

[26]As Donald Davie observes, Eliot sometimes deliberately juxtaposes written and spoken styles. See his "Pound and Eliot: a distinction," in *Eliot in Perspective*, ed. Graham Martin (New York: Humanities Press, 1970), p. 69.

[27]Cf. Eliot's Introduction to Valéry's *The Art of Poetry*, trans. Denise Folliot (London: Routledge and Kegan Paul, 1958), pp. xvi–xvii.

[28]Nicole Celeyrette-Pietri, "L'Ecriture et la voix," in *Cahiers du XXe siècle*, No. 11 (Paris: Kliencksieck, 1979), p. 221.

[29]Celeyrette-Pietri, p. 223.

[30]Christine Crow, *Paul Valéry and the Poetry of Voice* (Cambridge: Cambridge University Press, 1982), p. 250.

[31]Gerald L. Bruns, *Modern Poetry and the Idea of Language* (New Haven: Yale University Press, 1974), pp. 261 and 258–59. According to Bruns, a hermetic poem is "a self-contained linguistic structure," whereas the Orphic poet goes "beyond the formation of a work toward the creation of the world" (p. 1).

[32]Robert W. Greene, *Six French Poets of Our Time* (Princeton: Princeton University Press, 1979), pp. 12 and 19. Greene discusses and elaborates on Bruns' distinction between Orphic and hermetic poetry. The following quotation from Greene in this paragraph appears on p. 9.

[33]Michael Hamburger, *The Truth of Poetry* (London: Weidenfeld and Nicolson, 1969), p. 27.

[34]*The Letters of Ezra Pound, 1907–1914*, ed. D.D. Paige (New York: Harcourt Brace, 1950), p. 48.

[35]Ezra Pound, *Make It New* (New Haven: Yale University Press, 1935), p. 173.

[36]Hamburger, p. 47.

[37]Francis F. Burch, *Tristan Corbière* (Paris: Nizet, 1970), pp. 168, 169 and 170.

[38]Burch, p. 171. See also Michel Dansel's reference to the "réalisme, d'une essence bien anglo-saxonne" of *Les Amours jaunes*, in his *Langage et modernité chez Tristan Corbière* (Paris: Nizet, 1974), p. 154.

[39]Burch, p. 171. Cf. Edmund Wilson, *Axel's Castle* (New York: Charles Scribner's Sons, 1950), pp. 14–16; Burch refers to *Axel's Castle* at this point.

[40]Ramsey, p. 190; Henri Peyre, "Laforgue Among the Symbolists," in *Jules Laforgue: Essays on a Poet's Life and Work*, ed. Warren Ramsey (Carbondale and Edwardsville: Southern Illinois University Press, 1969), pp. 44–45; Michael Collie, *Jules Laforgue* (London: Athlone Press, 1977), p. 79, and see also pp. 84–89.

[41]See Michael Mason, "Browning and the Dramatic Monologue," in *Robert Browning*, ed. Isobel Armstrong (London: Bell, 1974), p. 248; Mallarmé, *Oeuvres complètes* (Paris: Gallimard, 1945), p. 300. Cf. also Ronald Bush's comments on Pound's attitude to the theatre (*The Genesis of Ezra Pound's Cantos* (Princeton: Princeton University Press, 1976), pp. 153–54).

On the question of acted and unacted drama in mid-nineteenth-century England, see pp. 240–52 of Mason's article; and in the latter part of the century in France—see Jacques Robichez, *Le Symbolisme au théâtre* (Paris: L'Arch, 1957), pp. 36–37.

[42]Cf. Wylie Sypher, *Loss of the Self in Modern Literature and Art* (New York: Random House, 1962), pp. 67, 86–87, and passim.

[43]Hamburger, pp. 59 and 60.

[44]Mallarmé, *Oeuvres complètes*, p. 304.

# Bibliography

### Primary Sources

Baudelaire, Charles. "Le Peintre de la vie moderne." In *Curiosités esthétiques*. Paris: Garnier, 1962, pp. 453–502.

Browning, Robert. *Browning: Poetical Works 1833–1864*. Ed. Ian Jack. London: Oxford University Press, 1970.

———. *The Complete Poetical Works of Robert Browning*. Ed. Augustine Birrell. New York: Macmillan, 1937.

———. *The Complete Works of Robert Browning*. Gen. ed. Roma A. King, Jr. 7 vols. Athens, Ohio: Ohio University Press, 1969–85.

Eliot, T.S. *Collected Poems, 1909–1962*. London: Faber and Faber, 1974.

———. "Donne in Our Time." In *A Garland for John Donne*. Ed. T. Spencer. Cambridge, Mass.: Harvard University Press, 1931.

———. Introduction to Ezra Pound's *Selected Poems*. London: Faber and Faber, 1928.

———. Introduction to Valéry's *The Art of Poetry*. Trans. Denise Folliot. London: Routledge and Kegan Paul, 1958.

———. *The Three Voices of Poetry*. 2nd ed. Cambridge: Cambridge University Press, 1955.

Laforgue, Jules, *Mélanges posthumes*. Paris: 1902; rpt. Geneva: Slatkine Reprints, 1979.

———. *Moralités légendaires*. Paris: Droz, 1980.

———. *Oeuvres complètes*. Paris: Mercure de France, 1925. Vol. IV.

———. *Poésies complètes*. Ed. Pascal Pia. Paris: Gallimard, Livre de poche, 1970.

———. *Selected Writings of Jules Laforgue*. Ed. William Jay Smith. New York: Grove Press, 1956.

Mallarmé, Stéphane. *Correspondance, 1862–71.* Ed. Henri Mondor and Jean-Pierre Richard. Paris: Gallimard, 1959.

_____. *Correspondance, 1871–85.* Ed. Henri Mondor and Lloyd James Austin. Paris: Gallimard, 1965.

_____. *Correspondance, 1886–89.* Ed. Henri Mondor and Lloyd James Austin. Paris: Gallimard, 1969.

_____. *Oeuvres complètes.* Ed. Henri Mondor and G. Jean-Aubry. Paris: Gallimard, Bibliothèque de la Pléïade, 1945.

Pound, Ezra. *The Cantos of Ezra Pound.* New York: New Directions, 1970.

_____. *The Letters of Ezra Pound, 1907–1941.* Ed. D.D. Paige. New York: Harcourt and Brace, 1950.

_____. *Literary Essays of Ezra Pound.* Ed. T.S. Eliot. London: Faber and Faber, 1954.

_____. *Make It New.* New Haven: Yale University Press, 1935.

_____. *Personae: The Collected Shorter Poems of Ezra Pound.* New York: New Directions, 1971.

_____. *Selected Prose 1909–1965.* Ed. William Cookson. London: Faber and Faber, 1973.

_____. "Vorticism." In *Gaudier-Brzeska: A Memoir.* New Directions, 1970, pp. 81–94.

Valéry, Paul. *Cahiers.* Ed. Judith Robinson. 2 vols. Paris: Gallimard, Bibliothèque de la Pléïade, 1973, 1974.

_____. *Cahiers.* 29 vols. Paris: C.N.R.S., 1957–61.

_____. "Histoire d'Amphion." In *Variété III.* 5th ed. Paris: Gallimard, 1936, pp. 85–96.

_____. *Oeuvres.* Ed. Jean Hytier. 2 vols. Paris: Gallimard, Bibliothèque de la Pléïade, 1957, 1960.

### Secondary sources

Amossy, Ruth, and Elisheva Rosen. *Les Discours du cliché.* Paris: SEDES, 1982.

Anderson, Kirsteen. "The Idea of voice in the Work of Paul Valéry." Diss. Cambridge University 1981.

Arkell, David. *Looking for Laforgue: An Informal Biography.* Manchester: Carcanet, 1979.

Armstrong, Isobel, ed. *Robert Browning.* London: Bell, 1974.

Aubailly, Jean-Claude. *Le Monologue, le dialogue et la sotie.* Paris: Champion, 1976.

Austin, J.L. *How To Do Things With Words.* Oxford: Clarendon Press, 1962.

Bailey, Helen Phelps. *Hamlet in France from Voltaire to Laforgue.* Genève: Droz, 1964.

Bakhtine, Mikhaïl. *Esthétique et théorie du roman.* Trans. Daria Olivier. Paris: Gallimard, 1978.

_____. *Problems of Dostoevsky's Poetics*. Trans. R.W. Rotsel. N.p.: Ardis, 1973.

Barthes, Roland. *Sur Racine*. Paris: Seuil, 1963.

_____. "To Write: Intransitive Verb?" In *The Structuralist Controversy: The Languages of Criticism and the Sciences of Man*. Ed. Richard Macksey and Eugenio Donato. Baltimore: John Hopkins University Press, 1972, pp. 134–45.

Barthes, Roland, Wayne C. Booth, Philippe Harmon, and Wolfgang Kayser. *Poétique du récit*. Paris: Seuil, 1977.

Bastet, Ned. "Valéry et la voix poétique." *Annales de la Faculté des Lettres et Sciences Humaines de Nice*, 15 (1971).

Bayley, John. "Character and Consciousness." *New Literary History*, 5, No. 2 (1974), 225–35.

Beaujour, Michel. *Miroirs d'encre: Rhétorique de l'autoportrait*. Paris: Seuil, 1980.

Benveniste, Emil. *Problems in General Linguistics*. Trans. Mary Elizabeth Meek. Coral Gables, Florida University of Miami Press, 1971.

Bernstein, Michael. *Ezra Pound and the Modern Verse Epic: The Tale of the Tribe*. Princeton: Princeton University Press, 1980.

Block, Haskell, *Mallarmé and the Symbolist Drama*. 1963; rpt. Westport, Connecticut; Greenwood Press, 1977.

Bonniot, Edmond. Preface to *Igitur*. In Mallarmé's *Oeuvres complètes*. Ed. Henri Mondor and G. Jean-Aubry. Paris: Gallimard, Bibliothèque de la Pléïade, 1945, pp. 423–32.

Booth, Wayne C. *The Rhetoric of Fiction*. Chicago: University of Chicago Press, 1961.

_____. *A Rhetoric of Irony*. Chicago: University of Chicago Press, 1974.

Bouché, Claude. *Lautréamont: du lieu commun à la parodie*. Paris: Larousse, 1974.

Bourjea, Serge. "Sang et soleil de la Parque: La Jeune Parque et l'éternel retour." *Revue des lettres modernes*, 498–503 (1977), 123–46.

Brooks, Cleanth and Robert Penn Warren. *Understanding Poetry*. Rev. ed. New York: Holt, 1950.

Brower, Reuben. "The Speaking Voice." In *Approaches to the Poem*. Ed. John O. Perry. San Francisco: Chandler, 1965, pp. 259–70.

Bruns, Gerald L. *Modern Poetry and the Idea of Language: a Critical and Historical Study*. New Haven: Yale University Press, 1974.

Burch, Francis F. *Tristan Corbière*. Paris: Nizet, 1970.

Bush, Douglas. *Mythology and the Romantic Tradition in English Poetry*. New York: Pageant Books, 1957.

Bush, Ronald. *The Genesis of Ezra Pound's Cantos*. Princeton: Princeton University Press. 1976.

Carleton, Frances. *The Dramatic Monologue: Vox Humana*. Salzburg; Salzburg University Press, 1977.

Celeyrette-Pietri, Nicole. "Deux font un." *Cahiers Paul Valéry*, 2 (1977), 143–58.

———. "L'Ecriture et la voix." *Cahiers du vingtième siècle*, 11 (1979), 207–27.

———. *Valéry et le Moi, des Cahiers à l'oeuvre*. Paris: Klincksieck, 1979.

Chassé, Charles. "Le Thème de Hamlet chez Mallarmé." *Revue des sciences humaines*, janv.–mars 1955, 157–169.

Chisholm, A.R. *Mallarmé's L'Après-midi d'un faune*. London: Cambridge University Press, 1958.

Christ, Carol T. "Self-Concealment and Self-Expression in Eliot's and Pound's Dramatic Monologues." *Victorian Poetry*, 22, No. 2 (1984), 217–26.

Cixous, Hélène. "The Character of 'Character.' " *New Literary History*, 5, No. 2 (1974), 383–402.

Claudel, Paul. "La Catastrophe d'Igitur." In *Positions et propositions*. 6th ed. Paris: Gallimard, 1928, pp. 197–207.

Cohen, Jean. *Structure du langage poétique*. Paris: Flammarion, 1966.

Cohn, Dorrit. *Transparent Minds: Narrative Modes for Presenting Consciousness in Fiction*. Princeton: Princeton University Press, 1978.

Cohn, Robert Greer. *Toward the Poems of Mallarmé*. Berkeley and Los Angeles: University of California Press, 1965.

Collie, Michael. *Jules Laforgue*. London: Athlone Press, 1977.

Crow, Christine M. *Paul Valéry and the Poetry of Voice*. Cambridge: Cambridge University Press, 1982.

———. " 'Teste parle': the question of a potential artist in Valéry's M. Teste." *YFS*, 44 (1970).

Culler, A. Dwight. "Monodrama and the Dramatic Monologue." *PMLA*, 90, (1975), 366–85.

Dansel, Michel. *Langage et modernité chez Tristan Corbière*. Paris: Nizet, 1974.

Davenson, Henri. *Le Livre des chansons*. Neuchâtel: La Baconnière, 1946.

Davies, Gardner, *Mallarmé et le rêve d'Hérodiade*. Paris: Corti, 1978.

———. *Stéphane Mallarmé, Les Noces d'Hérodiade: mystère*. Paris: Gallimard, 1959.

De Nagy, N. Christoph. "Pound and Browning." In *New Approaches to Ezra Pound: A Coordinated Investigation of Pound's Poetry and Ideas*. Ed. Eva Hesse. London: Faber and Faber, 1969, pp. 86–124.

Derrida, Jacques. *La Dissémination*. Paris: Seuil, 1972.

———. *La Voix et le phénomène*. Paris: Presses universitaires de France, 1967.

Drew, Philip. *The Poetry of Browning: A Critical Introduction*. London: Methuen, 1970.

———, ed. *Robert Browning: A Collection of Essays*. London: Methuen, 1966.

Dujardin, Edouard. *Les Lauriers sont coupés, suivi de Le Monologue intérieur.* Ed. Carmen Licari. Rome: Bulzoni, 1977.

Fairchild, Hoxie N. "Browning the Simple-Hearted Casuist." *University of Toronto Quarterly,* 18 (1949), 234–40.

Faral, Edmond. *Mimes français du XIIIe siècle.* Paris: 1910; rpt. Geneva: Slatkine Reprints, 1973.

Felman, Shoshana. *La Folie et la chose littéraire.* Paris: Seuil, 1978.

Ferrara, Fernando. "Theory and Model for the Structural Analysis of Fiction." *New Literary History,* 5, No. 2 (1974), 245–68.

Finas, Lucette. *Le Bruit d'Iris: essais.* Paris: Flammarion, 1978.

Flowers, Betty. *Browning and the Modern Tradition.* London: Macmillan, 1976.

Foucault, Michel. *Les Mots et les choses: une archéologie des sciences humaines.* Paris: Gallimard, 1966.

Frey, Hans-Jost. "The Tree of Doubt." *Yale French Studies,* 54 (1977), 45–54.

Fromilhague, René. "La Jeune Parque et l'autobiographie dans la forme.' " In *Paul Valéry contemporain.* Proc. of a Conference organised by the CNRS and the Centre de philologie et de littérature romanes de l'Université de Strasbourg. Nov. 1971. Paris: Klincksieck, 1974, pp. 209–35.

Fumaroli, Marc. "Rhétorique et dramaturgie: le statut du personage dans la tragédie classique." *Revue d'histoire du théâtre,* 3 (1972), 223–50.

Fuson, Benjamin. *Browning and His English Predecessors in the Dramatic Monologue.* Iowa City: State University of Iowa, 1948.

Greene, Edward J.H. *T.S. Eliot et la France.* Paris: Boivin, 1951.

Greene, Robert W. *Six French Poets of Our Time: A Critical and Historical Study.* Princeton: Princeton University Press, 1979.

Hair, Donald S. *Browning's Experiments with Genre.* Toronto: University of Toronto Press, 1972.

Hamburger, Käte. *The Logic of Literature.* Trans. Marilynn J. Rose. 2nd ed. Bloomington: Indiana University Press, 1973.

Hamburger, Michael. *The Truth of Poetry: Tensions in Modern Poetry from Baudelaire to the 1960s.* London: Weidenfeld and Nicolson, 1969.

Herschberg-Pierrot, Anne. "Problématiques du cliché." *Poétique,* 41–44 (1980), 334–35.

Hiddleston, J.A. *Essai sur Laforgue et les Derniers vers.* Lexington, Kentucky: French Forum Publishers, 1980.

Hobsbaum, Philip. "The Rise of the Dramatic Monologue." *Hudson Review,* 28 (1975–76), 227–45.

Honan, Park. *Browning's Characters.* New Haven: Yale University Press, 1961.

Houston, John Porter. *French Symbolism and the Modernist Movement: A Study of Poetic Structures.* Baton Rouge: Louisiana State University Press, 1980.

Howe, Elisabeth A. "Repeated Forms in Laforgue." *Nottingham French Studies*, 24, No. 2 (1985), 41–54.

Ince, Walter. "La Voix du maître ou Moi et style selon Valéry." *Revue des sciences humaines*, 129 (1968), 29–39.

Jackson, John E. *La Qeustion du moi: un aspect de la modernité poétique européenne*. Neuchâtel: La Baconnière, 1978.

Jackson, Thomas H. *The Early Poetry of Ezra Pound*. Cambridge, Mass.: Harvard University Press, 1968.

Jakobson, Roman. *Essais de linguistique générale*. Paris: Minuit, 1963.

————. "Linguistics and Poetics." In *Style in Language*. Ed. Thomas A. Sebeok. Cambridge, Mass.: M.I.T. Press, 1960.

Jespersen, Otto. *Language: Its Nature, Development and Origin*. London: Allen and Unwin, 1922.

Johnson, Barbara. *Défigurations du langage poétique: la seconde révolution baudelairienne*. Paris: Flammarion, 1979.

————. "Poetry and Performative Language." *Yale French Studies*, 54 (1977), 140–58.

Johnson, Wendell Stacy. *The Voices of Matthew Arnold: An Essay in Criticism*. New Haven: Yale University Press, 1961.

Kanters, Robert. "Paul Valéry et l'art dramatique." *Cahiers Paul Valéry*, 2 (1977), 39–48.

Kenner, Hugh. *The Invisible Poet: T.S. Eliot*. New York: McDowell, 1959.

King, Jr., Roma A. *The Bow and the Lyre: The Art of Robert Browning*. Ann Arbor: University of Michigan Press, 1964.

————. *The Focusing Artifice: The Poetry of Robert Browning*. Athens, Ohio: Ohio University Press, 1968.

Köhler, Hartmut, "Valéry et Husserl: le Moi et son oeuvre." *Cahiers du vingtième siècle*, 11 (1979), 191–206.

Kravis, Judy. *The Prose of Mallarmé: The Evolution of a Literary Language*. Cambridge: Cambridge University Press, 1976.

Kristeva, Julia. *Semeiotike: Recherches pour une sémanalyse*. Paris: Seuil, 1969.

Langbaum, Robert. *The Mysteries of Identity: A Theme in Modern Literature*. New York: Oxford University Press, 1977.

————. *The Poetry of Experience: The Dramatic Monologue in Modern Literary Tradition*. London: Chatto and Windus, 1957.

Larthomas, Pierre. *Le Langage dramatique: sa nature, ses procédés*. Paris: Colin, 1972.

Laurenti, Huguette. "Les Langages de la jeune Parque." *Bulletin des études valéryennes*, 6 (1975), 18–30.

————. *Paul Valéry et le théâtre*. Paris: Gallimard, 1973.

Lawler, James. *The Poet as Analyst: Essays on Paul Valéry*. Berkeley: University of California Press, 1974.

————. *The Language of French Symbolism*. Princeton: Princeton University Press, 1969.

Lazaridès, Alexandre. *Valéry: Pour une poétique du dialogue*. Montreal: Presses de l'Université de Montréal, 1978.

Lechantre, Michel. "L'Hiéroglyphe intérieur." *Modern Language Notes*, 87 (1972), 630–43.

Lehmann, A.G. "Pierrot and fin de siècle." In *Romantic Mythologies*. Ed. Ian Fletcher. London: Routledge and Kegan Paul, 1967.

Lejeune, Philippe. *Le Pacte autobiographique*. Paris: Seuil, 1975.

Levaillant, Jean. "La Jeune Parque en question." In *Paul Valéry contemporain*. Proc. of a Conference organized by the CNRS and the Centre de philologie et de littérature romanes de l'Université de Strasbourg. Nov. 1971. Paris: Klincksieck, 1974, 137–51.

Lotman, Iouri. *La Structure du texte artistique*. Trans. Anne Fournier et al. Paris: Gallimard, 1973.

Lucas, F.L. *Eight Victorian Poets*. Cambridge: Cambridge University Press, 1930.

MacCallum, M.W. "The Dramatic Monologue in the Victorian Period." *Proceedings of the British Academy*. Vol. 11. London, 1925; rpt. Nendeln, Liechtenstein: Kraus Reprints, 1976, pp. 265–82.

Martin, Graham, ed. *Eliot In Perspective: A Symposium.*. New York: Humanities Press, 1970.

Matthiessen, F.O. *The Achievement of T.S. Eliot*. 2nd ed. New York and London: Oxford University Press, 1947.

Mauron, Charles. *Mallarmé l'obscur*. Paris, Denoël, 1941.

Mermin, Dorothy. *The Audience in the Poem: Five Victorian Poets*. New Brunswick, N.J.: Rutgers University Press, 1983.

Miller, J. Hillis. *The Disappearance of God*. Cambridge, Mass.: Harvard University Press, 1963.

Mondor, Henri. *Histoire d'un faune*. 9th ed. Paris: Gallimard, 1948.

————. *Vie de Mallarmé*. 10th ed. Paris: Gallimard, 1941.

Noulet, Emilie. *Les Cahiers de Paul Valéry année 1934*. Paris: Jacques Antoine, 1973.

————. *L'Oeuvre poétique de Stéphane Mallarmé*. Paris: Droz, 1940.

————. *Le Ton poétique*. Paris: Corti, 1971.

Olney, James, ed. *Autobiography: Essays Theoretical and Critical*. Princeton: Princeton University Press, 1980.

Oster, Daniel. *Monsieur Valéry*. Paris: Seuil, 1981.

Picot, Emile. *Le Monologue dramatique dans l'ancien théâtre français*. Mâcon: 1886–88; rpt. Geneva: Slatkine Reprints, 1970.

Rader, Ralph. "The Dramatic Monologue and Related Lyric Forms." *Critical Inquiry*, 3 (1976), 131–51.

————. "Notes on Some Structural Varieties and Variations in Dramatic 'I' Poems and Their Theoretical Implications." *Victorian Poetry*, 22 (1984), 103–20.

Ramsey, Warren. *Jules Laforgue and the Ironic Inheritance.* New York: Oxford University Press, 1953.

———, ed. *Jules Laforgue: Essays on a Poet's Life and Work.* Carbondale and Edwardsville: Southern Illinois University Press, 1969.

Ransom, John Crowe. *The World's Body.* New York: Scribner's, 1938.

Raymond, William O. *The Infinite Moment and Other Essays on Robert Browning.* Rev. ed. Toronto: Toronto University Press, 1965.

Rees, Thomas R. "T.S. Eliot's Early Poetry as an Extension of the Symbolist Techniques of Jules Laforgue." *Forum,* 6–8 (1968–70), 46–52.

Richard, Jean-Pierre. *L'Univers imaginaire de Mallarmé.* Paris: Seuil, 1962.

Riffaterre, Michael. *Essais de stylistique structurale.* Paris: Flammarion, 1971.

Robichez, Jacques. *Le Symbolisme au théâtre.* Paris: L'Arche, 1957.

Robinson, Judith. "La Jeune Parque: poème de l'adolescence?" *Revue des lettres modernes,* 498–503 (1977), 33–55.

Ruchon, François. *Jules Laforgue: sa vie, son oeuvre.* Genève, Albert Ciana, 1924.

Ruthven, K.K. *A Guide to Ezra Pound's Personae.* Berkeley and Los Angeles: University of California Press, 1969.

Scarfe, Francis. *The Art of Paul Valéry: A Study in Dramatic Monologue.* London: Heinemann, 1954.

———. "A Stylistic Interpretation of Rimbaud." *Archivum Linguisticum,* 3 (1951), 168–92.

Schérer, Jacques. *La Dramaturgie classique en France.* Paris: Nizet, n.d.

———. *Le "Livre" de Mallarmé.* 2nd. ed. Paris: Gallimard, 1977.

Sessions, Ina B. "The Dramatic Monologue. *PMLA,* 62 (1947), 503–16.

Sinfield, Alan. *The Dramatic Monologue.* London: Methuen, 1977.

Smith, William Jay, ed. *Selected Writings of Jules Laforgue.* New York: Grove Press, 1956.

Sollers, Philippe. *L'Ecriture et l'expérience des limites.* Paris: Seuil, 1968.

Sonnenfeld, Albert. "Hamlet the German and Jules Laforgue." *Yale French Studies,* 33 (1964), 92–100.

Staël, Madame de. *De la littérature considérée dans ses rapports avec les institutions sociales.* Paris: Charpentier, 1872.

Starobinski, Jean. *Portrait de l'artiste en saltimbanque.* Geneva: Skira, 1970.

———. *La Relation critique.* Paris: Gallimard, 1970.

Storey, Robert. *Pierrot: A Critical History of a Mask.* Princeton: Princeton University Press, 1978.

Suillivan, Mary Rose. *Browning's Voices in* The Ring and The Book. Toronto: University of Toronto Press, 1969.

Sypher, Wylie. *Loss of the Self in Modern Literature and Art.* New York: Random House, 1962.

Tadié, Jean-Yves. *Le Récit poétique.* Paris: PUF, 1978.

Todorov, Tzvetan. *Mikhaïl Bakhtine: Le Principe dialogique.* Paris: Seuil, 1981.

————. "Les Registres de la parole." *Journal de psychologie normale et patho-logique*, 64 (1967), 265–78.

Tracy, Clarence, ed. *Browning's Mind and Art*. London: Oliver and Boyd, 1968.

Tynjanov, Jurij. *Problema Stikhotvornogo Jazyka*. Leningrad, 1924; rpt. The Hague: Mouton, 1963.

Weinstein, Arnold. *Fictions of the Self, 1550–1800*. Princeton: Princeton University Press, 1981.

Wilson, Edmund. *Axel's Castle: A Study in the Imaginative Literature of 1870–1930*. New York: Scribner's, 1950.

Wing, Nathaniel. *The Limits of Narrative: Essays on Baudelaire, Flaubert, Rimbaud and Mallarmé*. Cambridge: Cambridge University Press, 1986.

Witemeyer, Hugh. *The Poetry of Ezra Pound: Forms and Renewal, 1908–1920*. Berkeley: University of California Press, 1981.

Woodward, Anthony. *Ezra Pound and the Pisan Cantos*. London: Routledge and Kegan Paul, 1980.

Wright, George T. *The Poet in the Poem: The Personae of Eliot, Yeats and Pound*. Berkeley: California University Press, 1960.

# Index

# A Note About
# the Author

Before embarking on an academic career Elisabeth A. Howe worked as a linguist at the United Nations in Geneva and for the British government. She speaks French, Russian, and Polish. She received a PhD from Harvard in 1987, taught French at the University of Southampton, England, and currently teaches at Brandeis University.